YOSSARIAN SLEPT HERE

ERICA HELLER

Yossarian Slept Here

When Joseph Heller was Dad
and Life was a Catch-22

VINTAGE BOOKS
London

Published by Vintage 2011

2 4 6 8 10 9 7 5 3 1

First published in USA in 2011 by
Simon & Schuster

Vintage
Random House, 20 Vauxhall Bridge Road,
London SW1V 2SA

www.vintage-books.co.uk

Addresses for companies within The Random House Group Limited can
be found at: www.randomhouse.co.uk/offices.htm

The Random House Group Limited Reg. No. 954009

A CIP catalogue record for this book
is available from the British Library

ISBN 9780099570080

The Random House Group Limited supports The Forest Stewardship Council
(FSC®), the leading international forest certification organisation. Our books
carrying the FSC label are printed on FSC® certified paper. FSC is the only
forest certification scheme endorsed by the leading environmental organisations,
including Greenpeace. Our paper procurement policy can be found at
www.randomhouse.co.uk/environment

Printed and bound by CPI Group (UK) Ltd,
Croydon, CR0 4YY

With boundless gratitude to Richard Glass

and the late Warren Cassell;

and to my niece Ivy

and the grandparents who never got to meet her,

Grandma Shirley and Grandpa Joe

She believed once long ago in the country she had crossed a meadow to pick a few rhododendrons that she took to her family, the deep red ones. From afar they looked close together, each petal brushing against its neighbouring petal, but close up, that was not the case at all, each petal was on its own stalk, separate, surviving, the way it is with every living thing.

—Edna O'Brien, *Time and Tide*

Contents

YOSSARIAN
SLEPT HERE

INTRODUCTION

*A Jewish wife will forgive and forget, but she'll
never forget what she forgave.*

—Jewish proverb

"Joe *who?*" my mother asked without guile from her hospital bed.
She'd just read a card that had been tucked into a glorious bouquet
of freshly delivered flowers.

"Joe *Heller*," I told her. I was flabbergasted that she didn't know
or couldn't guess, but then we were in Sloan-Kettering. It was 1995,
she was dying, and although my parents had been married for
thirty-eight years, they had had a particularly acrimonious divorce
twelve years before and had not spoken since. So perhaps the fact
that she was scouring her brain for non-Hellerian Joes she might
know was not really all that startling. I reached over for the card
and read aloud: "My darling Shirley," it began, "I am so sorry. Joe."
I handed it back to her.

When I told her who'd sent the flowers, she spoke slowly and
without rancor. "Well, he *is* a sorry soul," she pronounced wea-
rily, crumpling up the card and dropping it into the yellow plastic
trash bin on the floor beside her bed. "But he sent you flowers," I
pushed, somehow hoping for more. "They're from *Dad*. Don't you

think they're nice?" I pestered, leading the witness. She stared at me, unruffled and unimpressed. "I get it. I understand," she said. "But really, how wildly would you like me to celebrate this? Should I hire jugglers?" Then she muttered something that I made her repeat twice because it was said so faintly, she closed her eyes and we never spoke of the flowers or of my father again.

By then my mother was bald and terribly frail. After her initial diagnosis a year and a half earlier, I'd moved back in with her at the Apthorp, the apartment building where I'd grown up, decamping from the Upper East Side to properly care for her for as long as was needed.

From the day I moved back in, whether my mother was home or, as she was with increasing frequency, in the hospital, my father was too stubborn and too shaken by the gravity of her illness to call or speak to her. Instead, he called me. Night after night he inquired about her with an array of questions that never varied: Had she eaten? Had she gotten fresh air that day? Was she able to sleep? What were the doctors saying? Had she taken all of her medications and had I remembered to give her all of her vitamins? What was her mood? Every night I answered him, increasingly baffled by his persistent interest and concern, but not, I suspect, as baffled as he himself may have been.

As my mother got sicker, had brain surgery, lung surgery, chemo, and radiation, I could hear how much more difficult it was for him to keep the fear from creeping into his voice. He knew we were going to lose her. It was only a question of when. Officially, they had lost each other many years before, of course, but it was obvious how deeply he was tied to her. They were still uncannily connected.

Even after years of silence, the truth remained that there'd never been anyone who'd known or understood each of them better than the other. There never would be. With Mom's death, this aspect of my father's life would be obliterated, and I sensed that fact very strongly during that time. To me, it could easily be seen lurking just beneath the surface—a surface customarily guarded and closed and, for the most part, ineluctably indecipherable.

When my father called me those nights he was not the blustery, famous author; the gruff, arrogant big shot; the smug, cocky fellow who sometimes showed up to friends' cocktail parties for the sheer fun of insulting them. He wasn't the caustic, clever master of the verbal arabesque who for years had answered the question "How come you've never written a book as good as *Catch-22*?" with the sly, Talmudic response to put any other to shame: "Who *has*?" he'd ask, genuinely wanting to know. He was not bombastic or self-satisfied during those nightly calls. He was only sad. He just wanted to talk, and I let him.

Then, about a month before my mother died, when she had gone into Sloan-Kettering for what seemed as if it might be the last time, one night when Dad called I was simply too exhausted to hold everything back that I'd been wanting to say to him ever since she'd first been diagnosed. I had never found the courage or the proper words to use with him before.

I blurted out that he simply had to communicate with her again *now*, or he would never forgive himself. "How will you live with yourself if you don't? How will you sleep at night?" I asked in an uncustomarily loud tone. He listened silently, and I could picture him sitting in his lemon-yellow study out in East Hampton where he lived, seething at the very notion of being scolded by his daughter. "Call. Write to her. Send flowers. Do *something*. There isn't much time left, and if you don't, I think you'll always be sorry," I fumbled, suddenly aware of and horrified by my own stridence. Now, understandably, there was angry silence. When Dad finally spoke, he was petulant, childlike. "I don't need *you* to tell me what to do," he growled, hanging up before I could respond.

It was the very next day when, sitting in my mother's hospital room, there had been a knock at the door, and an orderly had entered with the exquisite bouquet of flowers for Mom. From Dad.

When I arrived home that night the phone was already ringing. He wanted to know if she'd gotten the flowers and if so, had she liked them. I assured him that they'd arrived and had been magnificent. "Well, what did she say?" he asked with some urgency, and then it was my turn to be silent.

After the divorce, for years my father had begged, cajoled, and finally actually offered me a hefty bribe of ten thousand dollars in cash if I would only tell him my mother's secret pot roast recipe. It was handed down to her from her mother, my grandmother Dottie, and the meal was for him like kryptonite. It always made him groggy, feeble, and positively stupid with glee, turning his knees to jelly.

When my mother had closed her eyes in the hospital after receiving his flowers, what she had muttered to me, in fact, was: "No matter what, don't *ever* give him the pot roast recipe," and with that, she'd drifted off to sleep. I did not share this with him, take a sorrowful moment when he was so uncharacteristically humbled and vulnerable and make it even more difficult.

On the other hand, he never did get that recipe.

PART 1

Apartment 2K South

Starting small: In at the Apthorp,
but there was a catch

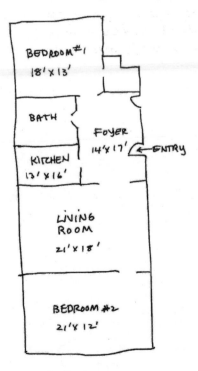

1952–1962

THE SORROW AND THE PITTI

It was certainly a strange quarter to have settled in. Small dress-makers, bird-stuffers, and "people who wrote" were her nearest neighbors.

—Edith Wharton, about New York City,
The Age of Innocence

In retrospect, my parents planting themselves at the Apthorp in 1952 made perfect sense. The Apthorp's history has an undeniably comic, often operatic eloquence, replete with notes both high and low. This made it the ideal place for Joe and Shirley Heller and their endlessly squealing infant, who happened to be me.

Since its construction in 1908, the Apthorp has been a quirky, iconic, and grand Manhattan apartment building rich in fascinating anecdotes and gossip; a limestone palace with an interior courtyard, built by the whimsical, shrewd robber baron William Waldorf Astor. Much later it became a fixture of the upper-crusty Upper West Side. But in 1952, there was a catch.

To begin with, the neighborhood was dangerous, ugly, and filthy. Respectability and astronomical real-estate prices came decidedly late to this once blighted area, and for much of its history, the Apthorp cast its shadow over a begrimed and dilapidated quarter teeming with junkies, prostitutes, pimps, muggers, and gangs. Just within its stately, wrought-iron gates, this was a Palazzo Pitti wannabe, lodged in the middle of Dodge City. Moreover, the Apthorpian thread of lunacy, recklessness, and absurdity began almost a century before the building itself was even erected, on farmland beleaguered by lawsuits initiated before the American Revolution, which weren't settled until 1902. The peculiar brand of Apthorp craziness is documented, pedigreed, cumulative, and exponential.

A favorite joke of my father's when I was a baby was to hide me up in a closet while my mother was out. When she'd return, he'd wait to see how long it took her to notice that the baby was missing. Several years later, when I was in grade school, my brother and I would sometimes play in the courtyard on weekend afternoons, and my father, at home writing, would tell us that we wouldn't be allowed back into the apartment unless we brought him a pizza. There was, in fact, a pizza toll. Our family did its part to uphold the Apthorp's crazy pedigree, and continued in our way for many years to come.

When the weather turned warm in our courtyard apartment, life inside bore a distinctive smell. The Apthorp beauty parlor was just beneath our windows, and while a courtyard breeze was a rarity, this meant, particularly on hotter days when windows were thrown open, that what blew in was the sulfurous smell of ammonia mixed with peroxide. The wafting scent floated inside the apartment and simply settled there. No matter what my mother served us for dinner, it smelled as if it were getting a permanent.

Drama and notoriety have always been quintessentially Apthorpian. Nora Ephron and her husband, Nicholas Pileggi, were residents for many years, and she wrote a prickly piece about it for *The New Yorker* called "Moving On, A Love Story," when they moved to the East Side in 2006, fed up with the Apthorp's maddening eccentricities, foibles, and runaway "fair market" rents. "Fair" can be such a flexible word.

My father wrote much of *Catch-22* in Apartment 2K South, early in the mornings and after returning home in the evenings

Courtesy of the author

Mom and me, 1952

from his pleasant but prosaic job as an ad writer. The apartment was cramped and had little light. Still, it was rich in distinctive detail, so it makes sense that the man who was about to invent a unique brand of circular logic lived in a second-floor apartment overlooking a circular driveway and courtyard. As he was about to introduce the world to a new kind of twisted, irrational rationality, he lived in a place that was itself completely idiosyncratic and extraordinary, and has only become more so with the galloping passage of time.

LOSE A MINK,
GAIN AN APARTMENT

"How did you find the chicken?"
"Underneath the potato."
—Typical waiter's joke told at Grossinger's
in 1945, from Tania Grossinger,
Growing Up at Grossinger's

In 1952, securing an apartment at the Apthorp, which extends from Seventy-eighth to Seventy-ninth Streets and from Broadway to West End Avenue, took only a deposit. And since the rents in those days were astonishingly reasonable, so were the deposits. You pretty much just showed up and if you wanted a place here, you got one. Rents were generally under two hundred dollars, and frequently half that price. And as long as you were hidden away in your apartment and never ventured out past the building's imposing gates into the violence and teeming squalor of Broadway, life was sublime. But my parents didn't start out on Broadway.

After getting married in New York in 1945, they departed immediately by train to California, where my father enrolled in the University of Southern California for a year and then transferred back east to New York University. He studied writing there and got his B.A. in 1948, and then his M.A. from Columbia a year later. Earning a Fulbright scholarship, he finished his education after he and my mother, Shirley, had spent a year at Oxford.

During their time in New York City, they'd lived in a brownstone just a few blocks from my maternal grandparents, Dottie and Barney Held. By the late 1940s, my grandparents had moved from Brooklyn to Riverside Drive and Seventy-sixth Street. The small brownstone apartment my parents rented was owned by one of my grandmother's card-playing friends, a woman named Pearl Marx, who was a chic and cunning businesswoman at a time when that was still considered uncommon.

This arrangement worked well, and my parents lived nicely—albeit under the surveillance of my grandmother's friend—for several months, until one night, when the house of Mrs. Marx more closely resembled that of the Marx *Brothers*. On a snowy winter's evening, when my parents went out for a late dinner and returned home to the brownstone, they passed by a man in the vestibule. He was nice-looking, well-dressed, and he actually tipped his hat to my mother as they came in and he went out. And just as he passed them, my mother noticed that he was carrying a mink coat and commented to my father about how much it looked like hers. Well, of course, not only did it resemble hers, it *was* hers. The instant they put the key in the door, they knew they'd been completely cleaned out. The following day they moved in with my grandparents on Riverside Drive and stayed there until my father took up a teaching position at Penn State University that spring. Their second hiatus from New York lasted from 1950 to '52, when they returned and were once again situated solidly in my grandparents' orbit.

In those early days the relationship between my father and my grandparents was simple and satisfying. They were Dad's biggest devotees. In fact, my grandmother in particular gave him not just room and board, not just money to live on while he completed his education, but she'd given him something far more significant: her one and only daughter.

Dottie Held, Grandma,
1949

Courtesy of the author

In the winter of 1945, when Mom was twenty-one, my grandmother had taken my mother and her younger son, my uncle, up to
Grossinger's, in the Catskills—the Jewish Alps—for a bit of fresh
air and winter recreation. My grandfather remained behind, working in the city. He was a partner at Queen Casuals Sportswear, and,
whenever he could slip away, a frequent patron of both Belmont
and Aqueduct raceways.

While checking in that afternoon at the hotel's massive front
desk, my grandmother spotted a skinny guy in an army uniform
clowning around with a few of his friends. He had a toothpick
stuck in his mouth and looked quite obviously pleased with himself. As he surveyed the throngs of guests milling about in the vast
lobby, all around him were girls his age, many with their mothers. It
was winter, and flocks of these girls were wrapped in fur coats and
wore expensive clothes and jewelry.

My grandmother suddenly caught sight of him, heard him talking to the man behind the counter and asking questions that seemed interesting. She could never put her finger on it afterward, what it was exactly that appealed to her. She only knew that she liked the sound of his Brooklynese; he was funny, sharp, and clearly very bright. Wasting no time and reaching him before any other mother might possibly do the same, she went right up to him, uttering these fateful words and thus rendering herself an instant cliché:

"Have I got a girl for you!"

In those days, people really said things like that. He stared at her. "Everyone I know has a girl for me," he told her. "Oh yeah? Well, this one has red hair and freckles," my grandmother countered. He scowled. "I hate red hair. And the only thing I hate more is freckles." And that should have been that, except where anyone else would have been finished, my grandmother was only getting started. As he signed the register and he and his pals picked up their bags, he passed by my grandmother and said: "See you later, Mom," and she always remembered how impish he'd looked when he said it.

He was on furlough after flying sixty missions in Italy during the war, a war which still had a full year ahead of fighting Japan. But this Coney Island kid, my father, was at last done with flying, and had come home to the U.S. by steamship from Naples to Atlantic City. And although he didn't know it yet, the day he arrived at Grossinger's he was confronted with two forces nearly as impregnable as any German battalion he'd encountered in the skies over Italy. The first was my grandmother, Dottie. The other was love.

That night in the smoky, jammed Terrace Room, the band pounded out the tango, the cha-cha, the mambo, and the rumba, and there was a dance contest. Seated with my mother, my grandmother spotted my father at a table on the other side of the room, again surrounded by friends, and headed right over without a second's hesitation.

She asked my father to be her partner for the dance contest, and he was so taken with her spectacular nerve that he agreed. The song was an

National Archives

Left to right: Lt. Clifford (pilot), Lt. Chrenko (copilot), S/Sgt. Rackmyer (tail gunner), Lt. Heller (bombardier-navigator), Pfc. Zaboly (not certain), S/Sgt. Schroeder (radio gunner), and S/Sgt. Ryba (gunner)—another 488th crew. The names here match the flight manifest for Dad's June 7th mission to Cencina, Italy.

Xavier Cugat hit, "Weekend at the Waldorf." They won the contest. With it came a bottle of champagne, and when they went back to enjoy it at my grandmother's table, Dad took one look at my mother and was besotted. Red hair, freckles, and all. The rest, as they say, is mystery.

They spent the week together up at Grossinger's, during which time he told her that he was going to be a writer, and not just a writer but a great writer; that he would write the definitive book about World War II. And then they wrote to each other when he returned to the air force base in San Angelo and she went home to Riverside Drive. My father called frequently and came and took her out as often as he could make it to New York.

Shirley Held had been born in the Bushwick section of Brooklyn, when homes there had porches and sprouted lush, carefully tended rose gardens. Mid-high school she was shipped off to board at the elite Highland Manor, which she and her schoolmates elegantly referred to as Highland Manure. I'm sure that my grandparents couldn't afford it and am equally sure that, as usual, my grandmother insisted on it anyway. When Dottie made up her mind about something irrationally extravagant, rationality never had a chance.

Following high school, my mother worked for exactly one half of one day in the shoe department at Bergdorf Goodman, a place she claimed not to have exactly minded spending time in. But she quit just before lunchtime the first day after overhearing two department managers making anti-Semitic jokes. Before leaving, she bought a pair of wholly impractical, bottle-green alligator pumps, the most expensive shoes in the department, and walked out with her red-haired Semitic head held high. Unlike people who actually earn money from working, my mother's retailing career *cost* her seventy-six dollars, and turned out to be her last formally salaried employment for the next forty years.

After about six months of courtship, with another push from Grandma (and after Dottie had chosen the engagement ring), my parents became engaged, planning to marry the following August. But midway, Shirley changed her mind. One night she told Grandma that she didn't really love my father and wanted to break the engagement. In her meekness, she asked my grandmother to write Dad, break the engagement for her, and send back his ring.

But asking my grandmother to intervene in this way was like entrusting Hermann Göring to light your Shabbat candles. There was no way it was happening. Instead, she sprang immediately to the phone, spoke to my father in Texas, alerted him to my mother's crumbling courage, and instructed him to get to New York *tout de suite*. My father was soon on a train, and when he arrived two days later on Riverside Drive—furious and ravaged by love, penniless, and unshaven—my mother took one look at her handsome, scruffy

Romeo, declared her love for him, and far from being canceled, their wedding was instead moved up several months, to October.

After Dad taught at Penn State University, when my parents were ready to move back to New York City in 1952, as far as my grandparents were concerned, there was no question that my parents' new apartment would have to offer security, perhaps a doorman. It also had to be affordable. And nearby. But from Grandma's perspective, everything was too far away, too expensive, too ugly, or sometimes all three.

Then one evening when my grandfather was coming home from work, he stepped from the Broadway subway and there it was, the Apthorp. Of course, he'd passed it several times a day on his way to and from the office, but he'd never given the place a single thought, assuming that the rents must be astronomical. Now, just out of curiosity, he wandered into the rental office to see if there were any vacant apartments, never expecting the favorable reply he received.

Both of my grandparents believed that my father's talent would someday catapult my parents far above their current standard of living, so picking an apartment at the Apthorp seemed somehow appropriate. Dottie felt deeply that we belonged there. It was not as posh as Riverside Drive, with a view of the Hudson River and your own sliver of sky overhead. But it was more than satisfactory.

My grandmother trotted over to the Apthorp rental office so early the next morning after my grandfather's initial inquiry that it was still dark when she arrived with her deposit check. Scurrying so quickly, she lost a heel on one of her shoes en route, but that didn't stop her. She found the super, woke him, and somehow convinced him to let her see the apartment my grandfather had been told about—the smallish one, on the second floor, facing the courtyard, available and waiting.

She sat down on a radiator in the empty apartment and never budged, waiting for the sun to rise so she could make out her surroundings. When it did, she was certain she'd come to just the right place.

My grandfather was usually the one who bet on horses, on long shots, and seldom, if ever, did they pay off. But here was my grandmother, with a new grandchild and a son-in-law just starting out in business, who nonetheless kept telling everyone that someday he would be a renowned writer who wouldn't need a regular job or a paycheck to support his family because his writing alone would sustain them.

Looking back now, Grandma's faith in Dad was nothing short of staggering. My grandmother trusted no one, took no one at his word, assumed the worst of everyone at all times. Through her shadowy lens, Dottie's cracked versions of things usually turned out, sadly, to be true.

But here was her cocky son-in-law, still with the toothpick. He had a way with a wisecrack, but what else did he have, other than an adamant belief that his own talent would end up being profitable?

Against all odds and her customarily unswerving judgment, she somehow swept aside her skepticism and chose to believe in him.

TWO TOUGH COOKIES, ONE RECIPE FOR DISASTER

I can only marvel at the pair of them now, my grandmother and my father, both so cagey and indomitable. They had a great deal in common, although neither would have agreed on that. Dancing brought them together initially, and then they did a kind of dance over the next forty years to music only the two of them could hear.

During the first years all was peaceful. These two powerful forces formed an alliance. My grandparents helped my parents out financially—after all, the GI Bill only went so far. But gratitude was not a mantle my father ever wore lightly, and in this case he knew instantly that, as the recipient of Grandma's generosity, he was at a definite tactical disadvantage. She wasn't shy about reminding him about his debt to her, and knowing him, it must have maddened him to know how meticulously she was keeping score.

In 1998, in *Now and Then: From Coney Island to Here: A Memoir*, Dad wrote:

> My mother-in-law, Dottie Held, was one of those culti-vated, modern women who knew the difference between turquoise and aquamarine. On the other hand, she also knew the difference between sirloin steak and top sirloin,

prime rib and top round, and that only first-cut brisket was suitable for a good Pot Roast.

Indeed, from the very start of his ardent internship of dedicated gluttony at my grandmother's table, this was a man who took his meat, and his meals, unabashedly seriously.

My father was known for his frugality. In contrast, neither of my maternal grandparents embraced reality when it came to money. His went to the ponies, and hers went to whatever happened to catch her fancy for a day or a moment. How they could afford prime rib or *any* rib, or had money to give to my parents, baffled everyone concerned. My mother's favorite cousin, Audrey, a snappy redhead now living in Florida, took to calling Grandma Mrs. van Upsnoot because she appeared to be (and wasn't) rich and had hallucinations of grandeur, but in truth was just posing. As for Grandpa, my grandmother's nickname for him was the Baron of *Haben Nicht*, the Baron of Nothing. She loved to tell all who would listen about how he wouldn't ever let her serve leftovers to him because it made him feel like he was living in a boardinghouse. Ordinarily, when it came to running the show he yielded to my grandmother, meek in the face of Dottie's willfulness, but not on this point. So Mrs. van Upsnoot and the Baron, both of whom had grown up poor a few blocks from each other in Brooklyn, were now living the life of moneyed people when actually they usually didn't have much money at all.

To be fair, Grandma had not had an easy time of it. Born in 1900, being the eldest girl in a family of eight children meant that whenever a new sibling arrived, she was expected to help take care of the baby and the house. Her brothers were typically boisterous, and their father, Max, he of the epically short fuse, would sometimes hit the boys when he arrived home from work in Manhattan as a tailor, then later as a jeweler. If the boys had done nothing wrong, this was merely a down payment for the next time they did.

Grandma's wedding day, when she was just seventeen, was a day like any other, meaning that she had had to get down on her hands and knees as usual and scrub the kitchen floor with newspapers as the family waited together to leave for the synagogue. Then, the second day of my grandparents' honeymoon in Atlantic City, they received a telegram telling them that my grandfather's father had died suddenly, and they returned immediately to Brooklyn. The honeymoon was over, in every conceivable sense.

As a housewife in Brooklyn, Grandma loved entertaining, and presided over many afternoons of card playing and mah-jongg. She was fond of telling the story of how sometimes she'd invite a woman she knew from Corona, Queens, one Josephine Esther Menzer, nicknamed Esty, to come by with her uncle, John Schotz, a Hungarian chemist known for whipping up batches of scented, velvety ladies' skin care creams. Esty worked hard for many years over a hot stove at home, perfecting her uncle's recipes, and when my grandmother invited them to stop by at these card games, Esty sold the ladies beauty products and Grandma said she always gave Esty and John lunch, which they sat and ate, gratefully, off in the kitchen. Esty, of course, turned out to be Estée Lauder, a self-made billionaire, and although Grandma never came right out and said that it had been her egg and tomato sandwiches that fortified Esty to go forth and conquer the frontier of women's skin care, I sensed that at times she felt it.

Apart from the inconvenient habit of always spending just a bit more than they had, my grandparents had other problems. Much, much later, after I'd been born, my grandmother told my mother about her suspicion that my grandfather was sleeping with various models at his Queen Casuals showroom, telling her that she had found lipstick-smeared handkerchiefs and matchbooks from nightclubs she and Grandpa had never visited. Was it true? He was such a docile creature it was almost impossible to envision him initiating any of this. Then again, he was also remarkably handsome. In the meantime, Grandma spent or overspent his money with what can most kindly be described as ebullient abandon.

She even employed a couple from Eastern Europe, Harold and Anna. Clean, quiet, and polite, Anna cooked and cleaned, and Harold was the chauffeur with his own car. Things worked out fine for a few months. Anna was hard-working, an expert cook, and Harold drove Grandpa to and from work every day. The arrangement changed the night my grandparents had a dinner party and Anna and Harold guzzled all of the booze before the guests arrived, then made a scene. In their sozzled merriment, they had also apparently emptied my grandmother's jewelry box. As soon as this was discovered, the police were called, and the two fired employees, reeking of gin, complained to the cop about the stingy, filthy Jews they worked for and what a lousy time they'd had in their employment. As luck would have it, however, my grandmother had happened to summon just about the only Jewish policeman at that time in all of Brooklyn. Harold and Anna took their act to jail, and Grandma got her jewels back. It turned out that they weren't even really from Eastern Europe, unless there's a town there called Secaucus.

In any case, it was clear to anyone within a tri-state perimeter that my grandmother offered my grandfather little, if anything, in the way of affection, companionship, or, heaven forfend, sex, which she counseled me from very early on was something she had only utter disdain for, wrinkling up her perfectly powdered nose and wincing at the thought of it. She was not without her yearnings, her cravings, and her addictions, however, and they proved every bit as tantalizing and irresistible to her as those perfectly proportioned Queen Casuals models parading back and forth in that season's smart white ducks may have been to my grandfather.

In fact, my grandmother was insatiable. Her lust was for jewelry, for antique, delicately gold-leafed china, for furs and cruises to Cuba with her friends, where she'd play canasta as the sun rose and set on her carefree revelry, chattering and happy on the gently rolling, sparkling seas. New York City was dotted with furriers, china salesmen, and jewelers who all turned chartreuse at the mere mention of my grandmother's name—indeed, they practically dove beneath their counters if they saw her or any of her relatives heading for their stores. Her perennial haunt, Jean's, an antique jeweler, catered to her whims for almost seventy years, putting up with her demanding nature, her frequent returns and exchanges, and steely determination to purchase things when she could clearly ill afford them. Armand, one of the owners, who knew my grandmother from the time she got married, told me that she single-handedly had aged him more than fifty years (in only about five) and that she alone had inadvertently invented both the layaway plan *and* the lay awake plan. "I called it that because the night after Dottie took something home from the shop I'd lay awake all night, worrying about whether she was going to return it, exchange it, break it, wake up the following morning hating it, or, mainly, ever pay for it. I let her take things home before they were fully paid because she was very persuasive," he told me years ago. "What could I do? Who could say no to such a woman?"

Well, one man could. And did. Grandma may have been childlike, narcissistic, part Ziegfeld girl, Evita, Auntie Mame, Lizzie Borden, Mussolini, and crafty riverboat gambler, but there was someone who couldn't be bullied by her into silence or submission. In him, she had met her match.

My father, unlike his mother-in-law, had been the coddled darling of his small Coney Island family. His parents, Isaac and Lena, were low-income Russian immigrants who had arrived here in 1913. Isaac, an agnostic with an affinity for socialist politics, drove a delivery truck for a wholesale baker. Lena never learned to speak English proficiently, and so it was my aunt Sylvia, my father's older sister by seven years, who would always have to go to school to meet with Joey's teachers or with his principal at P.S. 188 whenever he got himself into trouble, which proved often. But his kind of trouble was a different sort than that of most of the kids whose mothers were summoned to school: Joey wasn't smashing baseballs through school windows or bloodying noses in the schoolyard, he just refused to pay attention in class. The problem was that whenever he was called on by a teacher, he somehow managed to get the answer right anyway, which was demoralizing for the rest of the class. Couldn't daydreaming Joey at least pretend to be the smallest bit interested, the principal wanted to know? His mother declared, when he was still very young, that Joey had "a twisted brain" and would announce this proudly and often.

The first shock my father experienced was the death of his father, or more likely its aftermath, when Dad was only five. Isaac died suddenly from a botched ulcer operation, and among other things, this put the family into catastrophic financial exigency. Both my aunt Sylvia and uncle Lee, fourteen years older than my father, went to work. Struggling to feed her family, Lena took in sewing, Aunt Sylvia began a lifetime of employment at Macy's, and Uncle Lee made deliveries for a laundry, then worked for a while as a salesclerk at Woolworth's, then as a caterer's assistant. My father wrote that he felt somehow pampered and insulated from trauma during this time, and that the day of his father's funeral he was doted on and spoiled by everyone, given candy and money.

Certainly, it is only mere conjecture to suggest that this was when he began a lifetime of keeping secrets and choking off the excesses of certain difficult emotions. Still, he would only let anyone in so far into this strange place of his acquaintanceship, sometimes a dictatorship, where the currency was frequently sarcasm and a coruscating wit—snarling, brutish, yet often impossibly, improbably, delightfully, and deliriously funny.

A fine example of Dad's brand of humor was when friends of my parents adopted two small boys, younger than I, and one summer, when I was about twelve, we rented a house near theirs on Fire Island.

Fire Island, early sixties

Courtesy of the author

The boys were sweet, shy, and extremely well behaved. Nevertheless, more than once Dad bellowed at them, I think half-joking, while wagging a finger in their direction: "Both of you better behave, otherwise it's back to the orphanage!" They watched him, eyes wide with abject horror. Children had no amnesty when it came to the wicked barbs of Dad's idiosyncratic wit. If you showed up, whether you were four or forty-four, you were on your own, and the precision of Dad's gibes was almost incomparably masterful.

Ten years after Isaac's death, Dad's world shifted again when his brother, Lee, got married. During the ceremony, the rabbi referred to Lena as Sylvia and Lee's stepmother. In fact, Isaac's first wife had died when Lee was only seven, almost right after Sylvia had been born. These two older siblings were actually my father's half-brother and half-sister, only no one had ever thought to tell him. Lena had raised all three children as her own, and Sylvia said it had never occurred to any of them to mention it to Joey. As for Dad, he felt tricked, and some have suggested that thereafter he was engulfed in an anger said to have leaked into his work, already shaped by having lost his father. "I can let myself feel for people, and I can let myself stop feeling for them," he told writer and friend Barbara Gelb in a 1979 interview for *The New York Times*, "Catching Joe Heller." "It's easy, it's a skill—like an ability to draw."

During World War II, after Dad had enlisted in the army at nineteen, the morning he was to report to Penn Station on his way to Camp Upton on Long Island, Sylvia and Lena had walked him the few blocks to the trolley stop. They chatted as if it were any other day, then hugged formally and kissed each other's cheeks in farewell. To me, it sounded like surgery without blood. Especially when Dad wrote in a memoir that he had been "profoundly shaken (and tried not to show it)" when Sylvia happened to mention to him many years later that as soon as he had stepped onto that trolley car and it disappeared, Lena had collapsed, sobbing convulsively, inconsolable. Lena hadn't wanted Dad to detect the ferocity of her emotions, and those many years later, Dad didn't want Sylvia to realize the power of his own.

COLD COMFORT,
HOT BUTTERSCOTCH

*There is no more sombre enemy of good art than
the pram in the hall.*

—Cyril Connolly

I learned to speak and to read early, and at the age of three, garrulous and certainly more extroverted than I have ever been since, I was quite possibly mistaken for being "precocious," which seemed to be a notion my father enjoyed, and it was because of this, I think, that he and I spent many afternoons together. While I was small and Dad's mother was still living in a rest home out near Coney Island, the two of us would sometimes visit her. I remember little of Grandma Lena except that she had dark, thick whiskers on her chin and clammy hands with a frighteningly strong grip. She would take one of my small hands in both of hers, and I felt that if I ever saw it again, the bones would be crushed and dripping with her human moisture. We would take the subway all the way out there, a long ride, and I can remember the hard, cane-woven seats on the train. More than once, some kind of coil was jutting up and out and cut my leg, and when we arrived at the rest home I'd go immediately to the nurse's office. These were not trips I particularly looked forward to, but my father seemed to think my presence cheered my dour and failing grandmother. Her English was still shaky, so we could never have actual conversations, but that didn't prevent me from trying.

Meanwhile, when it came to preserving Dad's good will, whatever was questionably precocious about me at the time proved to be my undoing. I've been told by several reliable surviving family friends that an eerie turning point for Joe and me came one evening when I was not yet even four. My parents were hosting a dinner party. Ted, my baby brother, had just been born, and at some point during the dinner Dad started screaming at me in the room I now shared with my baby brother. My mother and a few guests came in and found my father yelling. "Joe, she's a baby," one friend told Dad, pulling him delicately away from me. I have spent more than a few moments since wondering what on earth could possibly have enraged him so. More likely than not, these family friends say, it was just the first time I had ever disagreed with him about something, anything, and voiced a thought or an opinion that contradicted his own. Suddenly it was open season; I had sailed from the gentle, protective cloak of my father's kindness over to the other side, the angry side filled with sharp-edged antagonism. And it had all happened in the time it took for my parents and their friends to sip their first martinis.

"I don't do children," my father said much later in a 1998 interview entitled "Bloody Heller" by Lynn Barber at the *Observer* in the UK. At the time I think he was telling her that he was not willing to exert the effort and expend the time and concentration necessary to pretend to be interested in other people's children. But I had the indisputable feeling that he was also referring to his own. Because I learned to speak and read easily and early, it was mistakenly assumed that beginning with nursery school, I would blaze a path of brilliance and accomplishment throughout my time there, outdistance the other students with significantly less effort. How do I put this? That was not the case. Not at nursery school, or later on, at P.S. 87.

In those days, there was no such affliction as a "learning disability." A child was either a good student or not. I was dreadful. The more I tried, the poorer I seemed to do. And once I fell behind in class, I was so overtaken by that most primal of distractions, terror, that from then on my poor performance just kept spiraling downward. Guidance counselors were consulted regularly to try to pinpoint just why I was so resistant to learning. I wasn't. I just lacked the tools for understanding how. What was interpreted as laziness on my part was in fact anything but. I was paddling twice as fast as the other kids, but somehow still drowning. Both of my parents were certain that I had "potential." They were just uncertain of what that potential was and whether it would ever be realized. This began as early as the first grade and honestly never changed.

My pal from the Apthorp (and good friend still today), Joey, aka Joe Winogradoff, and I had played together in the courtyard as kids, and we walked to and from school together pretty much every day. We also sometimes came over to the other's house for lunch. His mother, Bertha, was a sensational cook. Mine was not. Bertha, born in Russia, had left with her mother and two older brothers when she was two, living most of her life in Iran (Tabriz, then Tehran) before coming to the U.S. in 1948. When she arrived, she spoke no English, but was fluent in Russian, Farsi, and French, plus a smattering of German and Armenian. She found her way, married an American attorney named Solomon, they had Joe, and then her husband died when Joe and I were in the first grade.

In the third grade, when it became known that Joe was going to skip to fourth grade and I wasn't, a calamity of sorts struck. The simple truth was that Joe was a strong student and Bertha had instilled in him a far greater work ethic. Our mothers were friendly, and we often did our homework together at each other's apartment, so I could see how much better prepared he was for most things at school than I was. Evidently, so could the people who ran our school.

When my parents heard that Joe was skipping ahead and leaving me behind, my mother immediately made an appointment at my father's insistence to go and challenge this decision with the principal at P.S. 87. I can still see Mom as she set out that day, fueled with the urgent wish to right this flagrant wrong. Her defiant errand seemed borne of an oddly uncustomary optimism. It was a mild spring day, and for the occasion she dressed in her best Loehmann's tweed suit, and may even have had gloves on. Her soft red hair had been elegantly styled. Her makeup was flawless. She could not be deterred.

I was busy doing homework at the kitchen table that afternoon as I watched her leave, head held high. She nodded to me on her way out the door, as if to say, "Don't worry, I'll take care of this." But an hour or so later when she returned, her posture was different. It was as if she'd been snapped in half like a twig. She gazed at me with almost unbearable sorrow, her face now a murky sky filled with terrible clouds. She hugged me with exceptional force, and with her coat still on, spirited me up the street three blocks to the blessed halls of Schrafft's, where neither of us could ever stay gloomy for long. This was another lesson her mother had taught her, one she never forgot and which came in handy whenever anything in life hurt or disappointed us, or even when it didn't.

If you were sad, upset, if life had somehow let you down or your luck had just fizzled in some relatively inconsequential way, Dottie's philosophy, passed on to my mother, was get ye to Schrafft's. Beginning in 1958 for us, these outings were frequently teamed with a visit to a neighborhood theater to see *Gigi*, my grandmother's virtual cinematic obsession.

A glamorous, gilded soda fountain with a counter, Schrafft's was a tearoom and bakery, a place where women could dine alone in those days, and partake of an alcoholic beverage and not feel awkward. It was the dowager's Starbucks. The patrons were ladies at liberty, wearing fur stoles with the heads of various pricey weasels with glassy eyes and pointy ears. My grandmother herself owned several.

Our closest Schrafft's was at the corner of Eighty-second and Broadway. The New York City Ballet, founded and run by George

Balanchine, an Apthorp neighbor, was housed directly above it. I thought then, and now, how sad it was that those beautiful ballerinas had probably never gotten to know the high-caloric, lazy splendors of the palace of pleasure directly beneath them, the always astonishing sensation of that first taste of thick and actually *hot* butterscotch in a hot butterscotch sundae, or that first spoonful of cold vanilla ice cream, topped with a slight sprinkle of crunchy chopped almonds, served up in its regal silver chalice. The mostly unsmiling Irish-born waitresses in crisp maid's uniforms would take your order, and regardless of what time you arrived, you almost always faced a wall of elderly women hiding behind hats with thick netting, their stoles tucked around them, nursing an endless parade of Manhattans, draining them to the last dark amber drop. These cocktails were frequently accompanied by a sandwich, perhaps a crustless chopped chicken and vegetable, or else a platter of blue-point oysters. The food often sat untouched.

The day I found myself at Schrafft's with my mother following her letdown by my school's principal, I knew that Schrafft's was my consolation prize. But still, to me, the hot butterscotch tasted sweet, the ice cream delectably cold. My beautiful mother looked as if she might start crying into her strawberry ice cream soda at any moment, but I told her that things weren't really so bad, and at the time, I honestly believed it.

LONG BEACH, SHORT STOPS

In 1956, the summer after my brother was born, I was sent out to Long Beach, on Long Island, to spend part of the summer with Grandma Dottie. My grandparents had bought a small house there, and Grandma planned to stay through the summer. My grandfather toiled away in the garment district all week, and also most conscientiously performed his civic duty by lending support to the nearby racetracks. Grandpa came out to the beach on weekends, along with my parents and baby brother. The smell of french fries and suntan lotion will be forever comingled in my brain, because that summer, at the Malibu Beach Club, in and out of our cabana, those were the two omnipresent smells. In the local patois, we were known as Malibubians, and as such, my grandmother developed quite a social circle there, playing canasta and mah-jongg with a revolving cadre of hapless, well-intentioned victims. I take no particular pleasure in reporting here that she somehow found a way to cheat at both games without being discovered, and that it was she who, in that group, first proposed that they start playing for money. Soon, Grandma Dottie had quite the little racket going.

In those days she was mad for polka dots and roses, and everything she touched, wore, or surrounded herself with had to be one or the other, except for the huge green-and-white–striped awning she put up over her house's front door, making it look like a seaside outpost of Lord & Taylor. Her rose garden was lush, running the perimeter of the house, and she worked hard at it, actually getting down on her hands and knees in the dirt and working up a sweat. My Long Beach vacation was my first real experience with having secrets and practicing duplicity, two hallmarks of the Dottie/Joe dynamic I wouldn't learn about until much later.

Chevrolet manufactured 1.5 million Bel Air hardtops that year and each one sold for at least twenty-five hundred dollars, but Grandma Dottie got hers for nothing, or rather for a dollar, by entering and winning a raffle at her charity, the Manhattan League. The car was aqua (not turquoise) and white, sexy and sassy. It whispered "money" and was my grandmother's favorite fashion accessory. She wore it well. However, both of my grandparents were quite simply the two worst drivers imaginable. She was the fastest, he was the slowest, and both were forever being stopped by the police. Grandma zoomed through every red light, and there always seemed to be a policemen there to see it. There was even one fine summer morning when she took me to the supermarket and got a ticket both on the way to *and* from the store. As the cop was writing out the second ticket, he said to me: "This woman drives like Wild Bill Hickok."

"Grandpa can't know about these tickets," Grandma would say to me immediately after each of these incidents. I certainly never told him. (Nor did I tell him about the one day early in the summer when she had bought three houses and then changed her mind about all three.) As it turned out, several years later we learned that Grandma had never actually taken her driving test. She had simply sent one of the secretaries in Grandpa's office to take it for her and then paid the woman ten dollars to keep quiet. The drama of Grandma's double traffic-ticket bonanza was compounded that night when Grandpa, who had come out to Long Beach from the city, took me for a drive after dinner to get an ice cream cone. When he got a ticket for inching along like a broken-backed snail on Thorazine, his first words to me were: "Don't tell Grandma."

My next important Long Beach lesson, something I failed to comprehend for many years, came about because that summer, my grandmother's mother, Sadie, died. Crowds of relatives visited my grandparents' house every night for a week. In the Jewish tradition of shivah, clothes were torn and mirrors were covered. And there was always too much food.

The day of the funeral I stayed home with my brother, an older cousin, and a babysitter, and then later, when everyone came home, I was given dolls, lollipops the size of guitars, stuffed animals, boxes of Fanny Farmer chocolates, even a small strand of fake pearls from an uncle whom I'd never met. I was pulled from one lap to another, and many compliments were whispered with breath that smelled from coffee, cigarettes, and sometimes both.

When, in later years, people discounted Dad's account of his father's funeral as being fun or at least pleasant, I never did. I had learned that it was possible for a small child to feel happy on the day of a funeral, even if later on the force of the aftershocks proved mighty.

After the summer in Long Beach, it was back to the Apthorp, to Apartment 2K South, and the stifling New York City days. Most evenings my father would come home from work and change, we'd have a small, cold dinner, and then he'd disappear into his room to write. When he emerged, he would take us for a walk where the big prize was a Fudgsicle or lemony Italian ices. If he was feeling particularly munificent, he'd buy a whole bag of whichever he chose and we'd bring them home and store them in the freezer. This was a big deal, the jackpot.

The summer of 1958, we took our first trip to East Hampton, the town on Long Island where Dad ended up living during his final years. Getting off the train there that very first time, I remember red roses climbing everywhere, *more* roses, and the welcome feel of the bright, hot sun.

My parents had rented a little cabin for a week, and nearby, so had George and Miki Mandel, with their two daughters, Mayo and Laurie. George was Dad's oldest friend from Coney Island, and also a writer. We shared a rented car with the Mandels, and even though the Hamptons then were a vastly different place from what they are today, not necessarily for the wealthy, both families were on a strict budget. Our most frequent meal was hamburgers. Luckily, there was a luncheonette in town on Main Street with burgers good and cheap, and we'd eat them practically every night.

Dad and George were kicked out of there a few times for not wearing shoes. Shoeless or not, Miki Mandel recalls that we would all gobble up the hamburgers right there in the car, still at the curb. They tasted best that way.

GOTTLIEB TO THE RESCUE

*Joe Heller and I, for instance, have never had a
bad moment because he is perfectly detached.
When you're editing a manuscript with him, the
two of you can look at it as though you were two
surgeons examining a body stretched out upon a
table. You just cut it open, deal with the offending
organs, and stitch it up again. Joe is completely
objective, he has that kind of mind, even
immediately after finishing a book.*

—Robert Gottlieb,
Paris Review, Fall 1994 issue

When Dad started *Catch-22* in 1953, it was called *Catch-18*. Later,
he and his young editor, Robert Gottlieb, changed the title because
Leon Uris's novel had usurped the number with *Mila 18*. I can
remember nights at the dinner table with my parents tossing out
different numbers. "*Catch-27?*" Nah, my father shook his head.
"*Catch-539?*" Too long, too lumbering. I had no idea what they
were talking about. Thank goodness for Bob, Dad's über-editor at
Simon & Schuster; he was the one to come up with the unremark-
ably remarkable number 22. Along with Dad's redoubtable agent,

Candida Donadio, and Nina Bourne, who plotted the clever, quirky promotional campaign for *Catch-22*, these were the book's earliest disciples. Without them, not only wouldn't there have been a number, there wouldn't have been a book.

To hear Bob talk about it, this modest, soft-spoken fellow who eventually ran Simon & Schuster and then Alfred A. Knopf, and succeeded William Shawn as editor of *The New Yorker*, one might think that *Catch-22* had just tumbled from the skies one day fully formed, and that he had merely been there to catch it. In print he has said more than once that for an editor to call attention to himself and his contributions in an edited book is not only unseemly but irrelevant, but he's not doing it here, *I* am. My father and Bob had real camaraderie and shared an almost mystical respect. No ego was involved, regardless of where Bob's pencil flew or what he suggested deleting, moving, rewriting. To Dad, every word or stroke of this editor's pencil was sacrosanct.

"Nobody ever enjoyed his success more than Joe," said Gottlieb recently, affectionately, and he ought to know, having edited John Cheever, Salman Rushdie, Bob Dylan, Barbara Tuchman, Nora Ephron, Bruno Bettelheim, Toni Morrison, Jessica Mitford, John Lennon, and many others. Gottlieb was one of the few people Dad stood in intellectual thrall to. "Did Gottlieb call?" was often Dad's first question on arriving home once the *Catch-22* machine had been set into motion. Mom's answer, and whatever message Gottlieb might have left, could well determine the tenor of our evening.

"We had a great relationship and didn't have to see each other often," Bob told me. "Between us there was total trust. Like Yossarian, Joe was a complete realist."

Candida Donadio, deep-voiced, intense, and often madly inscrutable, made up the last third of this essential troika working with Dad. When I was a teenager, Candida invited me to dinner a few times down at her brownstone in the East Thirties. At the time she was married, and she and her husband kept birds, huge colorful ones. Were they toucans? Macaws? Forgive me, I do not know my birds. I can only tell you that locked into the bathroom when company came were several enormous, brightly plumed, loudly squawking things. However, Candida and her husband neglected to mention this the first time I visited. When I went in to wash my hands before dinner, it was at my own peril, and I was unexpectedly ensnared in a damp, noisy, faraway jungle in a Manhattan bathroom.

At one point when Dad was writing *Catch-22* (he wrote it for nine years, which turned out to be something of an average gestation period for his books), only once and quite late in the game do I remember him becoming discouraged, fed up with the writing process and how long it was taking to finish. This brief, uncharacteristic bit of self-doubt caused him to actually set the book aside and try to find distractions. I recall seeing him watching television in the evenings, but his boredom and exasperation was immediate. Within a week, he'd become so sullen that soon he was scurrying exultantly back into the waiting arms of *Catch*, telling my mother that he honestly couldn't imagine how anyone survived who didn't have a novel to write.

The Apthorp was where Dad dreamed and scratched and scrawled his slow and carefully chosen, spidery words onto index cards and yellow legal pads. He then typed them onto his rickety machine, hunting-and-pecking his way to more opulent times.

When *Catch* was finally taking off, about a year after publication, my parents, who had now moved us to a much larger, far grander apartment, would often jump into a cab late at night and ride around to the city's leading bookstores in order to see the jaunty riot of red, white, and blue and the crooked little man—the covers of "the book," piled up in towers and pyramids, stacked in so many store windows. Was anything ever again as much fun, I wonder, for either of them? They would come home giddy and very late and go to sleep with their heads still full of the potent magic of a dream poised right on the cusp of becoming true.

"WHERE THE HELL DID YOU EVER LEARN TO EAT LIKE THAT?"

While we still lived in our first apartment, 2K South, like any family, we had our share of routines. Saturdays, more often than not, belonged to my father's side of the family, and that meant frequent pilgrimages to Brooklyn to see my father's mother. His brother and sister and their families would join us and then we'd go out to eat. After Grandmother Lena died, we still went to Brooklyn to see Aunt Sylvia and her husband, Bernie, who lived on Quentin Road, and Dad's brother, my uncle Lee, his wife, Perle, and their son, Paul, not too far from there, on Avenue R.

Our Brooklyn jaunts usually began at Aunt Sylvia's, where we never got to see a single piece of furniture without its prophylactic plastic covering. Year 'round the couch and chairs were enshrouded in thick, cloudy plastic cases. They stuck to us in summer. My father always asked my aunt the same question, namely: "What are you saving this furniture for?" But all he ever got back was a chuckle. As for me, I remember being hungry there once and picking up a ripe-looking peach from a bowl on the coffee table, biting into it, and my teeth scraping waxy plastic.

Of course, I never really had much chance to build up an appetite on these visits. Make no mistake, they were quick, perfunctory, dispassionate charades at best. Saturdays were really all about food. At that point, my father was a man of, shall we say, robust and uncontrolled appetites. His intake was enormous. He could and frequently would eat two entire dinners and then, lurking like a ravenous wolf in the kitchen late at night, polish off two pints of ice cream, quickly, with élan.

Often on Saturdays, though, we would all end up at Lundy's in Sheepshead Bay, a gruesome name for a neighborhood that calls to mind a vision of a sea of bobbing, decapitated, woolly heads. Lundy's seemed to be the size of fifty-six football fields, always crowded and so noisy you couldn't even hear yourself order, which we did in great abundance. Starting with a "coupla plattahs a steamiz" (translated to "steamers"), sandy soft-shelled clams dipped first in hot water to clean them and then in drawn salted butter, we'd gobble them down, usually following them with lobsters, shrimp, and great quantities of hot, fresh-baked biscuits. Dessert was usually just-baked blueberry pie puddled with ice cream.

When it wasn't Lundy's, it had to be Nathan's, and Steeplechase, the amusement park in Coney Island next to the boardwalk.

Either before or after Steeplechase, and once or twice both, we'd make our way to Nathan's, a place my father had frequented all his life, beginning with his childhood in Brooklyn.

My mother, my brother, and I would each have a hot dog slathered in mustard, a Coke, and french fries that came in a cone-shaped cup with a long, thin, plastic two-pronged fork to spear them. At Nathan's, fries received the ultimate compliment: they were so flavorful, they didn't require ketchup.

As for my father, in those early days, before *Catch-22* and the onslaught of vanity that quashed his legendary appetite, he would circle the counters at Nathan's, pacing, thinking, studying it all, eventually settling on pea soup, a hot dog, fries, a slice of pizza, chow mein on a roll, and a hamburger smothered in onions. Notice there was no "or" in that sentence. He had it all, sometimes topping this feast off with a frozen custard and a box of Shatzkin's knishes to bring home to the Apthorp.

We watched him eat, mesmerized, as if he were the prize attraction in some exotic zoo. Once I remember asking if I could have a second hot dog. He stared at me, slack jawed, and actually asked, with a perfectly straight face: "Where the hell did you ever learn to eat like that?"

My father's appetite was celebrated and much talked about among his friends. Norman Barasch, the eminent TV writer, playwright, and mensch extraordinaire, who with his late wife, Gloria, has been a dear family friend for many decades, recalls meeting my parents in the early sixties through common friends.

> My first impression of Joe was his obvious wit, high intelligence, and his grilling me about how much money one could make in TV. I thought Shirley was very pretty, shy, deferential to Joe.

But my father could also be a petulant and determinedly boorish guest. Norman told me that at one dinner party at their home in New Rochelle, my father had eaten plentifully, taking three generous helpings of everything. He then sat around the table with the rest of the guests, grumbling that hosts never served enough food. He polished off four desserts and was still apparently starving and griping about stingy hosts and overly stringent portion control. Finally Norman, in exasperation, went down to his basement and retrieved a huge, rock-solid, frozen leg of lamb, which he then brought upstairs and slammed down onto my father's plate. Even Dad had to laugh.

My father took his eating so seriously that many years later, in East Hampton, when the wife of a writer friend refused to divulge the name of the New York City caterer she'd used for a recent party where Dad had sampled the tastiest chicken salad he had ever eaten, he hounded her for days. She would not relent. Soon, at another party, Dad cornered her husband while the man was standing alone and begged him for the name of their caterer. The husband told Dad that he'd love nothing better than to tell him, but was fearful of his wife's vengeance. Dad never spoke to the man's wife again. Chicken salad could be very serious business.

Dad was a distinguished eater, but he was also gloriously immodest. Right after *Catch-22* came out, he gave an interview to a foreign paper and when he saw the photograph accompanying it, he actually turned pale. It didn't help that the interviewer had described him as "burly." Immediately after, he joined a gym, went to a doctor, and figured out how to drop an enormous amount of weight and keep it off, pretty much permanently. The Locust, the Animal, Hungry Joe, the Beast, all his nicknames had seen his reflection through the veil of vanity. It had a double chin. For the rest of his days, his discipline—when it came to writing, to exercising, and to taking weight off and keeping it off—was sterling. If my parents were going on a publicity tour, he would stop drinking and eating bread and sweets for a few weeks, and then could do as he liked while away without significant consequence.

It sometimes takes nearly an entire lifetime to realize what you have and have not inherited from your parents, especially if you haven't been paying close or serious attention. To this day, for instance, just like my mother, the sound of a telephone ringing (or now, beeping) fills me with potent dread. I'm not positive, but she may well have muttered "uh-oh" every single time the phone rang during her entire lifetime, believing the telephone to be, primarily, an instrument created to deliver news of calamities and tragedies. And from my father I inherited, as I only recently realized, the tendency to growl "no" to pretty much any question put before me, automatically, thereby postponing my answer and guaranteeing sufficient time to properly contemplate and deliver my true response.

Grandma Dottie Held, an inveterate fabulist, oversaw it all, and had her own habits. She would never, at any age, go to see a doctor when not feeling well. "I'll go when I feel better" was her perpetual comment. However, when well into her nineties and bedridden in Florida, she thought nothing of calling for an ambulance when waking up in the morning bored and longing for a bit of fresh air and different scenery. There was no question, mind you, of the merest medical distress; she was fine. Calling 911 was just so much easier than calling a taxi. When I was in my twenties, I once asked Grandpa Barney if he realized how many fibs she told to everyone. "Are you kidding?" he asked, adding: "Of course I do. But I enjoy seeing what she comes up with. It's like watching Rachmaninoff play." Some might call this crazy, but we just called it Dottie.

PART 2

Apartment 10C

Across the courtyard and up in the world

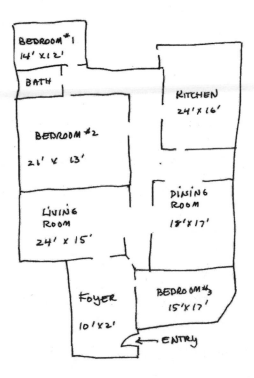

1962–1989

PRACTICE MAKES IMPERFECT

Should you fail to remit payment at once, I'll send my agent over and if you don't come across, she'll kick the shit out of you.

—Note sent from Joe Heller to a
defaulting magazine publisher,
recounted by George Mandel

The year after *Catch-22* came out, 1962, a much larger apartment became available on the tenth floor, across the Apthorp courtyard, and my parents grabbed it. It was huge; in fact, it looked to me as if twenty-seven jets could land comfortably in the living room alone and there'd still be room for a grand piano. The apartment did in fact have wings. In one direction was a bunch of rooms and in the opposite another. The coat closet alone may have been larger than our entire previous apartment.

The living room on the tenth floor seemed to scream "piano," so we got one, a Mason & Hamlin grand with a slightly cracked sounding board. Somehow it was decided that I'd be the logical one to take lessons. So one day, a petite, soft-spoken, gentle Russian woman named Essie Gilado arrived and began giving me weekly piano lessons, poor woman. I recall an endless amount of Scarlatti sonatas and the classic arguments with my parents about insufficient practicing. I struggled a bit learning to read music, although I could play by ear, and I remember having a lot of trouble mastering a particular sonata. One afternoon, right in the middle of my lesson, my father came in. He asked to sit down at the piano bench, then placed his hands on the keyboard and immediately played the piece through to perfection. Essie applauded. I gaped in stunned surprise. He didn't play the piano. In fact, as far as any of us knew, he'd never played *any* instrument. How could he possibly have known not only how to play but also so effortlessly and with such aplomb?

A year later I began taking flute lessons. I was about fourteen at the time and loved the word "flautist," and also found the pristine, silvery sheen of a flute majestic. However, I had to play it, not wear it. The fellow who came to teach me was a man who never took his hat off in the house. He wore one of those "von Trapp" numbers—green with a feather in it.

I would blow and blow and when nothing came out he would start screaming, chastising me that all he could hear was a hurricane. Then one day, right in the middle of my lesson, I suddenly heard the piece I was attempting to play issuing melodiously from directly behind me. Turning around, I was astounded to see my father, once again, this time playing a flute as if he'd played it for years. He'd secretly been studying, he said, so that we could play duets together. That never happened. Eventually I took some guitar lessons but quit before my father could pick one up, master it, and be booked at Carnegie Hall on a night when Segovia was otherwise engaged.

My father was always brimming with mischief. When my brother and I were small, at least once every summer while we were playing in either the courtyard or up in the apartment, at some point two or three snowballs were suddenly pelted at us. Dad would save snow from the previous winter and hide it in the back of our freezer. It was a joke that always amused him when, unsuspecting, we'd get bombed by one of those gray, shriveled ice balls. The bombardier of the Apthorp courtyard never missed his target.

LET THERE BE SHRIMP

The official pub date for *Catch-22* was October 10, 1961. A hard-cover copy cost $5.95 and 7,500 books were printed.

On Sunday nights, both before and after what became known as "the Book" to family and friends, we nearly always had dinner at Tony's Italian Kitchen just up the street from us on Seventy-ninth between Broadway and Amsterdam. It was an unpretentious place, inexpensive, and offered fairly good northern Italian food. To enter we'd walk down a few steps and arrive inside a dimly lit, usually

Tony's Italian Kitchen

empty bar area. Most striking, though, was that the restaurant featured an entire wall painted with a garish mural depicting the Bay of Naples during the violent eruption of Mount Vesuvius.

I have often been asked how the world changed for me, what was different for my family after *Catch-22*, and it's a question without an easy answer. When you are nine or ten you are not, for instance, focusing on *Publishers Weekly*, on foreign sales, or whether there is to be a next edition and, if so, on how large the print run will be.

One of the ways that life B.C. (Before *Catch*) and then after did change for me, though, was articulated in a language involving kicks and shrimp. Prior to "the Book," during the many years we ate at Tony's, if I tried to order a shrimp cocktail, I'd usually receive a sharp kick to the shins beneath the table from my mother. The kick was intended to stop me from ordering this because it was too expensive. Sometimes, to distract me, my mother would whisper that Faye Dunaway or Sandy Dennis was seated at a nearby table. I only had eyes for shrimp.

Frequently, I would ignore the kick. Then my mother would shake her head at me with such seriousness and, of course, attempted secrecy so that my father wouldn't see her, that at times I did abandon the shrimp and settled for a swampy bowl of lukewarm minestrone, the shrimp cocktail's lackluster step-cousin. Often, though, I would play dumb. I'd ignore both the kick and the exaggerated head shake and order the shrimp anyway. Then, with a squirt of lemon wedge, I would solemnly plunge each one into its spicy bath of ketchupy cocktail sauce, mixed with just a bit too much horseradish, and slowly and purposefully bite into each delectable treasure with visible pleasure. At such times my mother would regard me sorrowfully because I hadn't cooperated and had let her down.

After the publication and eventual success of *Catch-22*, the kicks under the table at Tony's suddenly stopped. My shins were safe. Shrimp cocktails lost their elite, exotic status and ordering them no longer brought disapproval or required the cooperation of unspoken pacts. It was in this way that it suddenly dawned on me that my father's book must have been successful.

The minute *Catch-22* was out the staff at Tony's, who'd barely noticed us all the years we'd been eating there, turned slavish and pandering. We were treated to such shameless favoritism that even at only nine years old, with the shrimp flowing freely, I knew enough to be a little bit embarrassed when our meals arrived on a wild gust of unctuousness from the head waiter, Jerry. Now Jerry buzzed around us for the entire meal like a demented wasp, and the food arrived with flourishes, delivered and bestowed upon us like he was performing in some intricate ballet.

I can vividly recall Jerry in his perpetually shiny tuxedo. He had a huge head and jet-black hair with a distinctly over-Vitalis-ed sheen. After *Catch*, Jerry's voice seemed to grow louder. "We have here the big author," he might say, pointing to Dad as he seated other diners, but in a voice faintly edged with sarcasm, suggesting that he might actually be thinking: "We have here the big idiot." He also relentlessly inquired about book sales and foreign projections and occasionally produced a copy of the Book for my father to sign for a friend or relative.

Once *Catch* was selling briskly, my father, too, began to upgrade and ordered steak pizzaiola with its accompanying mountains of spaghetti tinted with watery red sauce.

This, then, is one way that I knew my life had changed. Another way involved travels a bit farther afield. The summer just after *Catch-22* was published, my father was still working in advertising, but he decided to get us out of the city away from the hot weather, to a place decidedly less splendid than the ones we were to visit later on.

How on earth he'd ever heard of Uncle Morris's Motel, right on the highway in Morristown, New Jersey, or if he even *had* prior to depositing us there, I cannot recall. It was a place identical to every other American roadside motel. Everything about it was nondescript, unimpressive, with noisy ice machines that were usually broken, and an outdoor pool that was often closed for maintenance. It served no food. Instead, there was a diner located conveniently just across the highway. There was grass growing around the motel but it was sparse—dead and brown, like chopped hay. The vista comprised concrete, cars, and highway. Hardly a quaint, bucolic getaway.

In the summer of 1962, Mom packed some things for us and Dad rented a car to drive us to Uncle Morris's. He then left us there and returned to the city, Don Draper style, visiting us on weekends. Who knows, perhaps he'd just piled us into the car that day and started driving and stopped when he felt like stopping. Maybe it was that random. In any case, my mother didn't know how to drive at that time, so once Dad left us, there we stayed.

We shared one big room, chased the occasional butterfly, started a stamp collection without any real zeal for it, played lots of checkers, and Mom read tons of books. One can only speculate about how my father was keeping busy at the time, but chances are it wasn't with reading.

In the evenings, my mother would take one of my hands and one of my brother's and, halting traffic, march us across the highway to the diner for supper. I remember steamy chicken croquettes drowning in sticky globs of mashed potatoes. And Coke with lots of ice. My mother wore pearls and smoked Marlboros and I remember feeling, sitting in our red booth, that life was wonderful in that diner, especially when "Travelin' Man," by Ricky Nelson, nasal and whining, was played on our little tableside jukebox. Afterward, my mother would march us back across the road.

When Don Draperstein, my father, showed up on Friday nights, with his trademark Stim-U-Dent stuck into his teeth, he was greeted as a conquering hero. My mother, sleek and striking, would run out to him on her long, freckled, flamingo's legs when his car pulled into the driveway. And then my brother and I would grab Dad as he got out of the car and we'd tickle him and he would tickle us and we'd all giggle until we all grew bored, which generally happened quickly and abruptly.

Uncle Morris, a man whose false teeth clacked like castanets, would give my father a boisterous greeting. "So, genius, how many books did we sell this week?" he'd ask, clapping Dad mightily on the back. Proud that his little, unremarkable motel had somehow fetched a published writer, sometimes he would go and retrieve his very own signed copy of *Catch-22* from the torn corner of the pool table where he kept it. Then he'd read passages aloud to my father, who frequently laughed the loudest whenever Morris got to a part that he deemed particularly funny.

On Monday mornings my father would wake early, drink a hasty coffee, grab a doughnut or two from where they were laid out atop the pool table, and head back to the city to work for the week. Meanwhile, we were parked at a safe distance from him and would spend yet another uninspired week. In this way, he could enjoy his well-orchestrated, extremely compartmentalized life.

The following summer had a bit more zing. Early on, my brother and I were riding our bikes around the Apthorp's courtyard when two of the building's physicians, brothers, both of advanced age and with radically diminished eyesight, zigged when they should have zagged and, in their long, black boat of a Cadillac, overshot the courtyard driveway. The car went crashing into one of the four two-story-high iron-and-glass entryways. The quakelike impact could be felt everywhere throughout the building. All onlookers could see the rear of the Cohen brothers' car, with its front end lodged deep into the lobby. Very, very Magritte. For more than twenty years, that iron-and-glass canopy remained missing and with only three of the four canopies, the courtyard looked unfinished, or just cryptically asymmetrical.

Our family enjoyed the spaciousness of our lavish tenth-floor apartment, which was large enough to accommodate a Hollywood-style Thanksgiving, and at least one time that I can remember, that traditional feast was to be celebrated there, with Grandma Dottie at the helm. When I was growing up, holidays were often spent at the Upper West Side Karl apartment and then later on in Croton, where they'd moved in the late sixties. Dolores and Fred would cook for days, a feast that included Dad's favorite Karl dish, Fred's potato soufflé into which he put a stupendous amount of potatoes.

One Thanksgiving soon after *Catch-22* had come out, however, we were not invited, and this omission was significant, to say the least. Dad was nonplussed and called the Karls and told them—didn't ask—we would be "stopping by" before dinner, and when we arrived, they gave my parents drinks and us juice and produced, as always, lavish snacks. Dad kept looking past them into the dining room where the table was elaborately set for a large crowd. Finally, when it was apparent that we'd not be asked to stay for dinner and that their invited guests would soon be arriving, Dad broke down and asked Dolores, still incredulous: "You're really not inviting us for Thanksgiving dinner? How come?" Dolores, ever the master of the superbly crafted comeback and never afraid of telling Dad just what she felt, was fed up with the excesses of Joe's persona, of the Famous Author, and said to him: "Joe, if I wanted to invite a 'celebrity,' I would have invited Frank Sinatra." Although it was never discussed again, Dad got the message. We ended up eating at a restaurant that Thanksgiving and by the following year were happily back at the Karl holiday table.

But the Thanksgiving I'm referring to now, the Dottie Held Thanksgiving, was a bit later on, when my mother, a burgeoning Francophile, had gone off with a cousin for a week of cooking classes in Trouville, so my grandmother decided to come over and create the classic turkey dinner. While she could cook several things better than almost anyone, turkey wasn't in her repertoire. I remember my brother, Grandpa, and Dad watching football on television while I was presumably helping Grandma prepare the turkey. At one point Dad came into the kitchen to check on us and then stooped down to quietly whisper to me: "We're not going to eat until Christmas. This turkey's frozen." Then he put a finger to his lips in the universal "shush" gesture and tiptoed out of the kitchen. As instructed, I remained silent. Eventually, though, Grandma noticed that after a full day in the oven, the turkey was bewilderingly cold and mostly raw. She finally picked up the phone and called a friend of hers for advice, a very refined woman she knew from the Manhattan League. When she hung up, I saw that Dottie was aghast.

"You dumb bastard, you have to thaw it first!" this paragon of propriety had snorted uncharitably to my grandmother, who related this wisdom to us afterward. It was one of the few times that I ever saw this woman who loved to shock other people so much actually shocked herself.

HELLER'S COMPLAINT

George Mandel: *Do you think, as so many people maintain, that sex is clean and beautiful?*

Joe Heller: *No, and I'm glad it isn't. If people want something clean and beautiful, let them go to bed with a bar of soap. As that eminent financier and movie director Mel Brooks once said, if sex is so clean and beautiful, why can't you do it with your mother?*

—Interview, *Penthouse Magazine*, 1970

When I was about fifteen, my parents went to St. Martin to spend ten days together over Easter and left Ted and me in our grandparents' care. After *Catch-22*, when my parents could afford to travel, they always chose to fly separately, presumably so as not to leave us in an orphaned state when one of their planes fell from the sky. As I got older I wondered about this practice. Of course, their reason was plausible, but it should be noted that during World War II, my father slowly came to grasp the idea that during his bombing missions, people were actually trying to *kill* him. This left him gripped by an intense terror of flying afterward that never diminished. Days before even the shortest flight he would begin to panic: fussing, fidgeting, not sleeping, drinking a bit too much. He freely admitted it. Regardless of what airline he took or what class he flew, the skies for him were not friendly. Further, my mother was not the bravest traveler, either, when it came to sailing through the clouds. She was also a reluctant, jittery flier.

When my parents left for St. Martin it was to revisit a place they'd been once before. On that occasion, they'd been repeatedly attacked on the beach by horseflies, so I couldn't fathom then or now why they opted to try it again.

My uncle Lee, my father's older half-brother, was a talkative fellow who was good-natured but could ask you 197 questions in a minute and a half, all pinpointing the various aspects of nothing. At the time, he worked for the communications company MCA–Universal Pictures. I don't know what he did there, but I'm sure it entailed asking thousands of questions, and even if it didn't, I'm sure he asked them anyway. One perk my brother and I knew that he had, though, was the ability to send free telexes from his office. All we had to do was phone Uncle Lee, tell him our message, which, when our parents were away, we would do every other day or so, and then he would relay it to his secretary and *whoosh*, off it sped. On this particular trip, however, there'd been time for us to send only a single telex because, one morning shortly after they'd left, my parents suddenly flung open the front door and marched in together, having flown home *à deux*, unannounced and scowling, at least a full week early. My mother hovered nervously in the doorway while my father sat down with us, and my grandparents were quickly dispatched home to Riverside Drive.

As for Ted and me, we couldn't imagine what had brought them back so unexpectedly. Was someone sick? Had someone died, we asked. Dad's reply was perplexing, filled with horrifying anger. It had been the telex they'd received from us. We shrugged our shoulders and in all innocence had no idea what we had done. My father removed the crumpled telex from his jacket pocket, smoothed it out ever so slowly, and read it aloud. It said: "WE'RE BEATING OUR MEAT."

I quickly remembered that the Man of a Thousand Questions, Uncle Lee, had not asked a single one when we'd called with the text for this particular telex. We'd found it a bit strange, but at the time had just celebrated what we'd mistakenly supposed was good luck.

Meanwhile, "What the hell's been going on here?" Dad wanted to know. He told us that when they'd received our telex, they'd packed and checked out of the hotel immediately, racing to the airport so quickly that only when they'd boarded the plane did they realize that my mother had left the bath water running in the hotel room and that he had left behind his favorite wristwatch. Still, we didn't understand exactly what crime we'd committed. All we knew was that *Portnoy's Complaint* had recently been published, and we'd heard this expression on TV. Of course, we had no idea what it actually meant. We just thought that it sounded funny.

After this remarkably dramatic return home, all over a misunderstood telex, from then on when my parents traveled we were restricted to postcards and expensive, thus necessarily brief, phone calls.

Our stunning breach of propriety was never mentioned again.

THE INS AND OUTS OF THE APTHORP UPS AND DOWNS

The building my parents returned home to that day had elevators made of rich wood with extravagantly carved walls. Each was appointed with a small, velvet-topped bench inside and an accordionlike gate that had to be opened and shut for passengers. Our elevator operators were often Irish-born women in starched white blouses, with an elaborately stitched "A" on one collar. More often than not, they were a bit brawny and one or two were frequently so marinated in drink, that they barely managed verticality.

In those days, you might share the elevator with tenant George Balanchine, who lived in our wing, and some of his dancers. Over the years, the Apthorp has had its share of renowned singers, actors, film stars, directors, scriptwriters, rock stars, soap stars, talk show hosts, game show hosts, anchormen, news correspondents, writers, bankers, journalists, set designers, restaurateurs, and more psychiatrists than probably anywhere outside Vienna. The Apthorp also housed one state attorney general and at least two Miss Americas, one mustard heiress, and three world-renowned ballerinas. And of course, the aforementioned George Balanchine, who cannot be lumped together with anyone except perhaps the noted ballet dancer, longtime Apthorp resident, and former Mrs. Balanchine,

VANDENHEUVEL MANSION, LATER BURNHAM'S HOTEL, BROADWAY AND SEVENTY-EIGHTH TO SEVENTY-NINTH STREET

Where now there's the Apthorp, there once was a tavern

Tanaquil Le Clercq, who remained in the Apthorp long after Balanchine left its stage.

As for the very spot where the Apthorp now stands, it has always been a catalyst for contradictions. For instance, George Washington apparently was headquartered at the house that stood where the Apthorp is today during the Revolutionary War, following his defeat at Kips Bay. Word came one night that the British were coming just as Washington and his men were about to sit down to dinner and they made a brisk retreat. General Howe and his staff soon arrived, sat down, and ate the meal.

In 1833, a fellow named Tom Rogers, owner of Burnham's Tavern, a genteel establishment on Bloomingdale Road (which later became Broadway) and Seventy-fourth Street, leased the land where the Apthorp now stands from Baron John Cornelius Vandenheuvel, who had built his "country house" here, at Seventy-ninth Street. Vandenheuvel was a son-in-law of prominent lawyer Charles Ward Apthorp, and the house sat at the southern end of Apthorp's massive hundred-acre estate.

Mr. Rogers leased the house for six hundred dollars a year and named his new roadhouse "the Mansion." Popular and lively, it became a regular stop on the Broadway Stagecoach Line. This "line" consisted of one driver and one car, and would stop by once every hour. With a hefty fare of twenty-five cents, this was a luxury available only to the very rich.

William Waldorf Astor, known in his day, from 1848 to 1919, as the "landlord of New York," lived mainly in England, having renounced his American citizenship. For this, he was burnt in effigy in Times Square in 1899 by a violent, bloodthirsty mob.

Most of Astor's previous buildings, most famously the Astor Hotel, were designed by the elite, New York–based architectural firm of Clinton & Russell. When Astor envisioned an apartment building on the parcel of land he'd already owned for many years, he again turned for its design to Clinton & Russell. A twelve-story behemoth, the Apthorp began rising in 1906.

The Dakota had already been built in 1884, and stood in regal splendor at the corner of Central Park West and Seventy-second Street. The Ansonia, a gleaming, sprawling hotel that went up on Seventy-fourth Street and Broadway in 1902, was gargantuan, with four hundred baths, six hundred toilets, a dining room that could serve five hundred and fifty, and a roof garden with goats, chickens, ducks, geese, and a pet bear. The eggs were sold to tenants. The lobby had a fountain with live seals in it and the basement had a swimming pool.

Early days at
the Apthorp

This time, Astor had something a bit more urbane in mind, and no one was more familiar with the style and nuance of luxury than he. His earlier triumphs had been hotels, each larger and more flamboyant than the last. When the Apthorp officially opened in 1908, 104 families moved in, making it the largest residence of its kind in the world.

According to Ronald Blumer, Emmy Award–winning documentary filmmaker and Apthorp tenant since 1983, in New York in the early twentieth century

At the time, living in an apartment building was considered slightly disreputable. These places were called "French flats" and were thought to be the domeciles of randy bachelors and their mistresses. Respectable citizens lived in brownstones, town houses, row houses, with their own front doors and with nothing happening overhead or below that the master and mistress couldn't control. But these houses had their distinct disadvantages.

They were constrained by lot size and in this always expensive city, lots were typically eighteen feet wide and not very deep, resulting in a very limited layout, with light in only the front and back rooms. Only the wealthy could afford to break out of this constraining rectangle. Owning a house in the city came with other problems, too: repairs, the necessity for many servants, and the expense.

The Apthorp, which began construction in 1905, was an attempt to draw the upper middle class out of their houses. It was said to be the largest, most luxurious apartment building in the world, offering residences of ten or more rooms with expansive layouts, individual temperature controls for each room, and restaurantlike kitchens with huge gas stoves and iceless iceboxes fed by a central refrigeration plant in the basement. The building had its own electric generator, huge bathrooms, and, of course, its wonderful courtyard—a rarity in New York City. The apartments were ingeniously laid out to separate the entertaining areas from the private family areas and the servants' quarters. All on one floor, it was upstairs, downstairs, and then some. And in case you couldn't squeeze your visiting guests into your twenty-room apartment, the building offered to rent you rooms on the top floors for guests and their servants. In a short time, given the population pressures, apartment living became respectable in New York City and soon landlords stopped feeling that they had to offer such luxuries, or luxuries at all.

Elizabeth Hawes, in *New York, New York,* said this about the Apthorp:

Although its apartments were very private and richly elaborated—mosaic-tiled foyers, glass-paneled French doors, a Wedgewood-like frieze in the dining room, carved marble fireplaces in the salon—its sheer size gave it a public aspect. There were hundreds of house phones, ash bins, and mail chutes in the building, for example. On the top floor, there were 150 porcelain tubs, twenty boiling tubs, and twenty steam dryers in the laundry rooms—and as many irons in the ironing room.

The courtyard gave the property a distinctly European flavor and was evocative of royal residences, the piazzas of Italy, and the palaces of France. With its fountains and iron canopies, this carriage turnabout was the cherry atop Astor's very lush charlotte russe.

Astor built the Apthorp, but he moved to England and never saw it. Tashkent-born, Israeli-British businessman, real-estate tycoon, and billionaire diamond cutter Lev Leviev, a principal partner at the Apthorp today, had never seen the building when he helped to buy it in 2007. Oddly enough, he, too, lives in England.

HE COULD WRITE,
HE JUST COULDN'T SHOP

When it came to shopping for clothes, Dad knew that my mother could dress him better than anyone in the world. He not only let her, he delighted in it and trusted her completely. It was my mother who first introduced him to Turnbull & Asser in the early sixties, and it was the beginning of a long and very gratifying friendship. But first she had to wean him off Shirt King.

For a time, my mother's most fervent prayer each day was that my father would somehow resist the siren call of Shirt King on Broadway in the low Seventies. The shirts they carried were cheap and virtually all the same. Each was festooned with some large, unappealing motif invariably repeated in rows. But on those days when my father succumbed to the lure of Shirt King, he would arrive home grinning, hoping that this time he'd been triumphant. Like a small boy with a bad report card, he would hand the bag to my mother. She would then open it for inspection, usually already shaking her head "no," even prior to lifting out each shirt with two fingers, as if they'd been coated in poison. I remember one particular batch he brought home. The first appeared decorated with a herd of blood-red water bugs marching along on a sickly white background. The next had the same pattern but with keys—huge, clunky, rusty brown keys. The third was maps. Maps! Maps of the world repeated in brassy colors. The trash was instantly three shirts richer. Against my mother's withering glance, these shirts never had a chance. But Mom made mistakes, too, and wasn't perfect.

My father enjoyed recounting a cuisine-related anecdote about Mom and her early culinary shortcomings. During the year they'd spent at Oxford, when he'd had his Fulbright, my parents invited Dad's don and the don's wife over for dinner. My mother had evidently gone to a great deal of trouble to make sure that the table was lovely and the wine properly chilled. On a limited budget, she was preparing spaghetti and meatballs. Unfortunately, the don's conversation and remarks about T. S. Eliot were so engrossing that while listening to him, my mother stirred her sauce, oblivious to the fact that she was using a plastic spoon. Soon the plastic melted and disappeared into her vigorously percolating sauce. She was mortified, and dinner was relocated to a favorite pub a few steps down the road.

Christmas Eves when we were growing up, Mom would send Dad out to the supermarket to buy a cake or a pie, some special festive treat, and we would wait in tremendous suspense to see what he'd choose. The last dessert I remember was a pineapple cake with orange icing, chocolate sprinkles, coconut, cherries, and green Jell-O blobs in its corners, all topped off by candy canes and marshmallow bits and plastered with big meringue knobs pasted onto its sloping sides, in a bath of strawberry rum sauce. As he disgorged it from its box, we stared in fright. Who even thought to create such a grotesque mingling of flour, butter, and sugar? And who would select such a thing? Surely not even one other person besides Dad. Maybe he thought it'd taste good. Or maybe he just never wanted to be sent out again into the cold to a crowded store on Christmas Eve. If so, he never got his wish.

As far as Christmases went, Jewish or not, when we were children we had superbly decorated trees and stockings hung on the richly molded mantel of our nonworking Apthorp fireplace. And big Christmas Day celebrations with family and a great many presents from my parents and other relatives.

My mother, however, did not always fare so well with my father on holidays. In fact, regarding this, he had a "policy."

He gave her nothing for Mother's Day, claiming each year that she was not his mother, birthdays he usually ignored, and for Christmas, only Christmas, an occasion he always told us he deplored for the "pageantry," he had the curious habit, after *Catch-22*, of presenting her with a royalty check for her yearly Christmas gift, from whatever country happened to roll in right around the holidays. It didn't matter to him if it was a small check or a large one. She got what she got and was, overall, a great sport about this, but I do remember one year when she got Denmark and pouted just a bit.

Another time, I remember her opening her envelope on Christmas morning and her face flooding with sheer jubilance. It was the year she got Germany. Dad was big in Germany.

I always had a tough time with my birthday where Dad was concerned because he flatly refused, every single year, to agree with my mother about exactly which day I'd been born. He thought it was a month, to the day, later. "If you check your records, I think you'll find you're mistaken," he would tell me every year on February 1st.

What can you say after the first few years of this, when the woman who gave birth to you laughs each time and swears by the date on your birth certificate, saying every year, "It's not as if I wasn't there!" And what is there to do a month later when he calls to wish you "Happy Birthday"? If you are five, you say, "Daddy, you're being silly." If you're forty-five, you say, "Thank you." He once went with me to get my passport renewed in East Hampton, and, when I was filling out the forms, said to me: "I don't know why you insist on making yourself a month older." Birthday parties and dinners for me he sat through with some occasional annoyance, feeling that he was humoring us, not for what was taking place but rather when. He felt that just by being there he was adding to the fiction of February 1st. He yielded to my mother's judgment on many things, but on this he stayed firm.

A BROTHER BY ANY OTHER NAME

It was during this time, in the sixties, that a friend of my brother's, a neighbor of ours, decided Ted was due for a name change, came up with one, and Ted went along with it, to my mother's great consternation.

The friend's family lived in one of the three apartments on our floor and we knew very little about them other than the fact that the father, a short, cartoonish-looking man with an imposing handlebar mustache cloaking most of his face, was always seen carrying wooden furniture into the apartment and actually quite closely resembled illustrations we grew up with of Geppetto. The man owned a wood furniture business but whenever their front door was open and we got a glimpse inside, the entire place looked bare. What were they doing with all the tables and chairs he was forever pulling inside? Were they eating them? Converting them to firewood for a non-working Apthorp fireplace?

According to my brother, it was his friend who came up with Ted's new name, Zelmo, which may or may not have come from the basketball player at the time, Zelmo Beaty. Soon, when Ted's friends called the house, they would ask for Zelmo. Even his report cards signaled the change. "Zelmo needs to pay attention more in class," a teacher might admonish. The name change was perfectly acceptable to everyone except my mother, who kept saying that she'd given Ted a perfectly lovely name, and for this reason, seemed directly and personally insulted.

At dinner, sometimes drama ensued. As we sat eating our meat loaf/hamburger/meatball formula (all basically alike), for instance, my brother might ask my mother to pass the ketchup.

My mother, holding the ketchup bottle hostage, would then ask: "Pass *who* the ketchup?" If my brother answered "Zelmo," as he did more often than not, he and his meat paid a steep price and remained dry, ketchup deprived.

Ted enjoyed many privileges that Zelmo did not.

POWERFUL, EVERLASTING
LOVE x 2

*My friendship with the Hitch has always been
perfectly cloudless. It is a love whose month is
ever May.*

—Martin Amis, about his friendship
with writer Christopher Hitchens,
The Independent, January 15, 2007

Apart from writing, I believe that my father had two great and last-
ing loves in his life: my mother and Irving "Speed" Vogel.

Dad took his friendships very seriously and had significant,
enduring relationships with all the people who knew him longest
and understood him best. Most of his old pals are gone now, but
thankfully still around are George Mandel, Dad's beloved lifelong
compadre who went as far back as Coney Island and was more like
a brother, kindred spirits Dolores and Fred Karl, Norman Barasch,
Arthur and Barbara Gelb, and Per Gedin, Dad's Swedish publisher
and cherished confidant. At the top of this list, though, were Speed
and my mother. The more substantive, grittier issues he discussed
with George and with Fred and Dolores, but Speed was an alto-

gether different type of friend. Dad and Speed were alter egos to the end, their personas intertwined.

I believe mom and Speed were his rudders. My mother kept him safe, moored, and Speed kept him entertained. I'm not even sure in what order of importance they ranked. Neither was my mother, but she was smart enough not to care. Speed was a fact of life, and woe to the fool who ever attempted to come between them. A few fools did.

Mom was the one who indirectly, originally brought them together. She had gone to school in Brooklyn (prior to Highland Manure) with Speed's younger sister Connie. When during our first summer on Fire Island she spotted Speed, he was on the beach reading *Catch-22*. She remembered him and introduced him to Dad.

Speed was elegant, debonair, and diplomatic: all the things Dad was not. He was also handy. He could sew a button on a shirt, but also whip up a crème brulee. And he knew the best place to find *cinghiale in dolce-forte* in Florence—wild boar stew with prunes and chocolate—and what day was best to order it, even what time.

Dad and Speed Vogel, the éminence grise who actually was grise

Speed was notoriously calm and often quiet. He'd disappear for retreats in Armonk, New York, studying the teachings of the mystic and spiritual teacher George Ivanovich Gurdjieff. But as my mother once quipped: "If Speed was any calmer, we'd be sitting shivah for him." Over the years, I watched this facet of his personality, his implacability, drive more than a few women into livid frenzies because they wanted to provoke him, prove that they were affecting him by goading him into a loud, high-decibel fight. But Speed was the ultimate cool guy. It wasn't for effect. It was Speed. Dad, on the other hand, was not cool. He gnawed relentlessly at his fingernails and cuticles, and at times, according to my mother, screamed in his sleep, and that was when he *could* sleep.

Irving "Speed" Vogel, the quintessential bon vivant, born in 1918, was a metal sculptor and painter who also did pen-and-ink drawings and created collages from paint chips. He was formerly a textile salesman and married to a textile manufacturer. But when the marriage failed, so did the job. No big deal. He worked for a time for his friend, the architect Charles Gwathmey; then as a herring taster for Zabar's. He was also coauthor, with Dad, of the book *No Laughing Matter*, in which they alternated chapters.

Speed had several marriages but the last one, to writer and college professor Lou Ann Walker, in 1986, Dad said was the one he was meant for. They had a daughter, Katherine, and lived in Sag Harbor, Long Island.

Speed, who got his name because when he was a kid at sleepaway camp he took so long to tie his shoes, was also a founding father of the weekly gustatory extravaganza known as the Gourmet Club. From the 1960s through the 1980s, this club comprised Dad and Speed, along with Mario Puzo; writer and artist George Mandel; Ngoot Lee, another artist and advertising friend; the jeweler Julius Green aka Julie Green; theatrical writer Joe Stein; Mel Brooks; Zero Mostel, and select honored guests. The group would meet for food orgies each week in Chinatown, mostly on Tuesday nights. All wives, mistresses, kids, girlfriends, pets, anyone else, were banned. The location of these meetings was deliberately kept secret, and sometimes after their Chinese feasts they might head over to Little Italy for Italian ices. But the routine almost never varied. Or so everyone was told. Speed, who lived on Riverside Drive, drove his Jeep to pick up Dad, George, and Julie, all Upper West Siders, and then they'd head downtown and park at the Rickshaw Garage in the Bowery.

The Gourmet Club started when Speed met Ngoot Lee. At the time, they shared studios on the block of Bill's Flower Market, on Sixth Avenue and Twenty-eighth Street. One day Speed followed the aroma of Ngoot's cooking and was invited to supper. Soon Zero Mostel, another tenant with a painting studio in the same small walk-up building, would eat with them, too. Eventually Dad was invited and George Mandel and Julie Green and Mel Brooks and Carl Reiner and Joe Stein. Different members were accorded differing status. Finally, Ngoot complained that these guys just came and sat at his table and ate all his food, week after week, and had never once thought to take the poor guy out to dinner and give him a night off.

A Chinese banquet at a restaurant, timed to coincide with Mother's Day, was arranged to properly honor Ngoot, and he enjoyed himself immensely but then moped afterward, telling the guys that here it had been Mother's Day and not one of them had even thought to buy him a corsage. From then on he cooked less and instead took them to his favorite restaurants in Chinatown, places these "round-eyed men," as he called them, would never have found themselves. He would order for them in his native tongue, massive amounts that would disappear. Even though the Gourmet Club usually met on Tuesday nights, if a special guest were in town, like Mel or Carl, they'd either switch to a night that accommodated the man's schedule or else happily meet twice that week.

I've often thought that when Dad and Speed looked at each other they found their missing parts. What one lacked, the other had. Between them no skill was lacking. Their tempos and senses of humor were seamlessly complimentary. Dad worked hard so Speed didn't always have to. Speed cooked and dressed fastidiously so Dad didn't have to. Dad always laughed the loudest at his own jokes, it was his trademark, but other than that, Speed laughed the loudest because it was as if the joke had actually come from this witty Siamese twinlike configuration. My father was mercurial and it was easy to get on his nerves. But in all their years of friendship, I never heard a harsh word spoken between them nor saw even a moment's flicker of annoyance.

MARIO PUZO, AN AUTHOR YOU CAN'T REFUSE

I got my mother on the phone. She speaks broken English but understands the language perfectly. I explained it to her. She asked, "Forty thousand dollars?" I said no, it was four hundred and ten thousand dollars. I told her three times before she finally answered, "Don't tell nobody."

—Mario Puzo, on telling his mother
about *The Godfather* paperback sale

Sometime in the early sixties, Dad, George Mandel, and Mario Puzo started meeting, usually at our apartment, to develop and play a horse racing board game they'd invented called Horses. I remember nights when the living room was thick with cigar and cigarette smoke and ashtrays spilled over with empty red pistachio nut shells. When a game of Horses was in progress, the apartment was under siege. The battalion of men hunched quietly over the green felt game board seemed involved in something that was evidently deathly serious, as if they were defusing a live bomb.

This game, which proved so compelling, consisted of a racing oval and two decks of cards. George, being a painter and collagist as well as a novelist and magazine writer, "designed and created it, in whimsical decoration," as he wrote to me. The guys quickly became obsessed and playing became so seductive that games sometimes lasted an entire night. In the beginning it was rudimentary. For game pieces they used quarters. And since they were playing for money, they were savagely competitive. Soon they invited other friends to join: Mel Brooks, Speed, Alex Austin, Herbie Litwack, Julie Green. They were possessed.

According to Tony Puzo, Mario's oldest child, the only time they cheated was if someone's kid was playing. Then they fixed it so that the kid would win. Early on, Dad started to get bored with the game and wanted it to appeal to adults with a real gambling streak, so he came up with some inventive new ways to up the ante and make winning harder. These changes were adopted into the game's official rules and instructions.

George wrote a full-length piece about Horses for *True* magazine in 1972, explaining the addictive allure of this game and also the probable reason why it was never sold commercially:

> What happened was that we let the whole world play, on battleships, in prisons, even a home for the blind, and there were some Acapulco acquaintances of mine who gave up swimming for it, as well as alcohol and adultery.

In the same article, he detailed the rules of the game, showing the board and saying that all that was needed to play was

> . . . two decks of cards with the same back design, adequate betting chips, a game board (which anyone can improvise), a large-sized salami, abundant rolls or other compatible bread, mustard, halvah, beer, and things like that. The cards, chips, and board are standard, but substitutes can be made in the spoilables. We ourselves often replaced the salami with various cheeses or Peking duck and, instead of halvah, used ices.

I marvel now, thinking back to those times and to the players among them who were writers—not that each one's books took so many years to write, but that any books were written by them at all in their spare time, when not playing Horses.

Mario was a shy, humble man and yet, also, as the entire world knows, a reckless and extravagant gambler, the polar opposite of my father when it came to money. He and Dad had both been born poor but wore it differently. Of course, Mario had much more money, but that probably wouldn't have mattered. My father drove the same tan Buick Apollo, with a brown top usually covered in tree sap and the occasional bird dropping, for decades. It saw him through several books, presidencies, and houses. It got him where he wanted to go. Dad told friends George Mandel, Fred and Dolores Karl, and Kurt Vonnegut that he had "enough money." And that "Enough is all you need," but I believe he worried that he would outlive his money.

Dad called Mario a philanthropist because he provided such constant, excessive support to "needy casinos." Tony Puzo told me that he and his two brothers had estimated, not without palpable woe, that over the years Mario had probably lost at least $200,000 to $500,000 gambling.

He'd leave from his home in Bay Shore and fly to Vegas on a whim, drop forty grand, think nothing of it, and come home. Money was like water to this unassuming writer who gave the world the Corleones. One Christmas he ordered a whole stuffed cooked pig from Balducci's and paid a limo driver eight hundred dollars to retrieve it from the city and drive it to Bay Shore (which was just silly; Tony says he would gladly have done it himself, for a hundred). In fact, when Mario's kids were growing up, he was in the habit of bribing his children to behave. When company arrived, they'd act like angels, all five of them.

The truth was, Mario was far more pragmatic and clever than either of my parents. The closest things to actual bribes I ever got from Dad were, of course, the repeated requests for Grandma Dottie's pot roast recipe once my parents were divorced. When I was still small and then when I was a teenager, he'd also offered to pay me if, when I ever planned to be married, I'd elope and he wouldn't have to go to a wedding. The first time he offered I was only about ten and I had no idea what he was even talking about. He also told me, long before I had any, that I must never expect to introduce him to any of my boyfriends. That he didn't want to have to wonder or think about them hurting me or me hurting them, and that one day, if and when I met someone I wanted to marry, he would meet that person and I had better just hope and pray that he'd approve. I've always heard about doting fathers who live for that special day when they can walk their daughter down the aisle, but my father was just the opposite. That day, if and when it came, he would have much preferred to escort me to the nearest bank to present me with a withdrawal, and had been prescient enough to recognize that in himself decades earlier.

But money wasn't real to Mario. Once during the eighties, I was working at an ad agency on East Fifty-second Street and, after work one night, had gone over to the Doubleday bookstore on Fifth Avenue, a space now occupied by Prada. I was browsing the racks of new hardcover fiction when I heard several of the salespeople greeting Mario. He was a prodigious reader, I knew, always reading many books at a time. Apparently he shopped there regularly, buying pretty much everything. I said hello to him, we chatted for a few minutes, and he told me he had lost about $30,000 of some advance money he'd recently gotten, at a casino in Puerto Rico. I quickly calculated the time it would take me to earn such money at my advertising copywriting job and groaned. "Aren't you sick over it? How can you even get out of bed mornings after something like that?"

He looked at me squarely and imparted to me in a few quiet sentences what his son Tony says was pretty much Mario's *Guide to Gambling, Living, and Losing*:

"Look, kid," he explained, entirely matter-of-factly, "I didn't have that advance money before. Now I don't have it again. Nothing's different."

Officially, baccarat and roulette were Mario's games, sometimes craps. An old friend of mine, Tom Messner, at the time senior vice president and copy chief at Ally & Gargano Advertising in New York, reports having seen Mario at the Sands in Vegas once, in the eighties, during its decline.

> Mario was actually playing dice and roulette simultaneously, prancing nimbly while moving back and forth between the tables. I sat down at the roulette table just to point out to him, at an opportune moment like after a win, that he had actually made a mistake in his book *The Godfather*. "When you have Rocco Lampone do the job on Paulie Gatto, you have him and Clemenza drive back to the city on the Long Island Expressway. That was impossible. The expressway wasn't built until 1956 and the Gatto number was in the forties." He looked at me like I was bonkers, laughed, and just continued spreading his checks [chips] on the roulette numbers.

Whenever anyone in his family reproached him about the lost, gambled-away sums, Tony says Mario would say: "I may be losing thousands in the casino, but I'm making millions at my typewriter."

"Leave the gun, take the cannoli," Clemenza instructed his goon about the hit on Paulie Gatto.

$200,000 to $500,000 buys a lot of cannoli.

BLAME IT ON THE BOSSA NOVA

I was inconsolable early in the summer of 1963 when I heard that we had to leave for Beverly Hills for the rest of the summer. I was eleven years old, and we had just settled into a perfect Fire Island rental. The ocean was close by and I had a great summer ahead of me. Now Helen Gurley Brown was determined to ruin it.

My father had been recruited to rewrite the screenplay for the film version of *Sex and the Single Girl*, and would be paid a small fortune—five thousand dollars a week. We'd be staying at a bungalow at the Beverly Hills Hotel and everything from a car and driver to toys, meals, clothing, tennis lessons, even my father's mint-flavored, splintery Stim-U-Dents was going to be free.

When we arrived in L.A., a car was waiting to take us to the hotel. This seemed very grand indeed, but I was still leery. What was so great about Los Angeles, anyway? The sun was too glaring, the air too heavy, and the grass far too green.

In no time my brother and I learned the delights of something called "room service." We made friends at the pool, took some tennis lessons, and went with Shirley on a few movie studio tours. Along the way, I met Jack Benny, Natalie Wood, and Henry Fonda and went swimming one afternoon with my family in Tony Curtis's pool at his house high up in some canyon, although at the time, none of those names meant much to me. We also went to a taping of the TV show *Arrest and Trial*, with Chuck Connors and Ben

Gazzara, who turned out to be a neighbor of ours from Riverside Drive. I began praying for a glimpse of Terence Stamp. For my birthday party the previous year my mother had taken a group of my friends and me to go see *Billy Budd*, and he was the actor I most wanted to see. Apparently, though, Terence didn't hang out much at Uncle Bernie's Toy Store in Beverly Hills.

Some afternoons when Dad wasn't working we went to see my parents' friends Earl Hamner Jr., his wife, Jane, their kids, and their two dispirited-looking cocker spaniels, Clem and Chloe. Earl had written *Spencer's Mountain*, the book that would later be turned into *The Waltons* for television. We knew them from Fire Island. Earl was from Virginia, and spoke softly and slowly in a voice as warm and soothing as Schrafft's hot butterscotch. He may not have been Terence Stamp, but he did tell the most riveting stories.

I wrote to Earl recently and he sent me back this reminiscence:

> One summer in the fifties, we rented a small house on Fire Island in a community called Fair Harbor. The wives and children would remain there during the week. The fathers worked during the week, then sailed back to the island on Friday evening on the "Daddy Boat." We left at a painfully early hour on Monday morning to go back to the city on the "Death Boat."
>
> At the cottage next door was a family named Heller. As usual it is the children that establish communication, and in no time the Heller children, Erica and Teddy, and the Hamner children, Scott and Caroline, were wading in the surf, building sand castles, digging for clams, and trying to escape the wrath of our two neurotic cocker spaniels. Clem adored garbage and would look for nasty things on the beach to eat. Chloe was paranoid and suspicious of all people and snarled most of the time.
>
> The adults became acquainted over drinks on their deck or ours at the end of a long, hot day in the Long Island sun. Shirley, a pretty, warm, and cheerful woman, and

Jane, an equally pretty, warm, and cheerful woman, became friends immediately. Deep down I think we unconsciously chose our wives, somehow knowing they would tolerate the atrocious demands writers impose on them. Joe and I had chosen well.

On my first meeting with Joe he impressed me with his absurd sense of humor and his affection for Shirley and the children. From the first he and I looked at each other as if we might have come from different planets. The Jewish city boy, born and raised in Coney Island, and the Baptist country boy from the backwoods of Virginia, did not at first seem to have a great deal in common. But then, never missing a chance to drop self-congratulatory information, I happened to mention that I was a writer and had just published my first book.

My novel, *Fifty Roads to Town*, in one of the best-kept secrets in publishing, had recently been published by Random House. Joe then volunteered that in addition to writing copy at *Time/Life*, he also was working on a book. He described the book as a "little comedy."

It was later that year, on the Daddy Boat, that he confided he had finally read my book. "Beautifully written," he said, and then asked, "Do them hillbillies really carry on like that?" There it was—the country boy had written a beautiful novel, but the characters had been hillbillies. I had not known the phrase then, but it was my first encounter with "Catch-22."

Back in Hollywood, my father was being paid by the week and we didn't have to be back in New York for school until just before Labor Day, so he synched his work productivity precisely with our school calendar. We swam in the pool every day, ordered hot fudge sundaes for our friends and charged them to our room, went to lots of restaurants, and were in and out of more cars than I could count.

For my parents, returning to California this way was a kind of triumph. When they'd gotten married in 1945, at a temple on the Upper West Side, they left right away on a train for California because Dad had transferred to school at USC after having been there twice and liking it.

In *Now and Then: From Coney Island to Here: A Memoir*, Dad talks about that trip—how many days it took, how my mother got her hair and nails done on the train, about the week's honeymoon they spent at the Ambassador Hotel, and living without much money in a dingy rooming house. But always present was the exhilarating feeling that at any moment, around any corner might step Judy Garland, Van Johnson, Mickey Rooney, or Dorothy Lamour, even though they never did. Dad also wrote about being met at the trolley by Mom one day, on his way home from classes with his schoolbooks, and seeing her waving an envelope that was his acceptance for a piece in *Esquire* magazine, reworked from his original freshman thesis. And a check for two hundred dollars.

When this memoir first came out in 1998, my parents had already been divorced for more than ten years, and my mother had died in 1995. Yet the tender way my father portrays her and their first years together, along with the stories about the fun they had, screamed volumes:

> On weekend splurges we indulged ourselves in publicized glamorous haunts like the Brown Derby or Romanoff's in hope of catching a glimpse of some movie personality, any movie personality. (We scored only one, Rosalind Russell, and I would never have recognized her because of her tiny chin, but my Shirley did.)

"My Shirley," written by a man who might literally take years to craft a sentence and certainly didn't use any, certainly not these words, lightly.

But in 1963 they were back and seemed to be the darlings of L.A. Dad was being paid big money to dawdle over a movie script that didn't especially interest him. And this time around, my parents were at the Beverly Hills Hotel, not Mrs. Hunter's rooming house. (That sour-smelling place where the proprietress spent her days madly trying to convert my mother to Christianity while my father was in class.) They hadn't done too badly, really, after all. My mother had seen Sophia Loren in the hotel beauty parlor and sat next to her at the dryers. By the end of the summer, just as it was time for us to go back home to school, after being tanned and pampered and spoiled for two entire months, amazingly enough, Dad would type "the end" on his screenplay and we'd head home.

As for me, I hadn't seen any celebrities who meant anything to me and was extremely disappointed. The summer was winding down. Then, on our very last day, when we were all packed up and ready for the trip home, as we stood and waited for the car to come for us, I looked down the gravelly path for the very last time and saw something almost too spectacular to be real. Or some*one*: coming toward us were Eydie Gormé, singer of the hit "Blame It on the Bossa Nova," and her husband, Steve Lawrence, his hair pouffed up very high. Without thinking, I ran up to her and said: "I love you, Eydie," the exhilaration in my voice uncontainable, and then hugged her around the waist with such force I nearly tackled her to the pavement.

It was time to go home.

OF BOMBS AND BOMBOLONI

The past is the only dead thing that smells sweet.

—Cyril Connolly

When I was fourteen and my brother ten, in 1966, our parents took us to Europe for a summer of misery, unrelenting boredom, and torture. We suffered at places like the Ritz in Paris and the Gritti Palace in Venice while riding around in chauffeur-driven cars, and eating in the finest Michelin-starred restaurants. How could we have been punished so mercilessly? (And what, oh what, might I do now to be punished that way again?)

Dad was on assignment for *Holiday* magazine to go back and write about Corsica and the parts of Italy where he'd been stationed during World War II. He was also to meet with his editors at Bompiani, his Italian publisher, so we had been booked on a luxurious, all-expenses paid trip. Suddenly we were packing to go on the elegant SS *Raffaello* in first class. Meanwhile, I was the consummately bratty kid. I wanted to stay home and be with my friends. I nagged and whined and threw tantrums, hoping that somehow I might be allowed to stay behind with my grandparents for the summer. But I was doomed.

The trip across the Atlantic, in July, would take almost a full week, and when we arrived in Genoa we were to be picked up by the Karls, Dolores and Fred and their three young pigtailed daughters. The Karls were among my parents' oldest and dearest friends. Fred was a biographer, a Conrad and Faulkner scholar, among other things, and the Karls had spent one of Fred's sabbatical years from teaching at City College in France and were now spending the second in Italy. They had rented a house in Viareggio and we were to be stationed in the next town over, in the glittering, rarefied sunshine of Forte dei Marmi.

Once our ship left the Italian Line pier on the Hudson and was out at sea, my brother and I began playing Ping-Pong, and Dad always said afterward that we had played it right across the Atlantic. My always pretty mother now appeared splendidly glamorous, dressed up for dinner each night in the ship's formal dining room. My father begrudgingly wore a tux to dinner—he had little choice—but even though he was sardonic, bored, and faintly irritable, he turned out to be the life of the party at our table every night.

Ted on the SS Raffaello

Courtesy of the author

Meanwhile, the adorable young Italian waiters in their spanking white jackets all giggled when my mother spoke to them and I caught one of them blushing while trying to look down her celery-colored evening gown as he bent to serve her baked Alaska.

The ship offered Italian lessons in the afternoons in an enormous theater, and showed movies there at night, films like *Nevada Smith*, with Italian subtitles. My brother, Ted, remembers multiple showings of the Jane Russell movie *Waco*. I remember *Foxfire*, also with Jane Russell, whose indomitable chest was a frightening vision to a tender-aged girl.

Meanwhile, the only Italian I was interested in learning was *"Mi dia un sorbetto d'uva, per piacere,"* which is what I ordered: grape sherbet, morning, noon, and night, a delicacy I had never seen anywhere before and have never found anywhere since.

Each morning when we awoke, we found a little scrap of paper slipped underneath our cabin door, with the daily weather forecast. "It is raining. The sea is rough," it read one day, with the likely temperature range, in Celsius, listed next to it.

Once we arrived in Italy, we spent two months traveling, making trips to many places but always returning to the swanky but modest Hotel Byron, a little jewel in Forte dei Marmi. There were days when Henry Moore came to the hotel for lunch and we all sat outside, but of course I didn't know who Henry Moore was or what was so special about the enormous hunks of stone he selected from the nearby Carrara marble quarry. Or why any of the other world famous sculptors were said to have traveled there for the foundry. I couldn't really imagine why anyone would willingly travel there at all. I was homesick and bored. It was too hot. We had no television anywhere and no air-conditioning, and every two days or so we had to pack and be driven in some stifling car to some other hot, airless location.

On our days actually spent at the Byron, if we looked out our windows early in the morning with their crisply turned striped awnings, we could see right across to the beach as it was being swept and vacuumed, made so clean it seemed to almost glimmer in the sun. Late morning, matching striped beach chairs, hundreds, were put out in neat, perfect rows, at attention, like soldiers awaiting battle.

Every afternoon at precisely four o'clock, a seemingly ancient, sun-wrinkled little man would come around to the beach. Wearing battered, faded red sandals, he sold *bomboloni*, balls of crisply fried dough, dusted with sugar, hot in your hands, ambrosia in your mouth. Each day he wore the same radiant, toothless grin.

This was where we kept coming back to from Rome, from Florence, from Venice; from Bastia in Corsica, where we stayed in a creepy hotel that had not yet been finished—no toilets—and ate nothing but ham sandwiches and Coke that was hot from sitting in the sun for days in its bottle. We watched armies of salamanders slithering up our walls.

On one trip back from Rome, Dolores Karl remembers us arriving with a surprise for her and her family.

> One time when all of you were coming back from one of your trips out of Forte dei Marmi, you got off the train, got into a horse-drawn carriage, with not one horse but two, and before you went back to your hotel, Joe had the driver bring the horses and carriage right up to the windows of the house we were renting, and all of you were singing "O Sole Mio," as Fred ran to the window calling for the rest of us to come and see. We all stood there laughing like maniacs for at least ten minutes before you drove away to your hotel. Everyone from all the surrounding houses on our street came outside to see what was happening. Even now I can still see the laughter on everyone's faces.

In the evenings there, the Karls would usually come and fetch us and we'd all stroll around Viareggio, along the pier. According to Dolores:

> Fred used to say about that time: when we got into our car at night, he didn't even have to turn the steering wheel—it automatically turned toward your hotel. Don't you remember

the walks we used to take, almost every night after dinner, around Forte dei Marmi? Joe and Fred would usually walk ahead. We'd pick out a place to stop and have ice cream, and Shirley always wanted to stop in many of the shops so she could hear Italian spoken. I remember that time so well.

There was one thing on this trip that was irresistible, even to sullen, cranky me. It was the advertising planes in Forte dei Marmi that sometimes flew over us in the afternoons at the beach. One would come, seemingly from nowhere, trailing an ad behind it for a product—shampoo, candy, or toothpaste—and just as the plane flew over, down would rain a thick shower of goodies in plastic pouches containing a sample of the product, like parcels of treasure from the heavens. Every kid on the beach or already in the water would then try to retrieve one.

Now I'm wondering what Dad, a bombardier in World War II in Italy, must have thought as he watched those planes fly overhead, dropping their harmless, frivolous cargo. I asked Dolores if he had ever commented on it, but not surprisingly, she said no. Then I asked if during that trip to Italy, when we'd stayed for months, Dad had ever spoken about the war to her or to Fred. Her answer was instantaneous. "Joe never talked to us about his days in the war. We never asked him about it because we saw other people asking him to talk about it and he never would. 'No,' he'd say, 'everything I have to say about the war is all in *Catch-22*. I don't talk about it.'"

Apart from its endless selection of filigreed earrings, I could detect nothing then about Florence to merit our constant trips there, staying at the overcrowded Continental Hotel, laid practically at the feet of the Ponte Vecchio. Michelangelo, at that point, held no charms for me, nor did the fancy and festive lunches we sometimes treated ourselves to at Sabatini's when we'd hit town. Meanwhile, I nagged my parents every day, trying to get them to bring us home early, but that was not about to happen.

At one point we went to Lake Como and stayed at the Villa d'Este, so exquisite that even *I* had to work extra hard to seem blasé.

Looking back now, I can see that I was just impossible. The only time I laughed was when I really couldn't help myself, and that was when our very fussy, stilted waiter, when asked what accompanied the chicken that night, answered: "Mice." We made him repeat it three times and were on the edge of hysterics before Dad explained to us about maize. This was also when my little brother opened his mouth to ask a question that I still love to recall: "So who's the guy on the t in all the churches?" After clarifying his question, my parents explained to him about Jesus Christ. For me, though, he will always be the guy on the t.

Rome was dirty and noisy; it reminded me of Broadway. We didn't like the spaghetti, so we ate club sandwiches. At one point my mother went to get her hair colored in the hair salon at our hotel and midway phoned us because the non–English speaking colorist, misunderstanding my mother's request, had dyed her hair an arresting shade of bright purple. It was being corrected, but she would be late for the dinner reservation we had at a nearby restau-

A rare smile, Europe, 1966

Dad admires the Italian scenery, 1966

Courtesy of the author

rant. My father rushed us downstairs to the lobby and we sprinted to the salon just in time to be able to see my mother's hair transformed from an electric eggplant hue to the color we knew.

My parents dressed up and sometimes went out together in the evenings in Europe, and when I look back now I think they must still have been very much in love. They were not demonstrative, but they whispered a lot and laughed together often at private jokes. Sometimes I'd catch my father staring at my mother, looking as if he'd never in all of his life seen anyone so marvelous. They had a secret language, one not taught in theaters aboard majestic foreign ocean liners.

From Italy we traveled to France. Someone at *Holiday* magazine had arranged for us to have a car and driver, François, in a black fishnet shirt, who kept stopping at cafés for liquid refreshment, then driving faster and faster, taking hairpin turns while turning around to the back to speak to my mother, Ted, and me. I think he thought he was on the Stelvio. Meanwhile, by the time we arrived in Paris, my mother's face was quite nearly the same shade of purple that the Roman colorist had dyed her hair by mistake.

In Paris, we stayed at the Ritz. Mom went to a tailor she'd read about near the Arc de Triomphe and then we went up to the top to look out over Paris. For the flicker of a single moment I forgot to be phlegmatic. I was finally overcome by what I saw and was dizzy with almost incomprehensible joy, but I didn't let on to my mother. In a taxi later that afternoon, we happened to pass the Eiffel Tower as I was plunged deep into the by now almost crumbling pages of the copy of *Seventeen* magazine I'd dragged with me from home. As we drove past the Eiffel, my mother suddenly poked my arm, in weary exasperation, pleading with me: "Look, *please*, at the Eiffel Tower."

By the time we reached Paris, my poor parents were anything but amused

As for my father, to his extraordinary credit, he didn't completely give up on me until the following week when we reached Nice and I had them paged in a casino late one night, telling them that Ted and I were both very sick. For some reason, I had suddenly become afraid that they were going to gamble away all our money and we wouldn't have enough to get home. After that, he dealt with me differently. He was irate. Here they had been given the free trip of a lifetime and his ingrate adolescent daughter continued ruining every place, every stop, each meal, each moment.

From there, it was back to Italy, to Venice, where it was crowded and my mother didn't like our rooms at the Hotel Gritti Palace, so we changed them. One late afternoon, my father and I sat on the terrace of the hotel, overlooking the Grand Canal. I fanned myself melodramatically with a menu and he drank a Cinzano as he tore open the many boxes of mail that had just arrived from New York. He went through hours of it, silently, then opened something and, reading it, winced. Then he opened something else and winced again. He cleared his throat and reached into his jacket pocket for a Stim-U-Dent. He was quiet for a few moments, but then said to me: "I've just read your report card and it's a disaster. And I got a cable from my stockbroker that, if possible, was even worse." He had lost some large amount of money on something, perhaps Xerox or IBM. Then he suddenly clutched one of my hands resting on the table: "Do you want to go home? Do you really want to go home? Because if you do, I'm ready to send you. All alone. On a big ocean liner for a week. By yourself. I'll take you to Genoa this week and put you on and you can kick and scream the whole time. I'll be in London and won't care. Is that what you want? What do you say?" he asked. Finally I mumbled: "Well, I guess I'll stay." He stared at me coldly. "Well, I guess you will."

From Italy we went to Switzerland, a place I found very silly altogether, an observation I kept utterly to myself, and then on to England.

In London we saw Carnaby Street. Mom and I went to Biba, and we all had tea at Fortnum & Mason while I peeked around every corner hoping to see George Harrison. We also visited Madame Tussauds and ate very salty Chinese food upstairs somewhere, over a funeral home.

Then, finally, after months and months, we reached Southampton and boarded the SS *United States* for the long trip home. At last I was happy. I couldn't stop smiling. There were no adorable waiters, just big, beefy, red-faced ones, but that was okay. Then the ship sailed into a terrible storm and throughout our second, third, and fourth days and nights the entire ship lurched from one side to another. The furniture was all strapped down. Thousands of passengers, us included, stayed in their cabins throwing up, praying for instant death. We were not that lucky.

On the fifth day, weak but no longer queasy, Dad and I ventured tentatively up to the dining room. There sat all our waiters, smoking and playing cards. Dad and I asked if we could have something to eat. They gave us cheese sandwiches and sang us some Irish songs just as the sun started to poke through the brightening clouds.

Louvre, 1966. Mom looks at art. Dad looks at Mom.

As for my family and our summer abroad, we arrived home and into New York harbor early in the morning and passed right by the Statue of Liberty. Thousands of passengers applauded. We were finally, at long last, home.

When we reached the Apthorp, the place had never looked so beautiful to me. I cherished every crevice. Stepping from the cab with our many suitcases, my brother actually got down on the ground and kissed the pavement inside the front gate.

I shared his enthusiasm, but had not the slightest inkling that soon, very soon, it would be raining.

And the sea would be rough.

DID I DARE TO EAT A PEACH?

When the time came for me to switch from grade school to junior high in 1964, both of my parents refused to accept reality, preferring to believe somehow that even with my terrible grades and report cards that the posh New York City private schools would throw open their doors and accept me with open arms of cashmere.

My parents had decided that since my father was now a successful author and we were living in a grand Apthorp apartment, the appropriate school for me would be a private one. They contacted schools and went to a great many interviews. I lost track: Brearley, Spence, Birch Wathen, Walden, Columbia Grammar, Calhoun. None tossed us a crumb. And then someone mentioned the New Lincoln School, private but progressive, up at 110th Street, at the northern tip of Central Park. My father was sent ahead to scout the territory like a canary in a mine.

Remarkably, I started there in seventh grade and stayed until it was time to go off to college. A little more travel was involved than I was used to in getting to and from school each day; two, sometimes three buses each way. My third day on the Central Park West bus I happened to notice a man hiding behind a newspaper at the back of the bus and discovered, with incredulity, that it was my father. He'd been following me to school every day that week to make sure I knew where I was going and that I reached there safely.

During the years at New Lincoln, I fell passionately into a

classically unrequited love with my mysterious, avant-garde music teacher. I wallpapered my Apthorp room with tin foil and put red bulbs in my lamps, and began to iron my curly hair straight and Scotch tape my bangs every night before going to bed. I spent evenings on the phone with my friends. Although I wasn't especially interested in my education, my father was, and when I told him that I'd enrolled in a class in the ninth grade to study James Joyce, Thomas Mann, and T. S. Eliot, and he saw me reading *Finnegans Wake, Buddenbrooks,* and "The Waste Land," he went berserk and arranged to see the school headmaster. Dad felt strongly that throwing these writers at us at such a young age was merely New Lincoln's way of competing with other private schools and that by introducing us to these authors now, they would be spoiled for us later. He had a point.

By this time, Dad was teaching writing classes at City College and then at Yale.

There were many celebrities' kids at New Lincoln when I was there, but I certainly didn't feel like one of them. Somehow coming back to the Apthorp every day helped to keep me grounded, because most of my friends lived on either Fifth or Park Avenue. The Upper West Side was still suspect, although Central Park West was different, a bit like Fifth Avenue Lite. Susan Sontag's son, David Rieff, was in my class. In other grades were Zero Mostel's kids, Viveca Lindfors's son, and my friend Christopher Rauschenberg, Robert Rauschenberg's son. To me, my father was a teacher who had written a war book, no more, no less.

I had little interest in my classes, cut school a lot, and there were many hastily arranged parent-teacher conferences, but I couldn't deny that New Lincoln had some fascinating people who did intriguing things. On Christmas Eve in 1969, for instance, I went down to Park Row to visit Chris Rauschenberg at his mother and stepfather's place. Together with friends, we spent the entire night constructing a huge floor-to-ceiling foot out of chicken wire and papier-mâché. In the morning when it dried, we spraypainted its toenails.

©Christopher Rauschenberg

Big Foot—Christmas in high school with Chris Rauschenberg and friends

The late Warren Cassell, my seventh grade teacher and mentor, I credit single-handedly with getting me through high school. He wrote this to me last year:

> As you know, there were many progeny of celebrity parents at New Lincoln and, of course, you were one of those children, but I know you didn't feel you were among them.
>
> *Catch-22* was published in 1961 to mixed reviews, but it became one of my favorite books of all time—and, of course, to many other readers as well. When you landed in my class a few years later, you probably could have done nothing wrong, and I eagerly looked forward to parent conferences that year. Who knew that your dad would show up for the meetings! Was his celebrity so overpowering that I didn't think in terms of you having a mother? Not to give short shrift to your work and progress in school, but I did spend much of our conference time talking with your dad about *Catch-22*. You were doing just fine as far as I was concerned, and besides, how often would I get to talk to the author of my favorite book?

Several decades later, the very same Mr. Cassell had the pleasure of introducing Dad at a meet-the-author event at the bookstore he by then owned and ran, Just Books, in Greenwich, Connecticut. It was a highly respected fixture in Greenwich for many years, and more than a few people I know were bereft when Mr. Cassell retired in 2001.

While in the tenth grade, at one point I somehow diverted my attention from my music teacher and developed a crush on a classmate with a penchant for wearing Sgt. Pepper jackets. He had a wonderfully crooked sense of humor, which reached its full teen-age crescendo one evening as we spent the whole night talking on the phone. The sun set and the sun rose and on we burbled. The next night he invited me to go out with him for Chinese food with his favorite uncle, who happened to be Gene Wilder. The three of us had what I thought was a more than agreeable time, and then the next day at school, I asked my friend, as shallow, insecure, and narcissistic teenagers will, what his uncle had thought of me. My friend answered dryly: "He thought I could do a lot better."

I steadfastly boycotted Gene Wilder's movies for a good thirty years following that evening, until, as circumstances had it, my school friend and I happened to meet up once again. When I reminded him of the Chinese dinner and his uncle's assessment of me, all my friend could do was chortle. "I was teasing you," he told me then. "He never said that." I hastily arranged a Gene Wilder-thon for myself to make up for lost time.

There were frequent protests against the Vietnam War at that time, and it seemed that my New Lincoln class was always piling onto a bus and heading down to Washington, D.C., to take part in demonstrations.

My father, the aggressive provocateur who in reality claimed to care little about politics and the war and would eagerly tell people how he had never voted, told me repeatedly that these protests were a waste of time and energy. Imagine my surprise, then, when, on one of those trips, on a numbingly cold day, as I was lying in front of the Justice Department being teargassed, I happened to glance upward and there, just across the street, was my father, high up in a tree with Speed Vogel. He saw me see him. In the midst of all the chaos and burnt smoky air, I was hoping to get a ride back to New York with them, but no such luck. When the smoke cleared they had already gone.

One day soon afterward, Dad and Speed went to a pet shop in Queens on a whim. I'd begged for a puppy for years, and the entire subject was always postponed. Now Speed had gotten a basset hound and Dad a beagle.

Both puppies were named for Beatles songs. Our dog, Lucy, became a cherished part of our family and when she sprained her back and was paralyzed a few years later and had to be put to sleep, Dad ran to a coffee shop and got an order of bacon. He arrived at the vet's an hour before it was going to be done in hopes of tempting her with the bacon. But Lucy was too far gone. Dad came home with the bacon still wrapped in a crumpled paper napkin in his coat pocket. "If she had only recognized me or taken one bite of bacon, I would have brought her home," he told us. The house became a tomb for months after as we mourned her. Once, Mom walked by the hallway coat closet and thought she heard a strange, muffled sound. She opened the door to find Dad inside, crying. Against animals, he had no defenses.

Some time later, when we all began to feel that this state of doglessness was close to unbearable, we settled upon the idea of a Bedlington terrier. We went in a taxi to Staten Island one Sunday to retrieve a pup whom we named Sweeney, as in: *Tell it to* . . .

As Sweeney matured, Dad and he increasingly began to resemble each other. To accentuate their whitish gray, puffy topknots, Dad bought them matching red turtleneck sweaters. He doted on Sweeney in ways fascinating to witness. He talked baby talk to him, took him everywhere, walked him constantly, brushed and combed him every day and night right there on his desk, and in a supreme gesture of affinity, wiped his post-walk bottom religiously with a premoistened Tucks pad on their return home.

Meanwhile, with the specter of college looming, things did not look especially bright. I'd found math and science hopeless; but En-

Dad and his canine doppelganger, Sweeney, in the seventies

©Nancy Crampton

glish? In my junior year, my PSAT scores were so pitiful that I was sent to SAT tutors, two Dalton teachers, eighteen hours a week, in an effort to raise those numbers even infinitesimally. All day Saturday, all day Sunday, and every afternoon after school I sat, bent over my books. I worked hard and, Lord knows, so did the tutors.

My high school guidance counselor, the woman responsible for advising me on where to apply and ushering through my applications, was deeply concerned that she would not be able to place me. Anywhere. While my friends were visiting the Seven Sisters and talking about safety schools, I kept quiet. At New Lincoln we didn't have standard report cards but had evaluations instead. This was almost worse for me, because there were unlimited pages for the teachers to detail my vast range of academic shortcomings.

When the time came for appointments with our guidance counselor, we found that she'd scheduled us last. Mom, Dad, and I sat glumly out on the bench in the hallway as student after student, accompanied by one parent or both, filed in and out of her office, leaving with long mimeographed sheets of suggested schools, safety and otherwise, talking to one another with excitement.

When our turn came, the counselor explained that things were grim, but not necessarily hopeless. There was a school, actually a junior college, with an agricultural program: Itawamba Community College, in Fulton, Mississippi, which *might* be persuaded to accept me, on a trial basis. She handed Dad the little scrap of paper on which she'd written the school's pertinent information. "This name looks to me like the letters on an eye doctor's chart," he grumbled.

She nodded. What else could she do? We sat, stunned, silent. At last, my father fiddled with his Stim-U-Dent and, with barely disguised truculence, asked her: "Do you really think I paid tuition here all these years so that you could send my daughter"—pronounced "dawda"—"somewhere to learn how to grow fucking corn ("cawn")?" Needless to say, this meeting was even shorter than my college list.

What happened in the end was that Dad, in his way, came to the rescue. That year he was on a tour promoting his play, *We Bombed in New Haven*, which required that he speak at many liberal arts colleges and universities. This gave him an overview, and there was one, in the Midwest, smallish, good people, maybe, just maybe . . .

Mr. Cassell left New Lincoln in 1967 and I graduated in 1970, but I still credit him with the remarkable fact that I made it all the way through, for supplying the necessary momentum. As for his lovely Connecticut bookshop, a place he described as having been a "Dickensian refuge for the overprivileged, the literary, and those seeking intelligent Jewish help on their book selections," after he closed it, he moved with his wife to Portland, Oregon.

As for New Lincoln, it eventually merged with another private school and relocated to the Upper East Side. Then it closed. In its place today, at the northern edge of Central Park, sits the Lincoln Correctional Facility, a minimum-security work-release center.

If the view is lost to me, the joke is not.

MIKE NICHOLS,
A SUNDAY MORNING, AND THE
WRITER FROM CONEY WHO CRIED

One rainy Sunday morning in 1970, both parents were home and I had a few hours before I had to surrender myself to the SAT authorities, the Dalton tutors. The phone rang and my father got it, spoke in a low voice, and then told me that we had to dress quickly. The film version of *Catch-22* was ready, and Mike Nichols had called to ask us to come to a screening. My father was uncustomarily nervous. Although Buck Henry had written the screenplay, this was still Dad's baby, and he was about to see whether it had made it across the Santa Monica Freeway in one piece. Although he didn't stand to gain financially (he had sold the film rights for $150,000), his reputation was still in some overriding way being tested.

This occasion was so important that it was decided that the Dalton tutors could do without me that day. We piled into a cab and in the pouring rain headed down to Times Square and up into a seemingly deserted office building. The doorman unlocked the elevator for us, we went upstairs, and Mike Nichols was waiting. Dad and Nichols chatted briefly, and then my father took a seat, alone, in the front row, while we sat somewhere in the middle. Mike Nichols stood at the rear. We watched the film, and several times during it my mother reached for my hand and squeezed it. When the lights came back on, my father sat and conferred with Nichols. He looked relieved: The patient would live. On the cab ride home, Dad started to cry. He was so elated, he put two Stim-U-Dents in his mouth by mistake.

CRITICAL MASS

During the years Dad taught at City College and Yale, on his nights home he sat in his study with a red felt-tip marker, scribbling rapaciously in the margins of his students' attempts at writing, usually while listening to Bach. He didn't expect much from them—only for them to write their poems, stories, plays, and novels exactly as he would've written them.

It is hard to know exactly when and when not to disturb a writer in his study. I have discussed this with the children of other authors and was relieved to discover that this was a common family conundrum. Many people know exactly when their fathers leave and come home from work, but the ones with parents engaged in artistic professions have no clue at times when ideas are gestating or when their parent is simply daydreaming, staring out a window, leafing through a magazine. My father did not like to sit in his study with the door closed. It felt too confining. So we would pass by his wide-open door just off our apartment's mosaic-tiled foyer, on our way into or out of the house, glance in, and at times scan for clues, but seldom were any given. He might sometimes take kindly to an interruption. Sometimes as I passed by he'd yell out something like, "Where are you running?" as if he were feeling, touchingly, downright neglected. Five minutes later if you entered as he was staring off into space and tried to sit down to chat, he might fidget with his

Stim-U-Dent, grit his teeth a bit, and ask, "What makes you think that I'm just sitting here and not working?"

He often claimed that many of the City College students barely spoke English, so their writing attempts, to him, seemed especially dismal. By comparison he felt that the Yale students were more gifted but also more pretentious, their writing more self-conscious. City College did have one bright spot for him, however, apart from the ample paychecks, and it was named Wendy Wasserstein. He thought she was exceptional, though he never understood why her work seemed to be always handed in late, just after the class deadline. More than once she brought her assignments to him at home, where she would ring our bell and deliver them in person. Her margins were, I remember, remarkably free of his red-ink ramblings, but she was quite possibly one of few City College students of his who could claim that.

I once had an argument with him when he was about to read some of the work by his students and I'd seen him get out his red pen. It bothered me that he'd start befouling the students' margins immediately, without reading through an entire piece first, presupposing that criticism would be needed.

"How do you know you're even going to need that red pen before you've read something completely?" I asked.

"How do I know I won't?" he answered without looking up, continuing with his bloody, largely indecipherable scratchings.

I was in a position to receive pages and pages of similar critical hieroglyphics when I wrote a novel, in 1989, entitled *Splinters*, that was about to be published by William Morrow & Co. I sent Dad the galleys and they came back three days later, covered in that red felt-tip scribble, like a wild rash erupting. It made me feel like scratching. For many years my mother wouldn't read *Splinters*. "What if it's terrible? What will I say to you?" "What if it's not?" I countered, having learned at the feet of the master. A few years later she read it and told me that it was better than she'd been worried it'd be.

Meanwhile, "Not as bad as I expected," Dad had scrawled in those vulnerable margins. "And in some places good." He then proceeded to mark up every page with changes in punctuation and grammar and with corrections having mostly to do with historical references. "It may interest you to know," he'd written, "that Napoléon Bonaparte was born the second of eight children, not nine," which was actually helpful.

Somehow, without producing anything extraordinary, I had managed to exceed both parents' subterranean expectations. Then again, Dad was never one for doling out excessive compliments or praise—not just to us, but to anyone.

Once, my parents' friend Dolores Karl remembers Mom worrying over what she was going to wear to some formal occasion and my father saying to her, "You always worry about how you'll look and you're always the prettiest one there." This reassurance and flattery that he gave to my mother was so unusual, Dolores still remembers it today, perhaps forty-five years later.

From Joe Heller, that was a rave.

ONLY PARTLY TO DO WITH SEX

Before my graduation from New Lincoln in 1970, I applied to Lake Forest College, and was put on the waiting list. That meant that I'd learned the word "attrition," and also that for some or possibly most of the summer I wouldn't have any idea if, when, or where I'd be going to college the following fall. The notion of learning how to grow vegetables in Mississippi suddenly began to acquire its own peculiar charm.

In the meantime, it was summer, and we were bound for Fire Island. My father had waited until the last possible moment to rent a house, something he generally did that was dependably frustrating. He was undoubtedly hoping to seize upon some tremendous savings. The day after high school graduation was a Friday, and my mother opened *The New York Times* to look for a house rental in Seaview. Only two were available. One had only one bedroom, and the other appeared to be some kind of showplace, right on the ocean. The price, though, was so forbidding—seventy-five hundred dollars for the season—that my father, upon hearing it, thought we might have to take extraordinary measures and set our sights instead on Connecticut, literally a last resort for him. My mother was intrigued by the glitzy-sounding oceanfront house and was determined to go and see it and, not just that, but also to get us moved in there by the following weekend. The classified ad described an enormous place with two kitchens and an outdoor speaker system on the deck, adding that a recent film of note had been shot there. My father let out a hoot. "I don't care if *Cleopatra* was shot there and Liz Taylor comes with the price of the house, I'm not paying a penny over four thousand dollars, so save yourself the trouble of running out there and falling in love with it," he told Mom, but she ignored him. Tearing out the ad, she told me to hurry up and get ready. We had a train to catch.

By noon we stepped off the Long Island Rail Road in Bay Shore and caught the ferry. The owner of the house, an aggressive fellow, met us at the ferry slip and walked us up to his house. It stood majestically at the foot of the sea. The living room had over-size patterned pillows from India laid out all over the floor before a huge, ornate fireplace, and from the ceiling were suspended giant, colorful, genie-style lanterns. Everywhere in the house one could see the ocean, and I felt as if I were back on the bow of a huge ocean liner. My mother tuned out the owner's prattle and asked if a longer summer season were possible, one that included all of September, to which he said absolutely not. She asked if his dishes and linens were included in the rental and again, he said no. She told him that the house was lovely but the price was outrageous. Then she asked me to go down to the beach and wait for her. I resisted, because I sensed that she was going to begin bargaining with this man and I wanted to see how it was done, but she was adamant, so I left. Up at the house I could see them touring the perimeter and watched my mother pointing to something. Ten minutes later she came and got me where I was standing near the water.

"Well, we got it," she said to me in a low voice. "Let's get out of here before he has a chance to change his mind."

On the ferry back to Bay Shore, I sat in awe of this woman who was so personable and soft-spoken but who was also undeniably plucky. Who else would have dared tangle with that guy? Mom had left the Apthorp and my father that morning with a deal to close, and she had done it. It was not unlike the time she had gone to see the principal at P.S. 87 about me not skipping a grade when other students were, only this time she had succeeded.

When we came back to the apartment, my father had Sweeney on his desk and was combing him in long, patient strokes. The dog, with his perpetually quizzical expression, looked straight ahead. Their matching whitish topknots looked impossibly comical together.

"So how was the house?" he asked Mom, without looking up from his combing. She told him that it was outstanding.

"And we didn't get it for four thousand dollars, did we?" Dad asked Mom, sure that our trip had been the waste of time he'd anticipated.

"No, we didn't," she said. "I got it for us for thirty-seven hundred." He stared at her in unabashed wonder and set down his comb. "And," she added, "I got us all of September thrown in, *and* linens and dishes." Dad just kept staring.

"He wasn't adamant about his price?" Dad wanted to know. Mom lit up a Marlboro, took a puff, and answered, "Of course he was. But I pointed out to him that the season was about to start and he had no one for the house and that paint was peeling everywhere and the house was falling apart." She paused. "And I told him who you were and that the house would be filled all summer with rich, famous people."

"Jesus, I hope you were lying," Dad told her. Yet he was still marveling, astonished. Negotiating was something he had little interest in doing and, in any case, no knack for. Luckily he didn't have to. He had her.

We moved out to the house the following week. When we arrived everything about the place was perfect, even if the paint *was* flaking. We spent long, lazy days at the beach and at night, after dinner, Dad would turn on the klieg lights on the huge top floor deck and we would all sit quietly outside, usually with the warble of Bob Dylan in the air, drifting out to sea. We could hear and smell the waves in the inky blackness right outside our door.

Speed's house was just a few blocks over in Seaview, and the first time he came over he said the place looked like one giant sheikh's tent, and he was right. So for July Fourth, Speed surprised everyone and dressed up like a sheikh, flowing headpiece and all.

He walked around that way for a few days, to the beach, to the market. Everyone stared, but no one asked him about it.

In the middle of the summer, after waiting every day for word from Lake Forest's Admissions Office, I finally got the envelope accepting me for the fall. It included all relevant materials, including the name and phone number of the girl who would be my roommate, and it was decided that Mom would accompany me to college. In the meantime, we would shop for school clothes together in the city and prepare for my academic exodus.

Unfortunately, most of the shopping trips ended with us bickering. I wanted suede and leather and my mother wanted me to dress like a proper Lord & Taylor young lady. This led to battles, slammed doors, and nasty arguments. Somewhere around the middle of that summer I began to actively dislike her.

One sunny afternoon I remember talking to Speed about Mom out at the beach house—about both of my parents—as I was ready to leave for Lake Forest, Illinois. That conversation contained so much wisdom it took me years to grasp it.

Sitting on our deck drinking coffee while waiting for Dad to get off the phone, I asked Speed a question I sometimes wondered about.

"How do they get along?" I wanted to know, pointing to my mother. "She's bossy and thinks she knows everything."

"She *does*," Speed told me. To him it was that simple.

"But she's boring," I told him.

"Ha! Only to *you*, kiddo. You're an adolescent. You're supposed to think that."

Then he began to impart *The Romantic Wisdom of Speed Vogel* to me, all in a few sentences, in words that have never left me.

"Do you know the secret of your parents?" he asked with a wide smile. "It's only partly to do with sex," he told me, far overestimating my maturity.

"You mean how he doesn't kill her?" I wondered.

"Kill her? Are you kidding?" He laughed. "Don't you know how jealous the rest of us guys are of him?"

I shook my head, incredulous. "Hardly anyone will *ever* have what Joe has, and it's a lesson it wouldn't kill you to learn," he added gently. "Their sex is great, sure—"

"Please—" I put my hand up to stop him, not wanting any further elaboration. He talked right through it. He had a point to make.

"Your father has the luxury of having someone in the world who is more on his side than anybody else. Do you know what that's worth? You may not realize how that alters the universe for someone and how much that means, but it means everything." Of course I didn't.

Speed had clearly thought all of this through at great length. "Think about that," wise Speed said to me then, with a decisive nod, drinking the last of his coffee, closing his eyes, and tilting his face up to the sun.

Swami Speed could always look at the earth, at its madness and miracles, break it down to the simplest premises, and he was always, always right. Lou Ann Walker, Speed's widow, reiterated for me recently what I had always known. That Speed had adored my mother, considered her to be the perfect counterpart to Dad, thought that she was smart, funny, beautiful, Dad's one transcendent love. Lou Ann spent many years with Speed and with Dad, postdivorce, when Dad spoke candidly about his relationship with my mother. "Just read what Joe wrote about Shirley," she counseled me, referring to Dad's later books. "It's all there." I did. It is.

Speed's words about loyalty, about love, and about the exquisite luxury of having someone completely in your corner made sense then, and makes even more sense now. If only Dad had not forgotten, even temporarily, perhaps both of their lives might have turned out differently.

BLOODY HELL

In the fall, my mother and I flew to Chicago and then took a taxi to Lake Forest College. She planned to stay a day or two at a nearby inn until she felt I'd gotten settled at school.

I was anxious to meet my roommate. A member of the college's swim team, she was what was then referred to as a "militant lesbian," and only wanted to room with another swimmer. She quickly packed up her hats and cowboy boots and left me, shaking her head with a scowl, on the second day. "You don't understand *anything* and never *will!*" she said to me.

She was immediately replaced by a reed-thin, pale, giggly girl from the South who, I sensed, was just a bit off her pins. When I came back to our room on the fourth day of classes, I found her lying on our dorm room floor covered in blood, having smashed the fish bowl on our windowsill, in which her two goldfish swam. She had slashed both wrists. I called for help and an ambulance came quickly. Then I mopped up the mess. The following weekend, while my suicidal roommate convalesced, the college president's daughter hung herself. One morning the dean of housing summoned me to his office and told me that when my roommate returned, I was going to have to be very, very nice to her. While I sat in his office, the dean called my father, explaining to him what he had told me: that my roommate would be coming back soon and would require extra care and attention from me. All at once, I heard my father yelling on the other end of the phone, something he almost never did, telling the dean that I was not a psychiatrist and was not equipped to room with someone in such a precarious emotional condition, nor should I be expected to.

This was how I came to have my own room in the freshman dorm, by militant lesbian bias and suicide-attempt default. The year was off to a spirited start.

But I hated it out there, dropped out at the end of spring term, and tried to figure out what to do. Ultimately, I returned home and reinhabited my old room, soon beginning work at a menial job in downtown Manhattan: an awful job; about the worst I'd ever have.

My father, who generally disapproved of parents helping to get jobs for their kids, found this one for me. According to my parents, it was "just a job," something to do until I decided whether or not to resume college. But after two weeks it occurred to me that very likely the real reason my father had not only found me a job but had found me *this* job was because it would have me sprinting, not walking, back to academia.

The job, at a company called Facts, Inc., involved my sitting amid a long row of people among seemingly endless, similar rows, where all of us were charged with penciling in nine-digit CUSIP numbers for municipal bonds—all day, every day. "CUSIP" stands for Committee on Uniform Securities Identification Procedures. All I knew about CUSIPs were that I'd wake up and later go to sleep with meaningless strings of numbers still running through my brain.

The one saving grace of this horrible job was that our family friend, Dolores Karl, was the boss. Very early on, Dolores was something of a computer whiz. The company was owned by a man who was an old friend of both the Karls and my parents, so at least I felt comfortable working there. At Facts, Inc., I toiled alongside heroin addicts, teenage mothers, out-of-work actors, dancers, and singers, who, afraid of becoming rusty at their respective crafts, might suddenly break into a medley from *Gypsy* or a Shakespearean soliloquy. It was a fascinating New York assemblage where a stream of new faces could always be found.

I did make one friend at Facts, a woman named Nancy. Nancy spoke in a soft, whispery voice and wore her platinum hair in a massively teased updo planted high atop her head like a gigantic bomb. When she walked in her pointy heels, she took teeny, soundless steps no matter what kind of floor she walked on.

I brought her home to dinner at the Apthorp one night, and when I introduced her to my parents, they both simply nodded, and all through dinner said little and acted strangely removed. Then, when my mother was about to serve coffee, she steered me into the kitchen and suddenly couldn't stop herself from laughing. She whispered to me, "Your friend is a prostitute! You really had no idea?" Well, of course I didn't. But as soon as she said it, I realized it was true.

On Varick Street, nearby was an OTB, a dark, miserable place where mostly men would stand around watching horse races on screens. The floor was usually littered with used racing tickets and newspapers and if you didn't watch where you were going, you might step right into chewing gum, on a lit cigar, or walk onto someone's fresh vomit. Somehow I was appointed the Bag Lady of OTB for Facts, Inc., the one to whom everyone in the office entrusted their daily horse bets. I almost never bet myself, but enjoyed the walk over there each day and especially loved learning all the names of the racehorses, like Time for a Change or Baby Wants a Lollipop. Coming back to the office after these perambulations, under the merciless, bright white fluorescent glare, I'd distribute everyone's racing tickets.

By the summer, the CUSIP work had become so mind-numbingly boring that in some vague attempt to remain awake, I started writing them down backward. I remembered from the film version of *Catch-22* that Yossarian had censored letters and signed them "Washington Irving." (Or "Irving Washington," when the monotony became unendurable.) I could relate. In my struggle to remain lucid, the CUSIPs for something like Lubbock Texas Power & Light might suddenly conjoin with the Rancho Cordova California City Hall Facility Acquisition Project, or Alabama Power,

Georgia Power, Gulf Power, and Mississippi Power might have moved somehow, entirely unbeknownst to them, to Colorado, or Kansas, or Maryland, which was not good. Not good for Lubbock, the South, or for me. Finally, dear Dolores, in a voice choking with sorrow, had to sit me down one morning and fire me.

My coworkers were saddened. My friend, the whispery-voiced prostitute, looked like she would cry as she watched me clean out my desk. The young mothers gave me snapshots of their babies to take home and waved good-bye at the elevator with moist eyes. And the out-of-work actors, hoofers, and singers saw me off with a particularly rousing rendition of "Give My Regards to Broadway," with kicks high enough for the Rockettes—not at all rusty, I realized with relief.

As for me, it was Time for a Change.

By then my father had become friends with Philip Mayerson, dean of the New York University College of Arts and Sciences. I cannot even begin to imagine what promises were made, what favors exacted, but amazingly, I was accepted to NYU and would begin there in the fall, majoring in English. I was ready.

THE PRESIDENT RESIGNS, SHIRLEY BEGINS TO DEFECT

During my years at NYU, in the very early seventies, my parents bought a summerhouse, on Skimhampton Road in East Hampton. It was south of the Montauk Highway and very private, tucked away behind leafy old trees, which was a good thing, because at that point it was not much to look at. Still, everything that the house initially lacked was more than made up for by the land surrounding it. The property was dense, a parklike swath of green just out back, and beyond a lovely flagstone walkway and a wonderful heated pool. The price was right and both of my parents instantly fell in love with it, although Mom loved it a bit more because she could envision it transformed. Both my parents knew that my mother was a talented, if at that point uncredentialed, interior designer, who could brilliantly remodel the house using time, determination, and without spending too much money.

The first thing she did after buying the house was to find two gigantic porcelain foo dogs to place on either side of the collapsing front door, with huge pots of geraniums set on their heads. One was named Simon and the other Schuster; *Catch-22*, thus Simon & Schuster, had bought us the house. She patted each dog on the head for good luck every time she entered the house. Speed made a large tin bird and placed it in among the trees. My father told

Shirley repeatedly not to get too attached to the house since, if he ever divorced her, or predeceased her—something he always stated he had no intention of doing—he was leaving the place to the Animal Rescue Fund. This was a running joke that, notwithstanding my mother's affection for stray dogs and kittens, she never found especially amusing, perhaps because she sensed it might be true.

During the several years it took to renovate the house, my mother was frequently out in East Hampton while my father remained in the city or was otherwise traveling for work, giving lectures and readings.

Meanwhile, I was creeping along at NYU, striving, though stumbling along my way, to become a decent student. I worked hard, but was so distracted most of the time that I continually received terrible grades. I began to think that I might never graduate, and I'm sure if I was thinking that, so were my parents.

There was one very bright spot, however. I happened upon the most outstanding professor at NYU and believe that, were it not for her, I'd still be taking the train down to classes at Washington Square today. Her lilting name was Ilse Dusoir Lind. She was direct, wry, and brilliant, a Faulkner scholar and an established teacher within the English Department. Once I'd taken a class with her, I took every class that she gave, in women's studies, American poetry, and short stories. Suddenly, I was an insatiable reader. Professor Lind was the first teacher since high school who seemed to feel that I had an IQ above my shoe size, despite the fact that I was still such an unaccomplished student. Instead of taking regular exams, she let me write papers for her, and they always came back, just like my father's students' papers did, crowded with scribblings in the margins. Hers, however, were always effusive with extravagant praise. For one test, she allowed me to write a paper called "I, Bartleby," a version of the gloomy but also strangely hilarious Herman Melville story *Bartleby, the Scrivener*, told entirely from the recalcitrant copyist's perspective. In the margins of my paper, Professor Lind wrote: "Neat idea! You must write professionally." It was the first time *that* farfetched notion was ever suggested to me.

Armed with Professor Lind's encouragement and her list of cultural things to do, I went to London for the summer on a Sarah Lawrence program in my junior year, to live in a cement-block dormitory at the London School of Economics. I heard from my parents often. But where they both used to call together and babble simultaneously on phone extensions, now one or the other called me, and both seemed remote. My most powerful and lingering memory of this summer was the day I flew back to Kennedy Airport, August 8, 1974. After grabbing my bags, I went out into the area where flights were met and spied my father and mother on an escalator moving downward. Dad carried Sweeney, like a miniature self-replica, on his shoulder. They all greeted me and we got into the car to drive out to East Hampton, quickly, as I recall. A big night was ahead. Nixon was going to resign. He was abdicating that very evening, at 9:01, and we needed to be in front of a television set in time to see it. We loathed him.

In the car, the old Buick Apollo, tan with the brown roof dotted with its customary tree sap and bird droppings, I babbled about my trip, about visiting Cambridge and Oxford; about my class going to see *Cymbeline*; and rambled on interminably about Hampton Court. Yet none of my reportage seemed to be met by either of them with much enthusiasm.

By the time we reached Suffolk County I realized that my parents weren't speaking to each other. And by the time we reached the house in East Hampton, where we dropped off my bags and Sweeney, it was dark and we were hungry. We headed to a restaurant in town and ordered quickly because Nixon's speech was about to begin. At the table, my father kept glancing nervously at my mother, but she was ignoring him. I'd never, ever seen them behave this way. We had coffee and dessert and Dad told funny stories. One night, Dad recounted, he, Mom, and their friends playwright Murray Schisgal, his wife, Renee, and Dustin Hoffman and his then wife, Anne Byrne, had all piled into a car after dinner and then driven through the wealthy estate roads of Southampton, singing "Hava Nagila" at the top of their lungs. He looked anxiously at my mother but saw no reaction, so on he barreled, telling me that their maid, Viola, who by then was probably pushing 457 years old, had retired over the summer. And about how, when they'd come into the city during the summer for a week, the new cleaning woman, Euphemia, had stolen a handful of crystals from the dining room chandelier and had shown up for work the next day wearing them as earrings. When my mother confronted her, pointing to the empty spots in the chandelier and then to Euphemia's new adornments, the woman hadn't bothered to deny her pilfering. She'd only asked my mother if she might wear these "earrings" for the remainder of the day.

My father laughed tensely as he recounted these stories, but I wasn't listening. Nixon had begun to speak, and he and I turned our attention to the television in the restaurant's bar, where all of the evening's diners had relocated with coffee to watch the resignation. But I was also watching my mother. She sat stirring her coffee and staring down into her cup. When she brought it to her lips, I noticed the way my father was looking at Nixon alongside the way my mother was looking at my father. They were identical.

A SURPRISE PARTY WITH THE WRONG KIND OF SURPRISE

The previous year, when Dad was about to turn fifty, Mom decided to throw him a surprise birthday party. She loved giving parties and was good at it. Everything was always gorgeously done. But of all her parties, this was to be her true pièce de résistance.

Mom was surprisingly economical for someone who had trained at the feet of my grandmother Dottie—the fiscally deluded Lady Bountiful, aka Mrs. van Upsnoot—although perhaps it was *because* of this that she was always so frugal. Besides, my father wouldn't have had it any other way. When it came to this one particular party, however, she decided to spare no expense. After all, how many times would Dad turn fifty?

To surprise Dad with anything was always tricky at best. He may have often seemed preoccupied, but he didn't miss much. Then, of course, there was the problem of his friends, namely the Gourmet Club. Mom was certain that not one of them could keep a secret, and certainly not from one another. George? Speed? Mel? Mario? Julie? Ngoot, who by now was fluent in Yiddish? He could spoil the surprise in *two* languages. Our longtime cleaning woman, Viola, on the mirthful cusp of retirement, pronounced his name "Megoot," and she especially enjoyed the times each year when he'd come over to our house and make dinner. Typically, Ngoot would give Dad and Speed a shopping list. They'd go down to Chinatown and bring back about twice what he'd requested. Then Ngoot, with Viola's help, would prepare a lavish meal, and while they cooked they'd drink. The more Ngoot and Viola drank, the better the meals became.

For Dad's gala birthday party, my mother decided that Viola and Megoot would have the night off. They'd be among the guests at the party. Instead, she hired Donald Bruce White, a former television and Broadway actor who had become the caterer known as the Telephone Chef. His events were widely written up.

About 120 people were invited, including friends Saul Chaplin and Burton Lane, who would both play the piano. Mom had assembled an outstanding crew of bartenders and waiters. The birthday cake was so regally appointed it looked as if it would have been at home in a glass case at the Louvre. The guests were due at 7:00 and Dad was due around 8:00.

The day of the party there were thunderstorms with torrential rains. My mother popped around to see her close-to-saintly, longtime hairstylist and colorist, Pat, a man who also did my grandmother's hair and in almost fifty years of performing this delicate task had never once received an unkind or disgruntled word from her. Pat worked at the reliable neighborhood beauty parlor BetAl, a melding of the owners' names, Betty and Al. Pat couldn't be pressured or annoyed. He had endless patience and forever appeared to be in a good mood, or else just hid everything seamlessly. I pictured him going home at night and smashing plates, venting his day's frustrations.

By the time Mom arrived home from BetAl that day, all of the party food was supposed to have been delivered, so she was agitated to see that only a few waiters and bartenders were present, setting up the bar and filling the coffee urn. It was almost six o'clock. Mom called the Telephone Chef and learned that in fact he'd scheduled her party for a different night. Still, he said that he might be able to "rustle up" some food, "canoe over," and get something there in time. "Might?" "*Something?*" Mom was frantic. In the meantime, she, I, and the school friend I'd invited over ran out to every local supermarket to raid all the available vegetables for crudités, fruit, cheese, and anything else my mother could throw at the soon-to-be-arriving mob of guests.

In the end it all came together. A penitent Mr. White arrived and was visibly relieved that my mother wasn't the type to screech and shrilly castigate him. Somehow he produced a magnificent feast.

Astonishingly, Dad was astonished—and pleased. He couldn't stop beaming. One hundred and twenty-four people had RSVPd "yes," but it turned out that many people had brought others with them, so a head count at one point rose to 138. Luckily, somehow there was enough food and drink for them all.

Saul Chaplin, the friend, composer, and music director, played Gershwin. Burton Lane, a composer and lyricist, played Burton Lane. Viola and Megoot got smashed, took off their shoes, and danced a tango. All of the Gourmet Club members, those certified and not, patted one another's backs for having kept such a tantalizing secret. My friend and I watched the grown-ups having a great time. Mel Brooks and his wife, Anne Bancroft, came early

Still laughing, 1979

©Thomas Victor/Harriet M. Spurlin

and stayed late. Burton was there with his effervescent wife, Lynn, who wore a lavish, sleek white mink coat that both my friend and I modeled several times while the guests were eating dinner.

Dudley Moore and Peter Cook stopped by. Someone brought Farley Granger and Van Heflin, whom I'd never heard of, and nobody left until after 2:00 a.m., at which time my father, announcing that he was hungry, took my mother out somewhere for eggs, still euphoric, still under the party's exhilarating spell. I can still see his face. I'd never seen it so openly, buoyantly joyful, and never saw it quite that way again.

TOLSTOY, THE CIRCUS, AND THE GRADUATION THAT ALMOST WASN'T

It is a wise father that knows his own child.
—William Shakespeare

Professor Lind was a lifesaver, without question—accomplished, funny, rueful, and unbelievably perceptive. Unfortunately, I could not get through NYU and acquire a bachelor's degree in English by taking her classes alone. I needed to diversify.

In my senior year I discovered that I was exceptionally fond of the Russian short story and enrolled in any class that touched on that. One of my father's favorite short stories had been one by Tolstoy, spoon-fed to me way before I could understand and appreciate its biting message. Called "How Much Land Does a Man Need?", it depicts a poor yokel, driven by insatiable greed to own more and more land, and who, literally at the point of finally achieving everything that might finally satisfy him, collapses and dies. Six feet, from his head to his toes, for his grave, is all he needs.

As a senior at NYU, I actually did my work, passed my exams, and was beginning to see the light at the end of my academic tunnel with not a clue as to what I might do afterward. I had boyfriends, one of whom my father broke his rule and met when I had to have my wisdom teeth extracted and stayed home for a few days. My boyfriend came to our house and generously brought me flowers and books. He cut up toast for me into thousands of easy-to-chew slivers. My mother never forgot that toast cutting.

My parents were understandably thrilled when it looked like I was nearing graduation. We began having discussions, previously unthinkable, about my "future." Perhaps six months before my graduation, Dad took me to lunch one Sunday and earnestly discussed the possibility with me of becoming an advertising copywriter. He seemed positively jolly. "You like to write," he told me. "In advertising, you'll make a lot of money, work with people who are smart and clever, and if you finish your work you can go to the movies in the afternoon." That was his sales pitch. It sounded great to me, so I agreed to think carefully about it. But first there was the matter of my senior finals and graduation.

Somewhere in our discussion, my father quoted Shakespeare, and when I asked which play the quote was from, the tone of the lunch immediately shifted. He began rabidly quizzing me about Shakespeare's plays and sonnets, and when he realized that I'd read nothing, knew nothing, yet was still on the very verge of earning my B.A. in English, he became understandably unhinged. We left the restaurant abruptly enough for him to have forgotten to pay the check. Our waiter had to run out into the street and catch up to us for payment half a block away.

That night, still angry, Dad sat in his study, typing and retyping a letter to his friend Philip Mayerson, dean of NYU's College of Arts and Sciences, asking how it might be possible that his daughter, who was about to receive a B.A. in English, could do so without having read a single word of Shakespeare. Mayerson called Dad a few days later, upset that Dad was upset. The result was that I was to drop one of my classes and do an independent study in Shakespeare for the rest of the term with a professor he assigned to me. My highly accelerated Shakespearean mini-education completed, it appeared that I was finally going to be graduating at long last. Almost.

For the first time ever, the NYU graduation was going to be held at Madison Square Garden. Since the graduating class of the university numbered in the thousands, there was no question of each student going up to the stage to receive a diploma. Instead, each of the university's colleges picked one student as their representative. The chosen one would sit up on stage throughout the graduation exercises and receive a token diploma.

When Dean Mayerson phoned my father to ask if I might be the one to represent Washington Square College, the man who usually said "no" to things was surprised and excited and instinctually said "yes," immediately and without consulting me. I had never met the dean and was hardly the most exemplary or deserving student to occupy such an exalted position on such an august occasion and was not inclined to pretend I was, but apparently this had already been decided.

Before graduation, however, I had to take my final on the Russian short story. So far, I believed, all my exams had gone well. My father could actually look ahead, and not far, to the day when he would no longer be paying my tuition. And I could also see the day when I would be finished, forever, with school. It is difficult to imagine which one of us was more jubilant, not to mention relieved.

Graduation was set for a Friday morning, and my Russian test was literally the day before. I showed up early Thursday afternoon and felt ready. I was almost home free. By tomorrow at that time my entire academic career would be a memory.

The professor giving the test had a Moscovian accent with the timbre and cadence of a blaring foghorn. She handed us our exams and bleated: "You will please now to begin!" I scanned the test. It was passable. I began writing out the answers to the three essays carefully and calmly. I knew the material. There were no surprises.

I felt, in fact, rather like the man in Dad's favorite story—rushing, racing, running until his heart was bursting, to the finish line where the realization of every one of his life's dreams waited. I wrote about Pushkin and then Gogol. And then, rounding the final corner, when it came to Tolstoy, I took an index card out of my bag with a quote I'd written down and began copying it out to buttress an argument I was making. That was when I felt a heavy hand on my shoulder and in a second was yanked out of my chair. In the hallway, Professor Stolychnaya informed me that I'd been caught cheating. Not only would I be prevented from graduating the next day, I would in all likelihood be expelled.

"But look at my paper!" I said to her, nearly mad with desperation. I held the condemned test up to her eyes. "I *attributed* the quote to Tolstoy. I wasn't going to say it was *my* thought, my words. I very clearly indicated it was Tolstoy, not me." She was impassive, though, standing in the hallway with her two arms, like fat kielbasas, folded.

"I cannot believe you can be doing such a bad, terrible thing," she said to me with a look of disgust. "And here I thought you knew and loved so much the material." She looked at her watch, keeping track for the students still inside.

"I did! I do," I howled, beseeching her, imagining the next day at Madison Square Garden with the smell of the just-departed circus elephants and horses still ripe in the air. The thought of my parents, of facing them, telling them this latest plot twist, was unbearable. For once they were so proud of me. They had even invited Professor Lind to come to lunch with us following the ceremony, to the Italian Pavilion. It was to be a festive, triumphant occasion that would celebrate me for the first time ever. I pictured telling my parents, my mother wringing her hands, and my father, eyes blazing with fury, hearing the *ka-ching* of yet another year of paying my tuition. "What am I supposed to tell Mayerson?" my father would ask.

I was frantic. I explained to Professor Stroganoff that I'd been chosen to represent the college up on stage the following day at graduation. "Please reconsider," I pleaded with her. "I *wrote* that it was Tolstoy!" Sweat beaded on my forehead. She thought it over, and finally, after an eternity of clearing her throat and *tsk*ing me to death, agreed to "think about it." But where did that leave me? What about graduation? "Well, while you're thinking, what am I supposed to do about tomorrow?" I whined. "Ha!" she snorted.

"You think you are so wonderful smart. You can be finding the answer yourself, or maybe can be stealing one from Mr. Tolstoy!" she sneered, and then wheeled about and returned to her classroom, presumably to all of the students *not* plagiarizing Tolstoy, slamming the door shut.

What was I to do? Tell my parents about this transgression at the eleventh hour, or keep it to myself just in case she relented and decided in my favor? I went home and had dinner with them, and they were brimming with pride, so happy and excited were they about the next day. I excused myself three times during dinner to call the teacher in her office and leave a message, but she had left school hours before. That whole night I worried about showing up and about not showing up. Would the chair for my college sit empty up on stage? Or, if I went, would someone in the audience, perhaps even Professor Babushka herself, stand and bellow, pointing a finger in my direction: *"J'accuse!"*?

In the morning I tried calling the teacher again but got no answer. I thought of calling Professor Lind and seeking her counsel, but she was also so thrilled that I was finally graduating, I didn't have the heart to pierce her enthusiasm. Impossibly, I decided to keep quiet. Before we left for graduation, my father called me into his study to tell me that now that I was graduating, his work, as far as I was concerned, was done. "We can be friends from here on in, but any parenting obligations I had have been met," he announced with some mirth. "So it's kind of my graduation, too," he informed me.

We went to Madison Square Garden, on the heels of the circus that had just left town. I wore my purple robe and sat up on that brightly lit stage throughout the ceremony, waiting for the KGB to come and wrestle me off the stage in handcuffs, disgraced. At the appropriate moment, however, my name was called and I stood up as if in a trance. I collected my empty cylinder tied with a purple ribbon, the token diploma for a token student, having no clue whether or not I was indeed graduating.

My parents and Professor Lind savored my success and seemed incandescent with joy. We went to the Italian Pavilion, a place where several of my father's book deals had been sealed over lunch, and he toasted my graduation with champagne, thanked Professor Lind, and then we sat for hours, laughing and talking. That night my aunts and uncles all called to congratulate me, as well as my grandparents in Florida. Meanwhile, I harbored my dirty secret, as guilty as Raskolnikov. Not even guilty of the crime, I nonetheless awaited my punishment.

The Russian professor would not return my calls for all of June and July, although by then, she surely knew the outcome, and had probably known it all along. Finally, when the thirst of her inner sadist had been slaked, one day in early August, my NYU diploma arrived in the mail. By that point, though, I was ready to wring the teacher's neck. How could she have kept me in suspense for so long? Suspense was Hellerian anathema almost unparalleled in its destructive potential.

And to think that she'd thought I would try to take credit for that quote of Tolstoy's, from *Anna Karenina*, of all places.

And what was the quote? Well, it was:

Happy families are all alike; every unhappy family
is unhappy in its own way.

Now, where would I have ever come up with something like *that*?

THEY'LL *ALWAYS* HAVE PARIS, OR ONLY SOMETIMES?

During the course of that summer, my father enlisted the help of an old advertising associate whose ex-wife was not just a copywriter, but a big shot at the renowned ad agency Doyle Dane Bernbach. At this point I knew virtually nothing about ad agencies, but started to learn quickly. Apparently Dad wouldn't help me get a job (unless it was to try to get me to go back to college), but he would help me to meet someone else who might be able to.

The woman who helped me put my first portfolio together and became my friend and mentor was Diane Rothschild, and she did this with great care, humor, and patience. She showed up to our first meeting, lunch at La Cabaña on East Fifty-seventh Street, in pearls, Chanel pumps, and a black dress. With big eyes, straight, dark, shoulder-length hair and bangs, a baby doll voice, and a plan for my future, she was like Jean Shrimpton with an IQ of 12,987. A brilliant woman, she showed me samples of her work, and I later found out about all the awards she'd won and how revered she was in the industry. With her help, my spec book was put together and she got me a few interviews. In the meantime, I found an apartment on East Seventy-eighth Street and moved in.

My first interview was at Y&R, a top ad agency, with a bragging bully of a creative director who told me right away that he had no intention of hiring me. As I left his office, he told me to rethink things, become a nurse or a stewardess, or else go back to college, of all things, and get a degree in business management. I already knew from working with Diane that writing ads was fun and that, in fact, it was what I wanted to do. Besides, if Jean Shrimpton with a larger brain than the entire Y&R Madison Avenue building thought I could do it—and she seemed to—then a copywriter was what I was going to be.

I found a job the following week. On my first day, a dozen peach-colored roses arrived for me at my new desk. The card said "I told you so!" and was from Diane Rothschild, from the florist Irene Hayes, Wadley & Smythe. I had never heard of this shop, but my mother had, and if it was even possible, Diane rose another mighty rung in my mother's estimation. Chanel pumps *and* the right florist? My mother was right. Diane was spectacular.

During my third year in advertising, I was finally hired at Doyle Dane Bernbach, the place I'd hoped to get into all along. The cleverness and imagination of their work and the movies I got to go to in the afternoons helped.

Just after I'd started at DDB, my parents suddenly announced that they were going to go to Paris for a week, in winter, and they invited me to come. In fact, both were rather insistent, which I found peculiar. After all, our history of traveling together was, to all of our minds, less than dazzling.

It was a rare instance, too, that a publisher wasn't financing our trip. Dad was. We stayed at the slightly frayed but very appealing Left Bank hotel famous for its world-renowned literary and artistic clientele and gripping view of the Seine, the Hotel du Quai Voltaire.

Built in the 1600s as an abbey, it was converted to a hotel in 1856, and it was at this address on the Quai Voltaire where an exiled Oscar Wilde, among other notables, once lived; and in fact was the very place about which he quipped that he was dying beyond his means. This was also where Jean Sibelius stayed, where Baudelaire had written *Les Fleurs du mal*, where Richard Wagner composed

Die Meistersinger, and Camille Pissarro painted *Le Pont-Royal et le pavilion de Flore*, right from the window of his fourth-floor room.

My room had a panoramic view of the Louvre and the Seine, Notre Dame, the Tuileries, moving boats, and dusty, picturesque bookstalls. On its website today, the hotel is still described as "a totally French hotel, comfortable and classical, where discretion and serenity get the top priority."

My father had many business appointments and interviews. *Good as Gold* had just been published. A few years later, my mother's divorce lawyer would stand up in a New York City courtroom and call *Good as Gold* my father's version of *Mein Kampf* in terms of his marriage, but I always thought he got it wrong. He was one book behind—it had been *Something Happened*. On the eve of *Good as Gold*'s American publication, when writer Barbara Gelb, an Apthorp neighbor and old friend, had written her profile of my father in *The New York Times Magazine*, she wrote that he had married Shirley Held, of Brooklyn, in 1945, shortly after returning from the war.

> She was auburn-haired, slender, and vulnerable, and has changed very little. A mixture of gaiety and rue, she is as contradictory as her husband. Her loyalty to him is passionate, and the names of those who have presumed to write adversely of his work are tucked away in her mind, pickled in venom.

We didn't see much of my father at all that week in Paris. When he was around, he seemed edgy, and I quickly surmised that I'd been brought along as some kind of buffer. When my parents weren't bickering, it was only because one or the other of them had stormed off. On our last full day there, I took a bus to Chartres Cathedral, feeling nervous and unsettled about them, worrying about what was going on and what would happen—aware of the murderous glances, the smoldering resentments. Dad was drinking a little too much, and Mom's sarcasm was so sharp it could easily have sliced our Camembert. I was thinking about them when out of nowhere I fainted in the cathedral, sagging down onto the cold, hard floor. When I came to, nuns and priests were kneeling over me, speaking in strange tongues, and I really did wonder for a moment if I had died and gone to heaven or perhaps elsewhere, and whether the Jews, once and for all, had in fact been cataclysmically screwed.

NO NOBEL, BUT INSTEAD,
A LOVELY SWEDISH FRIENDSHIP

I cannot offer any true and complete accounting of my father's life and times, especially the good times, circa *Catch-22*, without mentioning that loyal champion of writers and devoted friend to Dad for over thirty years, his Swedish publisher, Per Gedin. Charismatic and quick-witted, with a superb knack for honing the ingenious, well-rounded anecdote, we met only once or twice over the years of their friendship but correspond to this day. Per was so loyal to my father that he didn't just give him the shirt off his back, he once even gave him the coat.

My parents traveled several times to Sweden on publicity jaunts and Per always entertained them generously. Meals, with ample rounds of excellent drinks, went on for many, many hours; the kind of languid lunches that might end when the dinner service was being set out. Per has told me that almost always, my mother excused herself after the main meal, offering a headache or stomachache as an excuse, and no doubt returning to their hotel happy for a break.

My mother was not a drinker in the sense that these two warhorses were, and the idea of sitting with them, eating for hours, listening to them talk about books ad infinitum, was not her forte. But my mother made deft excuses and left so frequently, according to Per, that he once actually sent his personal physician around to the hotel to examine her. The doctor found her in bed with the shades drawn and a warm compress over her eyes. "Since when is boredom an illness?" she asked him dryly, declining to be examined.

Meanwhile, the two literary fellows gabbed and guzzled away, delighting in each other's company, usually at Den Gyldene Freden—the Golden Piece—the famous restaurant owned by the Swedish Academy and once quite elegant, classic, and terribly expensive, but now, according to Per, taken over by tourists. In the 1970s, though, Per says, "Joe liked to go there. It seemed to him he was closer that way to the Nobel."

When Per came to New York, Shirley had a somewhat easier time of it. Sometimes the three of them went out to dinner, and then she just excused herself without fuss and went home. More often than not in those days, dinner or lunch was at the Russian Tea Room. When Dad and Per were there on Per's expense account, nothing was excessive, no amount of vodka or caviar or hours spent relishing each other's company in an opulent place where every day, all year round, was Christmas.

Per Gedin, Dad's friend and devoted Swedish publisher

©Cato Lein

One of Per (and Dad's) favorite stories concerned the time they ate a late lunch on a very cold winter's day, and from there, Per was to leave directly and go to the airport to return home to Stockholm. His luggage and fine sheepskin coat were both being held for him in the coatroom of the Russian Tea Room.

That afternoon, we ordered masses of caviar and vodka and had a great time. It was from there I walked away from my sheepskin coat, which Joe so admired and said he would very much like to have. Not "one," but "it." I had to leave for the airport and gave Joe my ticket for the coatroom where we both had our coats, and I left Joe both of our coats and just left with my luggage. Joe loved the coat but afterward, typically, complained for years that it was too small.

But my father was indeed grateful, and loved and wore that coat for more years than I can even count. And Per's generosity was soon rewarded with more than mere gratitude.

The next time Joe came to Stockholm, he surprised me with a small, very fine leather suitcase that he had bought for me at Crouch & Fitzgerald. It had a numbered lock and Joe asked me to open it. When I asked for the combination he told me it was the date corresponding to the date he and I first met, and he refreshed my memory. I was astounded that he had thought of and remembered such a date, never mind that he was sentimental enough to have thought to use this number for the combination, but it helped me over the next many years to understand him better. As for the case, I still use it and love it. More than that, on all numbered locks since then, even for my safes, it is always that date and number for the combination. And now that I've told it to you, Erica, you can open my safe and all my suitcases.

SO, WHAT THE HELL HAPPENED WITH *SOMETHING HAPPENED*?

"Joe, this is going to sound crazy to you, but this guy is not a Bill." He said, "Oh really, what do you think he is?" I said, "He's a Bob." And Joe looked at me and said, "He was a Bob, and I changed his name to Bill because I thought you would be offended if I made him a Bob." I said, "Oh no, I don't think he's anything like me, it's just that this character is a Bob." So we changed it back. It was absolutely amazing. How did it happen? I don't know. I suppose our convoluted, neurotic, New York Jewish minds work the same way.

—Robert Gottlieb, *Paris Review*,
Fall 1994 issue

I think by then, Mom's devotion to Dad had begun to dwindle. Perhaps she had found one too many letters in Dad's pockets, careless evidence of his dalliances, or perhaps it was the book that he had just spent thirteen years writing, the one that was due out the following month, *Something Happened*. In fact, I'm almost sure it was both. The book was 569 pages of hilarious but mordant, caustically wrapped, smoldering rage. It was also superb, depressing, and, many claim (including the author himself), that it was Dad's best work.

There had been arguments for years between my parents over it, over the fact that it so closely detailed someone who so resembled him and told, in the first person and in such harrowing detail, such an angry tale of one man's ennui, disgust, and scorching disappointment in, and dissatisfaction with, each member of his family, singularly and together, none of whom were named in the book. His depiction of marriage as a stifling, irredeemable purgatory that served as a home base for the protagonist's many liaisons was indisputable. But it was also my mother's concern for her children, I believe, that really precipitated the beginning of the end, the rupture rather than the rapture.

My father handed me the galleys one Saturday in August, in East Hampton, at lunch, but I waited a few weeks to read them. I knew that my mother was crushed by the slivers of it she'd read and I was in no hurry to join her. By then I was living on Sixty-eighth and Broadway, with a roommate, in the apartment my grandparents had occupied just before moving to Florida.

I feel confident in saying that it was not mere narcissism that led me to believe that the chapter entitled "My Daughter Is Unhappy" was about me. I cannot speak for anything else in the book. But there were years of verbatim conversations contained in it, and the dynamic between father and daughter—in all of its complicated, weary miscommunication and cutthroat struggle for the power that a father generally automatically holds—was strikingly familiar. The parental need, the perverse competition to "outfox" the child—was that, I wondered, universal?

So he looked at his daughter's future as a cold, empty grave? ". . . She sometimes seems so barren of hope that I find myself grieving silently alongside her, as though at an empty coffin or grave in which her future is lying dead already."

In the name of literature, is writing about anyone fair game? I wasn't sure, still am not sure. In this area, my sensitivities and sensibilities clash and no one wins. Reading Dad's galleys, I couldn't possibly believe that such an intimate recording of our life would soon be published, and I felt demolished. How much was true of what he'd written? And how could I ever know definitively? Even if some of it or most of it wasn't, the book was incontrovertible proof that such thoughts had at least filtered through his mind.

The day I finished reading his manuscript I went home and called him. He sounded nervous. "Well?" he asked. "What do you think?"

"How could you write about me that way?" I blurted out without completely thinking it through. But, of course, having had thirteen years to prepare it, his answer was ready. "What makes you think you're interesting enough to write about?" This meant that if I was interesting enough to write about, he had written terrible things. If not, the girl in the book wasn't me and I could rejoice in that, except for the fact that I was boring.

Was "My Daughter Is Unhappy" an observation or a goal? And how "happy" would anyone's daughter feel at reading such things about herself? When he'd tell me that I was too dull to be written about, my answer—"I don't think I am, but you evidently think so"—elicited a mere grumble, not surprising since we were still so much those people on his pages. Slocum could never, would never, have given an inch, and neither did Dad.

Lynn Barber, in her 1998 interview with Dad for the *Observer*, wrote:

> There are some truly harrowing scenes between father and daughter in *Something Happened*, the father clearly loathing the daughter and making no allowance for the fact that she is a child. He says dismissively, "I don't relate to children particularly, or even young people anymore—there's no basis for conversation."

That was the least of it.

• • •

Kurt Vonnegut Jr., a cherished friend of Dad's, reviewed *Something Happened* for the Sunday *New York Times Book Review*:

> What is perhaps Slocum's most memorable speech mourns not his own generation but the one after his, in the person of his sullen, teenage daughter. "There was a cheerful baby girl in a high chair in my house once," he says, "who ate and drank with a hearty appetite and laughed a lot with spontaneous zest: she isn't here now; and there is no trace of her anywhere."

As for my mother, she claimed never to have read the whole book, but I never knew whether to believe her. In any case, she refused to discuss it. On the most visceral level, I don't think she ever forgave him, nor did they resolve it, but I must assume that he had known this was coming for all of those thirteen years: the effect that this book would have on his marriage, that it would hobble it and beat it not quite to death, but almost. "Twisted brain" or not, this was not something that could possibly have taken him by surprise.

Meanwhile, the previous year, as had been our custom, Dad had called me up one Saturday morning to tell me that the final section of *Something Happened* was finished and to ask me to walk with him and his finished manuscript to Levy Brothers, a stationery store a few blocks away from the Apthorp. There he would make Xerox copies. This was something of a ritual. He would carry the box carefully, slowly, as if it might explode if held at an incorrect angle, and I would walk a half block or so behind him in case some sudden disaster befell him. In that case, I was to grab the box and run, although I doubted privately that in that instance I would be thinking much about his manuscript. After Levy Brothers, we would walk over to Seventy-ninth Street and Amsterdam, to Osner's typewriter repair shop, where typewriters were cleaned, oiled, and fixed. Typewriters there were a religion, and the shop had cared for the machines of Isaac Bashevis Singer, David Mamet, Alfred Kazin, Erich Maria Remarque, Roger Kahn, Philip Roth, Howard

Fast, and Murray Schisgal. Dad always went there when a book was finished to announce that he was done.

In the *New York Times* article published on September 16, 1982, about how various well-known authors protected their manuscripts, Edwin McDowell wrote that:

> Joseph Heller is another author who keeps his priorities well in mind. "When I wanted to Xerox the last section of *Something Happened* and mail it to my literary agent, I asked my daughter to walk with me to the store to get it copied," he said. "I figured in case a car hit me, if I got mugged, or if I dropped dead from a heart attack, the manuscript might still be saved." In recent years, Mr. Heller has hidden copies of his manuscript in the locker at the gym where he works out.

Of course, at some point in the near future, private copiers came along, making our short, nerve-wracking walks to Levy Brothers unnecessary. But I have a feeling that after *Something Happened*, he wouldn't have asked me to go again anyway and, in any case, I doubt I would have obliged.

LONG DAY'S JOURNEY NOT INTO WOODY'S PARTY

In December of 1979, I happened to be over at my parents' apartment at the Apthorp one weekend afternoon when the mail came, my mother opened it, and on a small, elegant, cream-colored card was an invitation to Woody Allen's New Year's Eve party. It was to be held at the very swank Upper East Side Harkness House, an architectural treasure. There had been much play in the press about how Woody had hand-selected the guest list, the caterer, even the paper for the invitation. Al Pacino would be there. Mick Jagger, Walt Frazier, Stephen Sondheim, Bette Midler, Lillian Hellman, Kurt Vonnegut, Meryl Streep, Paul Simon, Robert De Niro, Lauren Bacall. *Hundreds.* The list was endless. But Joe and Shirley Heller? I tell you, books or no books, this still confounded me.

At the time, my parents were preparing to leave on a trip to the Caribbean that would extend beyond New Year's, so there was no chance of them attending. It had all been planned months before, and they'd be traveling with Barbara and Arthur Gelb (also invited to Woody's; they were invited everywhere), who I later realized had been called on more than once to act as my parents' marriage counselors.

I had always hated New Year's Eve, the forced, synchronized gaiety of it, the cheesy, mawkish midnight kiss, and had had more than one fight with boyfriends over the years because when it came to planning and scheduling for that particular evening, I could never quite find it in my heart to cooperate.

But the sight of the Woody Allen invitation set my mind reeling. I held it in my hand, felt its formal, grainy heft, powerless to resist the sudden clarion call somewhere in the temporal lobes of my brain. In truth, I have no idea what happened to me, what astral force took hold; I only know that in the space of four seconds, my mind was racing. That was all the time it required, apparently, for me to metamorphose from Boo Radley, the Thing That Hated New Year's, into Holly Golightlyberg.

My father was sitting nearby at the time, drinking coffee and reading the paper. "Could *I* go?" I asked coyly. "Why would you want to do that?" he answered. I gave a reply he seldom heard from me and anyone seldom heard from him: "It might be fun." He peered out from behind his newspaper at me, not without amusement. "You figure out a way to go, then, and go. Have a good time." I wondered how I might possibly be able to pull this off. "Can I use your name? Can I tell them that this is okay with you?" I asked Dad. "Seems to me you would have to," he told me. "Do it. Go," he added. I was off and running.

I phoned the next day and accepted the invitation and planned to go with a friend. I explained that my parents would also attend later in the evening.

On New Year's Eve, an especially bone-chilling one, we arrived in the long line snaking down the block and over to Fifth Avenue. Limos lined up and out of them spilled endless fur coats and tuxedos. Flashbulbs popped everywhere. All of the local news channels had crews set up. In front of us were Howard and Mrs. Cosell, and we were so overpowered and transfixed by his toupee, we almost didn't realize that Arthur Miller and his wife were directly behind us. I clutched the invitation in my gloved hands and the line moved slowly. People were being screened very carefully, as if they were being admitted to a White House state dinner. Howard was getting impatient. "Let's move this thing!" he fairly bellowed at one point in that unmistakable voice. At last we reached the edge of the

Promised Land. Howard, his wife, and his toupee had gone in. We were up next. Two women asked us our names three times and then told us to wait.

Just then, a bespectacled man with a much written-in and crossed-out list of hundreds of names came running out, sprinting like doctors during emergencies on medical television shows. He removed his glasses and stared through us. "Why are you here?" he inquired rudely. Arthur Miller, just behind us, began to groan. I explained to him about how our parents, Mr. and Mrs. Heller, would be joining us there soon and about us having been given prior clearance, but he eyed us with disdain. At that moment, the voice of another gentleman came from behind and said, "Excuse me, excuse me," in a loud voice. "The Hellers are away with the Gelbs in the Caribbean and won't be back until next week! Go! Out! You're disgraceful!" My friend and I gasped with horror, but not as much as Arthur Miller, who then pushed past us and inside along with the rest of the legitimately invited guests, justifiably at the end of his rope.

It was arctically cold, it was 10:00 p.m. on New Year's Eve, and there we were, standing on Seventy-fifth Street. We glanced up at the festively lit, very tall Harkness House windows where Mick Jagger would be drinking champagne and Meryl Streep would be laughing, tearing into lobsters, and chatting at some point, certainly, with Woody.

In the end, we dragged our crestfallen selves over to Soup Burg, on Madison Avenue, with its drab, foggy windows, for a hamburger and coffee, and then spent a little time with Meryl Streep after all, if not quite the way we'd intended it, lining up for a midnight showing of *Kramer vs. Kramer* at Loew's Tower East. We made the best of it, eventually thawed, and drifted back down to earth from the glittering galaxy from which we had been ejected.

Later, in Andy Warhol's diary, he had written that this night, this party, had been "the best." Who could doubt it? It didn't help, though, when we saw the cover of the *New York Post* a few days later. Splashed all over it was the story about how the party caterer and a few of his friends at the party had, midway through the festivities, ducked into a bathroom and changed into formal attire, mingled with celebrities, talked to Woody in his tux and tennis shoes, gulped down spectacular champagne, and feasted on the very food they were supposed to be serving. We read in pitiless detail about the masses of delicate hyacinths set out in huge vases everywhere, the two discos. Breakfast, eggs and bacon, was served at 4:00 a.m. At 4:00 a.m., I was still tossing, still ashamed that Arthur Miller thought I was nothing but a pushy, classless slob.

When my parents got back to town, I told my father on the phone what had happened, and he couldn't stop laughing.

"Jesus, whatever made you think that they would let you in?" he asked.

"You told me it would be okay."

"Why would you listen to *me*?" he asked bemusedly. "What the hell do *I* know?"

LIMOS AND LYNX

My mother, alas, had not served in World War II, nor had she learned as expertly as her husband how to vanquish an enemy. Up until then, her own survival skills had never been seriously tested. She had an open face, and, as Barbara Gelb wrote of her in the *New York Times Magazine* in 1979, Mom was ". . . the only person I've ever known who can laugh and cry at the same time, and is, therefore, the perfect Heller heroine." Something she couldn't do was lie convincingly. Her mother, my grandma Dottie, tended to make up life as she went along, but my mother was a bit more pragmatic.

The one notable exception to this occurred in 1979. It was lunchtime and I was out on Fifth Avenue a few blocks from my office when I spied her coming out of what was then the Coca-Cola Building on the opposite side of the avenue. She got into a limo, bedecked in jewelry and wearing her lynx coat, a gift from my father that she loved dearly but almost never wore, as if she felt she had to protect it by keeping it at home in the closet. That day my curiosity was sparked, to say the least. A limo? The lynx? Shirley also almost never took a taxi. She once tripped climbing onto a bus, fracturing her ankle, and then rode the bus to the nearest emergency room.

When I called her that night to find out where she'd been coming from, she told me flatly that I was mistaken; that it hadn't been her. I kept at her about it for days, but she just kept denying it. The next time I saw her and looked into that ingenuous face and questioned her about what she'd been doing that day, she looked down and finally conceded to me, very quietly, that yes, I had seen her, and that the truth was she had been to see a plastic surgeon about a possible face-lift and had simply been too embarrassed to discuss it.

I never brought that day up again, but she did, twenty years later, inadvertently, when she happened to let it slip that, in fact, it hadn't been a doctor she'd gone to see that day at all. It had actually been a divorce lawyer. By then it was becoming clear that the glue keeping much of this family together was secrets, and that many or perhaps most of them were about to become seriously unstuck.

ALAS, THE CENTER WOULD NOT HOLD

On a chilly, wet, morosely gray Sunday afternoon in November of 1978, my mother broke an unwritten law and showed up at my apartment unexpectedly. It was the day of Erika Puzo's funeral in Bay Shore, Mario's wife, and I had assumed that both my parents would be attending. Apparently not. Neither my mother nor I were the type to be randomly dropped in on, and her unannounced presence was startling.

I noticed right away that she was tense and sweating. She sat down and lit cigarette after cigarette, chattering about nothing, room décor, my job, relatives we hadn't seen for a while. And the more she didn't talk about what was wrong, because clearly something was, the more dire I imagined it to be. The whole time she sat there, obviously disturbed and not acting quite herself, I kept wishing she would hurry up and tell me what was wrong so that we could discuss it. Rather, she prattled on, and just as I was about ready to scream with exasperation at her elaborate stalling, she began to speak in a great turbulent deluge. This was the day that she first told me about what was happening in my parents' marriage, when she pried open my eyes with a searing light.

As my mother explained it, my father had fallen desperately in love with a woman he had met several years before. She was a bug doctor (germs, not insects) who lived in Chapel Hill. Let's call her "Dr. Bugs." Mom said he had paid for her divorce, put her children into private school, and bought her a new house. The woman phoned him freely and often at the Apthorp, and although my father lied constantly these days, my mother knew just when and where he was with this woman. She said she'd hired a private detective, seen all of Dad's American Express bills for the past few years, as well as phone bills, and knew that more than once, when my parents had gone away on vacations, my father had stashed this woman in the same hotel, had even flown her with my mother on the same flights. I stared at Mom with bald incredulity. She had done all of her homework. She knew the ages, names, and Social Security numbers of every last one of Dr. Bugs' buglets. I was frankly stunned, but perhaps not for the right reasons.

Things had not seemed quite right between them by then for a while. Many years later, Arthur Gelb would write to me:

> In those difficult days when we were saddened by the start of the marital problems confronting your parents, they were shmoozing with us one evening in our apartment before leaving the next a.m. for L.A., where Joe was to make TV appearances for his new book. They were both seriously upset with each other and asked us to accompany them to L.A. to help enliven their depressed moods. We said we couldn't possibly leave our work here in New York so suddenly. So they left for L.A. the next day, and Barbara and I began feeling guilty over not going with them as their private psychiatrists. Barbara then told me, "What the hell, let's go." Without notifying your parents, we quickly made plane reservations, called the Beverly Hills Hotel, and, through *The Times*, managed to get a room right across the hallway from your parents' room. We arrived the next morning and Barbara rang the Heller room. Shirley answered the phone. Barbara said, "Hello, Shirley. Art and I decided you really needed cheering up, so we're planning to join you there as soon as we can get away." "When will you get here?" asked Shirley. "Sooner than you think," said Bar-

bara. Barbara hung up and we both dashed across the hotel hallway and knocked on your parents' door. Shirley opened the door and almost fell down. She and Joe couldn't stop laughing, and things did brighten for the moment.

My father was and had always been the most habitually playful of men. He flirted the way my grandmother dissembled. Both were hard-core: addicted to the *divertissement*. To be fair, my father was an equal-opportunity flirt—old women, young women, the homely and the beautiful, it didn't matter. He simply enjoyed the teasing, the bantering, the constant affirmation of his effect on people, like putting the key into a car to check whether the motor starts. A waitress might say at a coffee shop, "Your sandwich will be out in another few minutes," to which Dad might reply, "Oh yeah? And what if it's not?" See? Playful, jocular.

My assumption had always been that a man who flirted so openly with women in front of his wife and children, even with his wife and children's friends, had no need for actual affairs, let alone substantive relationships. I didn't accord it a lot of pondering, but that was only because it seemed so clear. He was just joking with people. He loved my mother. They had a strong marriage. Besides, other women took time and thought. It was an effort to keep se-crets and lie consistently. Wasn't he just a trifle too self-absorbed for the machinations of such tricky subplots?

That day at my aparatment, I listened to my mother and felt helpless as she started to cry and to tear at her hair and ask me what she was going to do if Dad left her. What was going to happen to her? She was fifty-five, and he had never "allowed" her to work or to develop a way to earn her own income.

When my parents met, my mother had also dreamed of having an artistic life. For herself. She loved playing the piano, had even talked about studying it seriously and possibly trying to have a mu-sical career. But that possibility ended abruptly and early on when one night, about a year after returning to New York from Oxford, while carrying groceries and wine home, my parents were walking along Broadway and my mother slipped and fell. A jagged shard of the wine bottle severed a tendon in her right hand. Of course, that was the end of the piano. Many years later, when she thought of going to school to get a degree in interior design, since it was something she enjoyed and everyone was always asking her for ideas and opinions about fabrics, room layouts, and furniture designs anyway, Dad told her that she was too old to start working.

Shirley eventually dried her eyes and pulled herself together. She took the crosstown bus home to wait for Dad to return from Erika Puzo's funeral, and was determined to have a serious discussion with him about what he wanted; a dry-eyed, honest appraisal of where they were headed and what was next. I was proud of her for being able to summon the necessary fortitude. Still, I awoke the next morning knowing what had to be done.

1980, THE MAN WITH A PLAN

At my request, my father met me for lunch the next day at Gin-ray, a Japanese restaurant on East Fiftieth Street near my office. I got there first, something that had never happened before, and Dad arrived shortly after. The minute he sat down, he burst into tears.

He proceeded to tell me that my mother's mental health had been unraveling for some time, that he still adored her and would never leave her no matter what—but that menopause had made her impossible to live with and that she was paranoid, delusional, and needed to be sent away somewhere for a good long rest. She had completely imagined Dr. Bugs, this woman he was supposedly seeing; someone who simply didn't exist. He wept into his miso soup. He raked a shaking hand through his tumultuous, leonine curls and told me, his voice faltering, tremulous, that his life had been hell for the past two years. He wiped his eyes with his napkin. He was a disaster. Some colleagues of mine sat at a nearby table, rapt, nakedly eavesdropping. I couldn't blame them. They had stumbled upon quite the spectacle.

"Do you understand what 'crazy' means?" my father asked me, crumpling in his seat and sighing loudly. When I told him that Mom claimed to have a copy of the deed for the house he had bought for Dr. Bugs in Santa Fe, and copies of plane tickets when this woman had, unbeknownst to my mother, accompanied my parents on holidays, he teared up again. I told him that Mom claimed to have photos of him with Dr. Bugs leaving various hotels on various continents; of him tossing her smallest children up into the air and catching them; picking them up from the expensive school where he had financed their education, in a pricey car he had also purchased for this nonexistent woman. I'd never seen these photos—I didn't want to—but I certainly believed they existed.

He looked ravaged. I began truly fretting about my mother's obvious mental and emotional fragility, and also began feeling terribly sorry for Dad. He looked broken. As if he hadn't slept since the Eisenhower years. Sliver by sliver, my heart went out to him, he who had so loyally stood by her.

But then, because I had decided to tell him this even before we met that day, regardless of whatever he was about to say, I told him for the first time, but certainly not the last, that every day people woke up and wanted to change their lives, that it wasn't a crime and that if he had indeed found someone else, had fallen in love and wanted to end his marriage, to change his life, just to please do it quickly, with some class, make arrangements for my mother's finances, be a mensch and not drag it out. Even as I spoke he looked at me, aghast, stung that I could feel the slightest need to even utter such ridiculousness.

"Haven't you heard even a word I've said?" he asked, leaning in toward me a bit, banging his fist on the table, upsetting the water glasses. "No matter what," he told me again and again, emphatically, smiling queerly, "I will never leave your mother. Never! Even if she has a psychotic break or drives me to have one. Even if she makes every minute of every day of my life intolerable. Even if I can't write or sleep or function, I still won't leave her."

And then about a month later he left her.

CLAUS IN THE HOUSE

People change and forget to tell each other.
                              —Lillian Hellman

I wish I could write here that this was the only lunch or dinner or slice of a mirthless afternoon or evening when I was to witness my father weeping and banging his fist on a restaurant table, in torment over his concern and resolute love for my mother. But it was just the first of many. Over the next two years, he maintained that my mother was imbalanced, hallucinating, that she'd invented an entire subtext to his life that was fantasy.

I finally believed him. In my defense, though, perhaps there *is* nothing defensible, others believed him, too. He was extremely convincing. In retrospect, nothing he said at the time made the slightest bit of sense, yet it all added up.

When he left my mother the first time, he claimed that she'd driven him out into the street, literally, with her madness, and that she must get urgent and prolonged psychiatric care. He took a studio apartment and told everyone that it was temporary. He had not wanted to leave, he claimed. Again and again, for two years, having no idea, really, of what the true picture was, I urged him to leave if that was what he wanted, to just settle things and move on so that Mom could do the same, psychologically and financially.

My mother's version of things, on the other hand, was that my father's decades of dedicated philandering had finally been brought to light. She had taken a shovel and had turned over the earth and knew where all the bodies were buried, and now, in order for my parents to stay married, he was going to have to change, something he was not prepared to do, not in the least and certainly not now, with Dr. Bugs in the picture.

As my mother told it, she'd first learned of the existence of Dr. Bugs when, according to my father, a call had come in from a certain film director who was flying into New York and wanted to meet with him the next day. After Dad left on the Jitney and came into the city, the same director actually *did* call the house and speak to Mom. She was on the next Jitney. She went to the Apthorp and confronted my father, who broke down, confessed all, and told her that he was in love. He began telling my mother then, according to her, about all of his affairs and indiscretions over the years with friends of hers, of theirs, students, writers, PR women, editors, butchers, bakers, candlestick makers. She said that, as he rattled on and on, his eyes and face had an odd, quiet calmness, as if he was relieved not to have to pretend anymore. Unburdening himself, he stood straighter, relieved. She was, of course, shattered.

My father denied this incident, the discussion, the litany of names, all of it, telling me for the first time ever that Mom, like her mother, Dottie, was an accomplished fabulist.

Meanwhile, Mom was a wreck. I remember visiting her at the Apthorp, walking through the thick curtain of cigarette smoke that clung to everything, noticing the piles of newspapers everywhere with crossword puzzles filled in. The place seemed cavernous when bereft of my father's presence. It was just room after room, hallway after hallway, leading to more rooms and more hallways, all empty of everything but cigarette smoke and a palpable despair. Crosswords, coffee, and cigarettes: those were, I think, the only things helping her get her mind off Joe in those days; off Dr. Bugs, and the torment of wondering if and when he might come back. He did. Several times. But only to leave again. "He just wants people to think he's a nice guy. He's *not* a nice guy," she would say to me defiantly. He wanted to leave but didn't want the responsibility of leaving, so he was making life so unbearable that she would have to throw him out once and for all. Then he could act, she claimed, literally put out, even though he had only accomplished what he'd set out to do in the first place.

She called me constantly, at work and at home, early in the morning, late at night—all day, every day—to talk about my father. It was always the same conversation, the same repetitive dirge. I began to dread and avoid her. A few times she showed up, again unannounced, at my apartment with folders and files, photographs, receipts from meals and vacations Dad had taken with Dr. Bugs, but I always, without exception, refused to look at them. I had made the decision to believe Dad, and then, having chosen that side of this devil's bargain, allowed everything presented rationally to me on the other side to be filtered through my prejudgment.

My mother went into therapy with a woman who, of course, would neither speak to me nor my father, nor divulge anything about my mother's treatment. I had met her, though, and recognized her on a crosstown bus one night, where I interrogated her from Third Avenue to Broadway with unanswerable questions. All my questions were about Dad. What should he do? Why was Mom doing this to him? How was he to deal with her in this state? By then almost no one would listen to my mother except someone who was paid to. Her story was not one any of us cared to hear. Eventually some of her friends became resentful toward her and paused their friendships. *How could she do this to Joe?* they asked her. I became impervious to her stories. There were a few times when I almost began to believe her, but then I would see my dad again—he would declare his love for her, his terror at her hallucinations, and his determination to fix their marriage—and I chose the version that sat best with me, his version.

My brother, Ted, was always unfailingly kind to her, but I was my father's daughter. Dad never wanted the messy detritus of other people's problems and neither did I. Looking back, I know I picked the side that was more comfortable for me, although, in truth, both were wrenching. However, I deserted Shirley, a sinking ship, just hoping that she was getting the care and help she needed and that maybe, just maybe, it might be in time for her to repair her marriage.

At some point during this very fragile period between them, before Dad left for the last time, when Mom was finally too furious and disgusted with him to exhibit her customary devotion, they attended a cocktail party together. While at this party, my mother referred to Dad, in the company of many, including him, as "the mogul." Arthur Gelb said about it:

> The mogul story, of course, illustrates Shirley's quiet, biting humor and is revealing of your parents' sometimes edgy relationship. And it's not hard to understand Joe's ire and embarrassment, illustrating his private insecurities—despite his remarkable renown as a writer.

In mocking him publicly, my mother had crossed an invisible line, broken the back of her loyalty to him. This was not, of course, the point of her. My mother thought that explanation ridiculous and would say: "He's in love. You'll see. That's what all of this is about," but I would shake my head, dismiss her words, and resume my life.

After the second time Dad left my mother and then returned again, he entered therapy for what I believe was the only time in his life. The doctor was highly esteemed, famous, a big name at his hospital. Big shot or not, my father was bored with the experiment, and when it came time for the doctor's August vacation, only a few months into their work together, the doctor (according to my father) asked him to please make no changes in his life until the doctor returned after Labor Day. My father agreed. The next day he packed up and left my mother for the last time, and soon fired his agent, antagonized his editor, and cut loose his CPA.

As for my mother, for the first time in her life she was alone. She had no work. She was not famous—the celebrity in the couple—so was quite literally on her own.

From the minute Dad left the third and final time, there were old and cherished friends who had been to her home for decades who now looked down when she passed, without acknowledging her. There were not many to offer her kindness, compassion, advice, or encouragement. Most of us were too busy feeling badly for Dad and were annoyed with her for tinkering with our delusions about their robust marriage. It was in this way that Dad drew a curtain around my mother, isolating her from friends and from other family members. Even my grandmother, by then no longer a great fan of Dad's, told Mom to knock it off and get him to come back already and then let him do whatever he wanted.

In another way, though, my mother was far from alone in her newly separated status. The Apthorp is a huge place and couples break up all the time. Phyllis Raphael, then my parents' next-door neighbor who was also at the time divorced, once picked my mother up from the floor of the lobby during the early days of my parents' schism after Mom had fainted. Two months later, Mom picked up the ordinarily feisty literary agent Lucy Kroll, now in the throes of her own divorce, from the same lobby floor after she'd collapsed. Did Lucy revive yet another jilted Apthorp wife at some later point? The circular logic would hardly surprise me.

Once Dad had left permanently, he stopped asking me about Shirley, although after my meetings with him, *she* would call me repeatedly with questions, most of which I'd never thought to ask him. Who was doing his laundry? Had he learned how to make his own coffee exactly as he liked it? Who, these days, was making him laugh? As for my father, his back story regarding my mother, once he had left her for good, began to take on a slightly different tinge. It became increasingly difficult to ignore the fact that the man was furious, consumed by rage, behaving as if he'd been scorned and was in fact the spurned party. No longer was there the merest inquiry or trace of concern for her well-being. I watched it happen. Bit by bit, the caring, sensitive, and devoted husband was metamorphosing into a great concentration of seething, blistering ire. When I'd see him, it was clear that this anger now engulfed and eclipsed all else.

My father was for the most part still in Joe World, different now because, whereas my mother had once been there to share it, now he shared it with his fury. And yet when we sat in restaurants together, I felt her absence so acutely in his life, it was tempting to ask for a place setting for her at the table.

Once, in 1985, years after their divorce, my father, always up for a bargain and a lover of coffee shops and diners, asked me to meet him at Mortimer's, a place in my neighborhood for the pedigreed. When I arrived, Dad was already eating his meal. As with many of his antics, I felt not particularly slighted. It was rude, but also amusing. I asked him a few times during that period why he couldn't just wait to order when I arrived, especially since I always arrived on time. But the great Talmudic thinker was, as ever, prepared: "Why should I be forced to sit here and not eat just because I'm here and you're not?"

That night at Mortimer's, we were talking about my grandmother's very excellent recipe for pot roast and about how much he missed eating that dish. As usual, he offered me ten thousand dollars in cash to divulge it, and as usual, out of allegiance to my mother, I turned it down. He told me that Speed had done his best to replicate it but had failed. Now Dad was asking me why the hell I wouldn't give it to him, for the umpteenth time, saying that Mom would never know. I responded that *I'd* know. Just then, a very tall, ghoulish-looking fellow in an expensive hound's-tooth sports jacket stood up from his table and made his way over to us. He had impeccable posture, and looming over us as he did, he seemed strangely self-important. "Joe Heller!" he said. "May I shake your hand?" My father put down his knife and fork and offered his hands to the man, saying, "Here, you can shake both." I stared at the gentleman in startled surprise, with my mouth open.

"I love what you write. Every word of every sentence of every book," our visitor gushed. "You have very good taste," Dad told him, picking up his cutlery to signal that the exchange was over. He was about to be bored; not quite, but nearly. I could see him teetering on boredom's precipitous edge.

The man returned to his table and my father to his food.

"How does it feel to be praised by an attempted murderer?" I inquired.

"Huh?"

At the time, the *Vanity Fair* piece about this man was everywhere, *he* was everywhere, there wasn't anyone who wasn't talking about Clarendon Court, the reportedly overinsulinized hypodermic needles, and wildly rich stepchildren. How oblivious did someone have to be not to realize who the man was?

"Who was that?" Dad finally asked.

"Claus von Bülow."

"No shit," Dad said, his eyes ablaze with devilment, craning his neck now to get a good look at von Bülow at his table, impressed; I was just never entirely sure by what.

HELLER EXEUNT

I had never heard of Guillain-Barré syndrome, but one Sunday in the winter of 1981, some months after my father had left Mom the last time, he awoke in his apartment on West Fifty-seventh Street one morning, and began getting dressed to meet Norman and Gloria Barasch, his old friends in from California, for brunch. He discovered that he had insufficient strength in his fingers to button his shirt. His condition deteriorated quickly, and an ambulance soon brought him to Mt. Sinai Hospital, where a nurse called to tell me that my father had been admitted. She said that he could speak but that he was "paralyzed all the way down," something too surreal to even attempt to envision. Tests would be required to determine what had been the cause. She asked me to notify my mother, which I did.

By the end of the next day, my vocabulary increased with the name of a pernicious and relatively rare paralytic disease, a viral infection of the nervous system, devastating and sometimes fatal, or so the doctors explained. My mother was badly shaken by the news that he was sick, very sick, but at first I think she may have mistrusted the whole thing, because by then they both mistrusted each other about everything. Everything she did now, he interpreted as some underhanded way to chisel money out of him in the approaching divorce, and everything he did, she suspected was a way to avoid paying her.

By then it had become virtually impossible for them to have even a short, civil conversation, and so finally they'd wisely stopped trying. Then one night, near the end of the first week of several he remained in intensive care, my father asked for a phone and for me to dial my mother. They spoke quietly, and in between his words I listened to the rhythmic sounds of the many machines helping to keep all the patients alive. They buzzed, beeped, and clicked. One large machine had a wet kind of suctioning sound. All other guests had left for the evening, and except for the machines and my father's almost whispery voice, the place was eerily quiet.

My father was telling my mother, slowly, because it still required great energy for him to speak and also to enunciate, how sick he was and how weak and defeated he felt. She listened. For the first time in years there was no rancor. When he had finished speaking, I could tell from his side of the conversation that my mother had told him that they were still married and that whenever he was released from the hospital he should come back home and that she would take care of him. That the only important thing now was for him to recover, and that then and only then should they try to sort out their marriage and figure out what was next—if they should remain separated or divorce. These were extreme circumstances, she'd explained, according to each of them later. Their hostilities deserved a break.

Sitting at the edge of his bed, I held the phone to his ear and saw tears begin flowing slowly down his cheeks. He cleared his throat a few times before speaking. "I would like to come home very much," he told her, "but that would be regressing." Because his speech was so garbled and his *R*s and *V*s so gutturally mangled, an effect of his illness, it was necessary for him to repeat this several times until she finally understood. If my heart stopped a bit at the notion of them speaking again, calmly like this, at her offer and the tenderness of his tears, at the specter of any kind of even temporary rapprochement, it then broke a little after hearing not only what he said but also the finality with which he said it. In those few quiet moments, their paths were charted and were clearly about to lead them out and away from each other for good. There was to be no thaw in their relations, and also no discussion.

But Shirley was still, amazingly, not defeated. The next day, while I was at work, she somehow shelved her years of escalating rage and any lingering pride, pulled herself together, and went to the hospital to visit Dad, to revisit what they'd spoken about the previous evening on the phone. This, however, was not to be. Two of Dad's friends met her at the door, like Don Corleone's henchmen, and begged her to go home, telling her that Dad didn't want to see her. He didn't. Both friends told me afterward that they had felt terrible doing it; they had each known both of my parents for over thirty years and didn't feel that they should get involved. But Dad was sick and his wishes should be honored. One friend offered to see her home, but she declined. I imagined her in the hospital elevator afterward, standing there as if in the grip of some sickly dream, getting down to the lobby of the hospital and then feeling faint, reaching for a chair and sitting down to steady herself, waiting for the reality of what had just happened to catch up to her day's cautious, impulsive dreams. My parents never spoke again.

Six years later, however, they stood together again, though clearly very much apart, literally on opposite sides of *my* hospital bed at Mt. Sinai. I'd been wheeled back to my room following a mastectomy. From time to time, I opened my eyes from the depths of my very deep, morphine-befogged sleep and saw them both turned away from each other. By then they were divorced, their hearts hardened entirely, with no more outward emotion shown than two pieces of furniture placed arbitrarily in a room. No words passed between them. From that day forward, they saw to it that they were never again in the same place at the same time. Such things can be arranged in life with great effort and reserves of energy, if one is only willing to expend them. They were.

If this were not bizarre enough, during the time that my father was a Mt. Sinai patient for Guillain-Barré syndrome, before he became a Rusk Rehabilitation patient some time later, my grandfather, the close to angelic Barney Held, my mother's father, was also admitted to Mt. Sinai, for prostate cancer. Grandpa Barney was a mild-mannered, soulful, faintly failed man who lived only to make his children and grandchildren happy. He was someone utterly without sharp corners or rough edges, incapable of a single nasty retort. Growing up, I could never understand where this benefactor of goodness and gentleness had come from. I could be the most re-calcitrant boor and he would still call me "doll." I could have shown up wearing the Lindbergh baby on my head and Grandpa would have said, "Nice hat." In fact, in the more than twenty years since his death, I still think of him every year on Kentucky Derby day. The week before he died, of bone cancer, in 1986, he awoke one morning and felt the overwhelming urge to make a last trip to the Gulfstream Racetrack. My grandmother tried to prevent it—he was impossibly weak—but he was uncustomarily belligerent and would not be deterred. He was picked up at home by a cab and taken to the track, but felt ill by the third race and fainted by the fifth. He always claimed that angels had gotten him home that day, because he had no memory of anything after fainting. Angels? At Gulfstream? I was only immensely glad that he made it home.

Now my mother was going daily to Mt. Sinai to visit her fa-ther but was forbidden to see her husband of thirty-plus years, also there.

I remember clearly the day of January 21, watching the hos-tages being freed from Iran on the wall-mounted television set in my grandfather's hospital room. His roommate moaned in un-imaginable pain. It was a great day for the hostages, but one not so great for this man, or for my mother. I glanced at her, watching the television as my grandmother bawled out one of the Jamaican nurse's aides about something inconsequential. My mother looked crushed.

The night before New Year's Eve I went to visit Dad at Mt. Sinai after work. He was still in intensive care. When I got there, I flicked open the curtain separating him from the patient in the next bed and then, once at his bed, flicked it closed again. And with that one, sharp, thoughtless motion of my wrist, that one movement and moment, I learned that my father's pose for the past several years had all been one colossal lie, a masquerade—because there, standing beside Dad's bed, was the "nonexistent" Dr. Bugs. I knew that because he introduced us.

All in a split second, I keenly felt the folly of my ways, understood what had been my resolute blindness. I saw right through the armor of my mother's aloneness, the elaboration of my father's spectacle, down to its finest, most intricate detail. In word and deed it was perhaps his finest creation, a masterpiece that would sadly never make it to the printed page. I thought of the energy that it had required of him, the willfulness of sustained deception and nuanced performance, and it engulfed me. I felt impossibly sad for both my parents. I still felt love for him, this man who had been so weakened by disease that he required feeding from a nose tube, and would need months of rehabilitation just to be able to sit up again in bed. I felt for him, but I also felt for my mother, wondering immediately what I was going to say to her about this; how I ever could even begin to make it up to her.

Meanwhile, nothing my mother had told me about this woman prepared me in the least for what I saw standing next to his bed, giggling. I had interrupted a discussion, apparently, about the rickety condition of his finances.

In the bedlam of his final separation from my mother that year, Dad had forgotten to reinstate his medical insurance policy, which would have amounted to all of $132. Instead, his illness, with a month and a half at Mt. Sinai, some of it in a private room with private nurses, then months spent at Rusk, were going to amount to in excess of $120,000 of out-of-pocket expenses. This was catastrophic for him, and he talked about it often to some of the visitors who came to visit him: George Mandel, Speed Vogel, Mel Brooks, Mario Puzo. Without loans, taken and repaid from friends, things would have been far more dire for Dad than they already were. And yet, he was now joking with Dr. Bugs about his lapsed policy and how he was destined for the poorhouse. I noticed that he laughed a bit more about it than she did.

Dad introduced me to Dr. Bugs without embarrassment or the slightest hesitation. He did this without any apparent awareness of the gravitas of the occasion or of how it recast the drama of the past few years. Perhaps he was just greatly relieved at no longer having to pretend. Meanwhile, I took in the whole experience of her, the gum energetically chewed, the wine-stained peasant blouse, the purple suede, high-heeled boots with tight jeans tucked in at the knee.

When I pulled myself together and put on my coat to leave that evening, I asked my father when we might be able to speak privately. He told me to come back at noon the following day.

As I was leaving, I heard Dr. Bugs ask my father: "How the fuck do you take a crap if you're paralyzed?"

At that point, I had many questions for him myself, but that was not among them.

THE GIMLET-EYED JOURNALIST, THE ANTSY NOVELIST, AND THE PREDICTION THAT CAME TRUE

Years later in 1998, when my parents were divorced and the charade over, in Lynn Barber's *Observer* interview, Dad spoke about the end of his long marriage.

Barber wrote:

> He once rebuked an interviewer for calling him a "womanizer," explaining that "a womanizer is someone who is passionately attracted to women. I wasn't." But if he wasn't attracted to women, why did he sleep with so many? "I'll tell you why. First of all, there were not that many. And second, it was part of the male culture. It was not a sexual drive, it was just . . . I was in New York City working in an atmosphere where men did that, we'd have parties and a couple would go into a room together. I think twice I fell in love—it lasted a year—I never had a wish to end my marriage, and when summer came and I went away with my family for the summer that was usually the end of it, a very peaceful ending. Those were what I would call affairs, the others were just individual sexual encounters. It was a

delightful phase; it mostly started after *Catch-22*, and I felt very good about myself. Looking back, I don't feel so good about it, because the effect on my wife was devastating. I regret much of the outcome. On the other hand, I enjoyed very much the experiences, and if I had to do it all over again, I don't know which I would do." He says his wife, Shirley, never accurately detected his affairs, but she knew he was unfaithful.

The truth is, he did not accurately know what she accurately knew. Some years before, as cliché an occurrence as in any marriage, she had come upon a crumpled, handwritten letter to my father in the jacket pocket of a suit of his on its way to the dry cleaner. The note was written by a saucy, famous French novelist and alluded to the affair they had recently had while he was at a speaking engagement in London. With her customary flair, the author had written at length about her love of the pair of sexy, expensive ostrich heels he'd sent her as a gift after returning home. My mother read the letter, filed it away in her brain, and put it back into Dad's suit pocket.

It was certainly not the only letter of its type that she found over the years, she later told me. It was just by far the best written.

Like many women I have known who are sage about others but willfully astigmatic about their own foibles, when a newly famous author and his shy wife came over one morning to my parents' home in East Hampton a few years before my parents' breakup, my mother looked into the woman's face and instantly read her future. They had never met before. The writer had phoned and asked if it might be all right to come by with his wife and kids. He was clearly in awe of Dad, the older, more established writer. He looked around the house as if he were in Versailles, although it was a simple place, far less opulent than most in the area. The four of them had coffee in the kitchen while a friend and I tossed a ball to the couple's children out back. The younger writer, already a huge success and about to become even more of one, was, according to my mother, clearly impatient about becoming much more famous much more quickly. She found the nakedness of his ambition daunting.

At one point the man's sweet, unpretentious wife said something and the younger author waved her words away like flies. As my parents watched them leaving, backing out of the driveway, my father said that the man was about to enjoy phenomenal success. He was correct.

My mother, meanwhile, had one thought in her mind, but kept it to herself. "I give that marriage, at most, a year and a half," she told me later. She wasn't off by much.

PART 3

Apartment 5B South

Bittersweet on Broadway/Shirley goes solo

1989–1997

SHIRLEY'S NEW HUSBAND

After my parents separated permanently, for a time I became my mother's new quasi-husband. There's no other way to describe it. I escorted her everywhere, made decisions for her, offered advice, listened to her, endlessly, every day about my father, consoled her hourly if that was what she needed. It took time for both of us to forge this new, post–Dr. Bugs relationship of ours, factoring in my immense guilt over having believed my father that Mom was a hallucinating maniac rather than a very miserable wife.

At some point that year, each of my parents hired a divorce lawyer and began preparing a strategy for arbitration, as well as running up outrageous legal bills. As time passed and my mother grew increasingly frightened about how she was going to manage financially, and as Dad became increasingly determined not just to divorce but to annihilate her, the likelihood of a full-blown trial began to loom.

Meanwhile, Dad was still recovering from his illness. He was confined to a wheelchair, with still a long way to go toward full recovery. While he was at Rusk, Speed lived in Dad's midtown apartment, dressed in his clothes, opened his mail, and paid his bills. That was the basis for their jointly written book, *No Laughing Matter*. It is often referred to as a "book about illness," but I always thought of it as one about friendship.

Money, as always, continued to preoccupy Dad. This was exacerbated by how much the illness had cost him in even more than monetary terms, and how much it still restricted and defined his life. The fact that he was now willing to pay a lawyer to go after my mother in court said much.

For Dad, the matter of settling with my mother had nothing to do with who would get Uncle Chaim Yankel's frying pan (if there'd been an Uncle Chaim Yankel and he'd had a frying pan). The suit against my mother had become something far more primal and enormous. He was now out for blood, behaving as if he were the spurned party, which, evidently, he somehow felt that he was. His weapon of choice, not surprisingly, was an attempt to withhold money. If at that point a judge had determined that my mother was to live out her last years destitute in a cardboard box on Broadway, on one dollar a year from my father, he would still have felt the sting of injustice. Nothing at that time would have felt fair or reasonable to him.

Friends spoke to him and explained that if he never settled with my mother, this action would go on and on and lawyers' fees would ultimately deplete them both. He knew that; he was far too smart not to. But he was in no mood for detente. Was some underlying wish of his at work then, was he trying in some way to keep himself connected to Mom by prolonging this relationship, even though it was through deprivation and contempt? When it was over and they parted, there would be nothing left to hold them together. The only communication they would ever have again would be through lawyers mopping up the mess. Was that why he insisted on protracting this costly vendetta? Like anyone, I can only turn off the sound and look at the picture. It was quite a picture.

Regardless of reasons or intentions, there was no way my parents were going to settle the terms of the divorce out of court. As for my mother, she felt that any further cutbacks in her already economical lifestyle would be unconscionable to expect from her at this point in her life; and yet, the reality of a divorce at that time, 1981, in New York City, where the husband worked and the wife did not, practically guaranteed an income for her from my father, but would also likely require some downsizing. Dad was asking to keep the East Hampton house while "giving" my mother the Apthorp apartment, which was, of course, only a rental.

In the midst of all this, my grandmother Dottie decided to fly up to New York to try to talk some sense into her hard-headed son-in-law. She had lunch several times with Dad, but each one seemed to go worse than the last. After their third meeting, Dad not only refused to ever speak to her again, he discontinued the small monthly allowance he'd been sending my grandparents for many years. That bit of money had helped to cover some of their medical expenses as they arose while they grew older. No one ever knew precisely what transpired at that last lunch, what Dottie had said or done to provoke him. Later on, she only told me that she should have "killed him when [she] had the chance." Oy. "He was right there. I could have smashed his brains to smithereens with a frying pan."

"You'd be in prison," I told her, knowing it wouldn't help to quell her hatred.

"Who would put an old lady in prison?" she asked seriously.

Grandma returned to Florida ahead of schedule, though behind in her checkbook, and my father was filled with a fresh wave of loathing for my mother for having unleashed the wrath of Grandma upon him.

There was another issue that prevented my parents from seeking an out-of-court settlement. My mother was claiming that my father had committed adultery with Dr. Bugs and that he had provided this woman with large sums of money over a span of several years. Dad absolutely refused to acknowledge my mother's assertion in the divorce papers and was now back to his old song about my mother imagining this woman who had never existed. As incredible as it appeared that Dad would revert to this, it was his only defense, I suppose, against having to give my mother what he felt was "all" of his money.

Eventually my mother's lawyer asked me to testify on her behalf, because there was in fact nobody else who'd go on legal record claiming to have actually met Dr. Bugs. To me, it was an eviscerating possibility. The prospect of going into court and opposing my father, whom I loved even if I didn't always understand him, was crushing, but what choice did I have? I had deserted my mother when she'd most relied upon my support. I could not abandon her again.

Once I knew I'd be called as a witness, I phoned Dad and let him know. I begged him to settle and end this trial, but his response was gruff and hostile, and at some point immediately following our conversation he decided that it was no longer enough to merely ruin my mother in court—he would also have to pulverize me. I could tell that he was seething from his subdued tone of voice.

I nevertheless knew that I had to testify. I was terrified about what my father's lawyer would do to me on the stand, but my mother's attorney, a benign and courtly gentleman, repeatedly assured me that attacking someone's child in a courtroom was an unwise tactic and that it would be unusual for it to be employed. "I'll ask you a couple of questions, then the other guy may ask a few, politely, and that'll be that," he promised.

If only. My mother's lawyer asked me three quick practice questions about Dr. Bugs, which I answered calmly. And then in the courtroom I faced my father's attorney. Dad had hired a tanned, cutthroat, manicured fashion plate with blue-black hair. With a sarcastic grin, he immediately began roaring at me with questions that my father was furiously scribbling and handing to an aide to give to him. At various times I turned to the judge, an elderly man who seemed impervious to the fact that an attorney in his courtroom was grandstanding. "Is it necessary for him to shout at me?" I asked the judge, perhaps three times. Twice the old bird waved away my words, and only the third time said, "No, but if I can stand it, you can stand it." The lawyer's loud, bombastic interrogation lasted roughly two hours and covered areas of my life that were not only irrelevant but also extremely private. My father's bag of tricks was overflowing as he quickly, masterfully jotted down his questions. I held to my story, though. I had to, and I simply waited for the inquisition to end. I couldn't look at my father, bent over the table where he sat, scribbling faster and faster.

Oddly enough, even on that day, no doubt the worst ever of my parents' marriage, it never occurred to me that they no longer loved each other. I merely considered that this love had been transformed into something malignant.

I left the courthouse exhausted, and the next day awoke with a fever of 103 and couldn't stop shivering. At the trial's end, the judge outwitted all involved by granting my mother a settlement high enough to madden my father and low enough to guarantee that her last years would be spent nervous and afraid, terrified over how she would manage.

As for what became of the notorious Dr. Bugs, I assumed that she'd soon become my stepmother. My mother had an altogether different theory, however. Her scenario was that Joe had depleted all of his resources during his illness, leaving Dr. Bugs without hope of a prosperous future with him.

Several years later, standing in line at a deli one morning, I felt a tap on my shoulder and turned to see the tanned face and blue-black hair of my father's attorney. I held in a gasp. What was there possibly for us to say to each other? But he was all sweetness and charm. The tanned, manicured hand stayed on my shoulder as he flashed me a bright smile and told me that he and his wife thought of me every day. Seeing my incredulous expression, he explained that they had thought my name, Erica Jill, was so lovely that they'd given it to their daughter. I dropped my coffee on the floor and ran for the exit.

My next experience in a courtroom came when I was called for jury duty, where it was my divine luck to sit on a panel in which the two opposing counsel were named Mr. Fox and Mr. Wolf. Mr. Fox had a pointed muzzle and gray hair and was far more cunning than Mr. Wolf. He was ferocious, bigger, taller, planted on longer legs, with sharp-angled, erect ears. Every time the judge requested anything of "Mr. Fox and Mr. Wolf," I had to stifle my laughter. In that case, the vulpine/lupine absurdity was entirely delicious, and yet when I looked around, no one else seemed to think that it was funny.

My mother always claimed that the entire divorce trial had been a sham because the judge had clearly been enamored of Dad, but I saw no evidence of that during the one day I was there. Meanwhile, two of my parents' friends, who sat in the courtroom on the trial's final day, told me that just as my father was preparing to leave, the judge actually asked him to please autograph the copy of *Catch-22* he'd brought with him from home. Dad evidently signed it, and honestly, I'd give anything to see what he wrote.

As for my parents and their divorce, there was no fox and no wolf, just two sad, furious, exhausted people who had come to the end of a very long and wild ride. Well, almost.

THE NURSE IN THE
LIME-GREEN SWEATER

*Many a man owes his success to his first wife and
his second wife to his success.*
—Jim Backus

In 1984, with the divorce behind them, both of my parents began
reshaping their lives. Dad lived at the house in East Hampton, and
with the help of Speed Vogel, a physical therapist, and a brutal rehabilitation agenda, made an extraordinary recovery. It should also
be noted here that he had the assistance of an able, voluble Mt.
Sinai nurse. And that when she met him, as he himself wrote later
in *No Laughing Matter*, she thought he was Norman Mailer.

They were married in 1987.

During the first years, I hunted for common ground between
us, but soon realized that the cartographer hadn't yet been born
who could pinpoint a single inch of it. She was younger than Dad,
not Jewish, favored gold chains, lime-green sweaters, and cerulean
eye shadow, and was fond of such non-Hellerian activities as line
dancing and playing bridge. Whereas her husband, if he had played

a hand, it would more likely have been turning the pages of some great novel or *The New York Times*.

It was hard not to feel bad for her; after all, even the nimblest mind was hardly a match for Joe when in a cutting mode. Per Gedin said that the first time Dad brought her to Sweden, he introduced her with: "This is my wife. She thinks *Catch-22* was a movie." (At such moments, she might have wished she *had* married Mailer.)

When Dad died, after his funeral, which played out like broad farce from one of his novels, there was never again any need for direct contact between Dad's wife and me.

The cartographer didn't need to have been born. Our locations were finally fixed, and the distance between us would remain vast.

MILO MINDERBINDER AND THE CASE OF THE MYSTERIOUSLY VANISHING SLIPCOVERS

Following the divorce, my mother began reclaiming all the dropped stitches of her life, trying to fuse them all together into something workable. She worried incessantly about money, spent as little as possible, but continued fretting nonetheless. When friends of hers began a catering company with parties in the Hamptons the following summer, she signed on as a server, a waitress. We both chortled and referred to her as Mildred Pierce, but there was little to laugh at when she was hauling heavy platters of food around in ninety-eight-degree heat at someone's beach estate, someone who more than likely had been entertained by her a few years earlier on Skimhampton Road.

When the time came to actually divide up my parents' many, many years of belongings, predictably, nothing went smoothly. Many of the larger pieces, chandeliers and armoires, for instance, that my mother had put into the East Hampton house had belonged to my grandmother. On the couches in the living room were slipcovers that my mother had had made by a woman who was an exquisite seamstress from Spain, now living in New Jersey. My mother, who always knew precisely who to go to for any aesthetic task she needed performed to her exacting specifications, had found this woman through her tailor, and the seamstress did not disappoint.

It was the era of chintz and my mother chose boldly. The first thing everyone commented on when entering the house on Skimhampton was the couches, and even my father, usually above such prosaic details as home furnishings, would tingle at the fulsome praise. After all, he had chosen the woman who had chosen the chintz.

But, of course, whenever it had come to dressing or decorating, my father had always been proud of my mother's unusual but unerring eye. That never changed. For thirty-seven years, when it came to furnishing an apartment or a house or choosing a necktie, my father had always depended on my mother for her expertise. Friends called her to get fashion advice and coaxed her to give them tips on how to spruce up their cottages, apartments, mansions. Later, much later after the divorce, my mother finally attended a program in interior design. She received a degree and then became a professional. But she found then that, as with many things, the joy was extruded from the experience when it was necessary rather than optional.

But now the thought of those Skimhampton Road slipcovers was gnawing at Shirley. Along with the many heirlooms from her side of the family that my father now owned, the idea of his also having those slipcovers agitated her. And so one breezy summer afternoon when my mother happened to read in a local paper that Dad was away on a speaking tour in Kansas, she rented a car and, with her cohort and old friend Roz Perlman and the ever-loyal, intrepid, now-retired Viola, drove out to the house in East Hampton. In those days, front doors were still left unlocked, so the women had no difficulty slipping inside, unzipping the prized chintz covers, and spiriting them back to the city, where by nightfall, they replaced the ones on my mother's Apthorp couches. She claimed later to have slept soundly that night for the first time in weeks.

Several years later, my mother realized that Apartment 10C had come to feel like a gigantic, empty mausoleum and that she could actually do with far less space. She tuned in to the well-known Apthorp grapevine. By then it was an extremely popular place to live. Apartments were frequently being traded in many apartment buildings then for unofficial cash deals. It was done all the time. You bribed someone to get in and then, when your needs changed, you bribed someone again. Once you were in, though, you were in. Young couples with growing families traded up, buying more rooms from divorcees and widows wanting to pocket some cash and consolidate.

Mom looked at some two-bedroom apartments. The current tenants wanted to pay her to swap, but for a while she found nothing that she felt was suitable. At the same time, she began taking the Hampton Jitney out to Amagansett, East Hampton, Southampton, and Bridgehampton once or twice a week to look at houses. She selected and then unselected more than a few places. The truth was, she badly missed being out there, and if she was trading down at the Apthorp, a weekend house was going to be her reward. Unfortunately, her budget dictated that the new house was not going to be what she'd been accustomed to. Eventually she found something just a bit beyond her price range, a sweet, newly built place north of the Montauk Highway in Bridgehampton. It had a splendid, airy feeling and a pool. The house was made especially lovely by its lush, green surroundings. It sat in the middle of horse farms, potato fields, and tall grasses that rippled in a breeze. The first night we spent there after the closing, there was a huge thunderstorm and lightning struck the well. The sound was reminiscent of the one made during my childhood when the doctors Cohen had smashed the Cadillac into the Apthorp canopy. "Why did I buy a house?" my mother asked the plumber who showed up the following morning, charging her more to repair the damage of one bolt of lightning than she was used to spending during an entire year in the city on her apartment. "What was I thinking? Who did I think I was?" she kept asking the man over and over again, as if he had any answers.

After the divorce and my testimony against him, my father had implemented what I came to regard as the Big Freeze. The Mondo

Froideur. My calls went unreturned. Letters were sent back to me unopened. I was excommunicated. This went on for months and was, of course, distressing, but I knew that Dad functioned on some invisible, unfathomable inner cycle with me. He had to make his point about the divorce and the trial, and there was nothing I could do to hurry along the trajectory.

But then one morning in July of 1988, the year my mother bought the house in Bridgehampton, I was sitting in my office in the city when my father called. Without the benefit of any small talk he asked me if what he'd heard was true, that Mom had gotten a place in Bridgehampton.

"Yes," I answered.

"So, what's it like?" he wanted to know.

"Nice."

He seemed flabbergasted. Clearly this was not something he'd ever planned on having to confront, the proximity of her out there, practically in his own backyard.

"How can she afford it?" he grumbled, starting to grow angry, realizing that something in his plan to keep her on a very short financial leash had obviously been overlooked.

Not a word was offered about the time-enforced silence between us, nor the reason for it.

"Well, if you want to come out and stay for a weekend, come," he offered amiably. "Bring anyone you want." Now *I* was the un-comfortable one. "Mom has a house. I'm taking a few weeks off over the summer and staying there."

He tried again. "Well, I have a pool. Come and swim in the pool."

"Mom has a pool," I told him then, at which point I could feel the anger rising in him, the confusion and exasperation at not being able to see the entire picture although it was right in front of him. He knew that Mom had moved to a smaller apartment and that, in those days at the Apthorp, that often involved money.

"Heated?" he finally asked lamely, grasping, about the pool. "You know mine is," he added, confident then that he'd won.

That entire summer he kept imagining he saw Mom, even

when she was in the city. "I saw your mother at the fruit market yesterday," he might call and tell me. "Tell her that that shade of blue she was wearing does nothing for her." I would try to change the subject, since I knew for a fact that Mom had been in the city that whole week. Still, he saw her everywhere. At the market, the beach, the pharmacy, at a Southampton gas station. Now that he knew she might be out there, he looked for her constantly. And kept finding her, even when she wasn't there.

Later that summer, in the middle of August, I took my summer vacation and spent it out at Mom's. We put in an herb and vegetable garden, tons of hydrangeas and roses, and two very puny, scrawny weeping willows. The flowers and herbs and vegetables flourished as if in a science-fiction saga. Overnight, basil plants barely reaching our ankles were now taller than we were. The salty breezes smelled of licorice and of roses and of horse manure from the nearby stables. During the course of this gardening extravaganza, both my mother and I were diagnosed with Lyme disease, something my father claimed to his dying day didn't exist. My mother's case was mild; she took Doxycycline and it was gone, but it did nothing to help me, so eventually I received daily IV treatments of antibiotics at Southampton Hospital.

The summer after that, nothing grew, nothing. Ever again. The soil was studied, we'd used the correct insecticides, and received house calls from nearby nurseries. No one could explain the phenomenon. It was a mystery. The two shriveled weeping willows had much indeed to weep about.

One day during my daily treks to and from Southampton, I happened to look out the living room window as I was getting ready to go. Sitting just across the road, parked right past our driveway, was a new-looking white car. Dad was seated behind the wheel, just staring ahead, down Scuttlehole Road, toward Sag Harbor. As soon as he saw me at the window and realized I'd spotted him, he drove away.

Still, he continued to call me and tell me that he had just seen Shirley at a Southampton coffee shop or leaving a tag sale. Once he called me at my office and said: "Tell your mother she's a terrible parallel parker," claiming to have just seen her botching the job in Amagansett, when at the time I knew she was in California visiting a cousin.

Back at the Apthorp after the summer, my mother found that from then on, living alone there proved not to be quite as challenging as she worried it was going to be when my father first left.

The only incident I can recall where she may have been decidedly out of her element was the following Christmas, after she had just left the gargantuan 10C for 5B South, after distributing Christmas money to the staff. The day after her envelopes had been given out, one elevator man, the meek but evidently lovestruck Mauricio, was so overcome with gratitude (though my mother, with her cautious frugality, had given less than most tenants), that the next time she entered his elevator, he put his arms around her, impulsively dipped her backward, and kissed her full on the lips. He was instantly contrite and babbled his apologies profusely, in Spanish and in English, but the damage was done. My mother may have reverted to using the stairs from then on during Mauricio's shifts, or else to scaling the side of the building; in any case, she was never in the elevator alone with him again. To me he only mumbled his sorrowful regrets the next time he saw me, shaking his head and throwing up his hands in exquisite desperation. "Your mother, she is a beautiful woman," he told me, pale and trembling, overcome, even as he sought to make things right. The following month he was transferred to another side of the building. My mother had never said a word to management about him, and I think the move was his idea. He was genuinely mortified.

Following what we thereafter referred to as "the Mauricio Incident," my mother continued to pull her life together. Now when I'd visit her, I'd find her bed cluttered with design books, graph paper, and rulers. She started to go on trips with friends. She slowly regained her equilibrium and was determined to live her life by stepping around the postdivorce detritus rather than splashing around in it. It took real mettle, and at last I began to see and fully appreciate what she was made of.

Two friends, two writers, two highly coveted slipcovers

Mom was no longer the celebrity's wife, and in many circles, both in Manhattan and in the Hamptons, this rendered her a nonentity. Still, she pushed ahead. She stopped smoking. She received commissions to decorate homes in East Hampton and in Ridgefield, Connecticut. She spent time at nurseries, at lunch, shopping, and at the movies with old friends like Dolores Karl and June Ferrin. Her humor was perhaps a touch more brittle, more wry and self-deprecating now, but the thing is, the old girl was back.

She had Dad's chintz slipcovers, yes, but for the first time it began to dawn on me that she might actually still have quite a bit more.

CURRIED TUNA, VALIUM, AND CANCER

There is no droll or winsome way for me to write about having cancer. I can only recount what happened and then what happened because of what happened.

About thirty years ago I had to change gynecologists, since mine was retiring. The one I found was an elegant, soft-spoken fellow in a large practice on Upper Fifth Avenue. He was patient, took the time to actually explain things, and when something was worrisome to him, he proceeded carefully. He was not prone to drama, although he did—and does—delightfully resemble Omar Sharif.

At one of my yearly checkups, he discovered something anomalous in one breast. I took the breast to several doctors affiliated with different hospitals. There was a lump, I had a biopsy, and it was determined that it was cancerous. We discussed a lumpectomy and a mastectomy, the cons and pros, if that word can be used in this context. When determining my course of treatment, my surgeon told me that whatever I opted for should be determined by the level of risk I was willing to live with. Since I knew only too well that I was equipped and prepared to live with exactly none, I chose to have a mastectomy. My left breast would be removed and reconstruction with a plastic surgeon would begin simultaneously.

At the time, I was living on East Seventy-eighth Street with my boyfriend, also a copywriter, and I was far more comfortable dwelling on his problems, which were considerable, than on my own. He drank too much, gambled too much, had ten children, biologically or adopted, and three (angry) ex-wives. He was terrifically funny, told a great story, and was somehow, to me, quite appealing. He also had a catastrophic degenerative disorder of the central nervous system. I had lived with him for several years—the lease on the apartment was in my name—but for at least the previous year, I'd been trying to figure out a way to get him to move out. He was, to put it mildly, reluctant to relocate. I wasn't ending the relationship because his neurological illness had progressed. I was ending it because drinking made him bitter, sloppy, and dishonest.

Over the years my father had slowly relaxed his rule about not meeting my boyfriends. In fact, he'd met this one on several occasions and quite liked him. He fell for the whole Damon Runyon demeanor, the suspenders and the homespun stories peppered with scintillating slang about casinos and racetracks, all served up in a sort of shy, self-effacing wrapper. My mother detested him from the minute she first met him, telling him: "I wouldn't trust you as far as I could throw you," adding, "How far would *that* be, do you think?"

But Dad? It was love. He knew that this man drank too much and gambled away our rent money, yet whenever we'd say good-bye to my father after a lunch or a dinner or a weekend out at the beach, Dad would slap him on the back and say about me, "I don't know how you do it. You must be a saint to put up with her." How many saints get so drunk that they tell you they accidentally washed their underwear in the dishwasher the night before, and not just that, but how delicate and forgiving Cascade can be on pastels?

In general, up until then, my father had usually been fairly perceptive about the men in my life. He wasn't overly curious or interested to know who I was seeing and, of course, had early on told me not to expect him to be. From time to time, though, while my parents were still married, I would bring people over for dinner at the Apthorp. After the divorce, those dinners took place in restaurants. One guy, who happened to be anorexic, arrived at dinner with me, Dad, and Mrs. Dad, ordered a full meal, tasted everything, and then moved it all around his plate in a well-rehearsed routine. But little got past Joe.

As we were putting on our coats, he leaned over and whispered to me about this guy: "What's the matter? He doesn't like food?"

Arriving home from my breast surgeon appointment the day after my mastectomy had been scheduled, I was very much hoping that Nathan Detroit would be elsewhere. When I got upstairs, thankfully the apartment was empty, and the first thing I did was call my mother. Then I called Dad.

At the time I was between jobs. It was late May, and I had six weeks until my surgery; six weeks in which to dread the mastectomy, and even more than that, what the postoperative pathology report would reveal. Somehow, the only thing I wanted to eat was curried tuna from a tiny shop in Southampton. My mother was out in Bridgehampton but returned to the city immediately with some for me. She was the one who managed to extricate me from my soured relationship, found my ex someplace to live, and actually moved him in, at great cost to herself.

The day I received the date for my surgery, my mother and her old friend June, from upstate, drove in from Long Island, picked me up from my apartment, and returned to Mom's out in Bridgehampton. Our first night there, when I realized how overwrought Mom and I both were, and that we'd never be able to sleep, I called Dad. He and I were getting along pretty well at the time, and when I told him that I was so frightened that I thought I'd never be able to sleep again, he offered me Valium. The upshot, which in retrospect does manage to seem amusing despite the circumstances, was that Dad put twenty-five Valium into an envelope and left it in his mailbox. Then Mom, June, and I drove over at around midnight to retrieve the package. We parked on his property. All around was pitch-black that night—no stars, no discernable moon. Total quiet on the road. One light was on in his kitchen. As Mom dug deep into the mailbox to pry out the envelope, I peered around a corner and saw Dad sitting at the kitchen table, running a sharp knife around the rim of half a grapefruit and dividing it into sections. Then he quickly speared the juicy, fleshy triangles, one after another, and popped them into his mouth.

THE THEATER OF RAGE

It was astonishing, but from the very beginning of my bout with cancer, my mother became enraged. She was furious—at *me*. The terror about the cancer and my impending surgery never left me during those days for even a moment, but I've come to believe that somehow it was an even greater trauma for her. And because I figured that there was no place for her to unburden herself of her extreme sadness and outrage, in some primal, transmuted form, she kept handing it all back to me. My father was stunned and upset, that was clear, but there were no tantrums. That was my mother's domain.

The night before my mastectomy, my father called me to say that I'd have to work out a "system" for my parents to visit me during the few days I'd be in the hospital so that there would be no overlapping. I then got furious at them both. My mother was at my apartment at the time, and I told both my parents that I was having serious surgery and that working out a "system" would be between them. Enough was enough.

I was not outstandingly brave. I threw up and paced the entire night before my operation, just trying to focus and imagine it all being over. When two friends arrived at 5:00 a.m. to take me to Mt. Sinai, I looked down at my feet and wondered how they were ever going to walk me into that hospital for something I so badly wanted not to have to do. Still, they got me there, and the surgery began on schedule. When I awoke in the recovery room hours later and was brought back into my room, both of my parents had shown up, along with my father's wife. They were all together, but not speaking. Both of my parents were obviously angry and unhappy about having to be in the same place at the same time. All rooms for this surgery were private, so Joe and Shirley could glower at each other freely, without distraction, except for Dad's wife, who never stopped fussing.

Over the next five days in Mt. Sinai, while I began to heal and waited for the pathology report to arrive, both of my parents visited every day but never again together. My father seemed abnormally shy and was peculiarly quiet. Meanwhile, whenever Mom came by, she usually managed to pick a fight with me, and ended up leaving and slamming the door, telling me that I was "impossible." This was significant, because perhaps for the first time ever, I honestly couldn't understand why. I mean, I *wasn't*. I hadn't challenged or provoked her in any way. I mostly lay in my bed wrapped in layers of clammy bandages, on painkillers, with tubes and drains plugged in from all directions, or else I walked the dimly lit halls, slowly, dragging my IV along with me like a wobbly rag doll. Friends visited, but their visits were exhausting.

I was unprepared for the savagery of my mother's fury. She phoned me every night in my room and we usually argued about one thing or another; she often ended the conversation by slamming down the phone while I was still speaking. Years later I found out that she had been so distraught about my surgery and frightened about my diagnosis that after each one of those calls, she would call my grandmother in Florida, sit on the phone, and just sob.

It took months for her anger to ebb, but it did, and eventually we became friends again.

JOYEUSES FÊTES? ALMOST

In 1993 Mom decided that she wanted to go to Paris for the holidays, that it would be impossible to feel lonely and forgotten at such a festive time of year in the world's most magnificent city. Since the divorce, Christmas in particular had made her feel morose. The twist, though, was that she wanted to go with me.

Sometimes a trip just doesn't work. It happens. And when it does, it's obvious from the instant you set out that nearly everything about the whole escapade is not going to work out—not your mood, not the sky, not all the hours about to roll by in weary, unsmiling determination. You want to stop somehow and sneak back home, cancel your attempt and start over, exactly the same as before, but another day, a different time. But it can't be done. It's too late.

So there we were, two sour-tempered, bickering travelers in a taxi on our way to JFK, just two days before Christmas. I was cranky over the breakup of yet another romance. Work wasn't going well. I wanted to write a book but couldn't. I didn't especially like where I lived, and that annoyed me. By the time we reached Queens, Mom and I were squabbling. I don't think we said a word to each other on the entire flight.

I recognized that we were at a full-blown trans-Atlantic impasse when, just prior to landing, a French businessman, standing up in his seat directly in front of me, took out a deodorant can from his briefcase and liberally sprayed his underarms *with* his shirt on.

When neither Mom nor I looked at each other to acknowledge it or laugh, I knew that the whole trip was going to be abysmal. We arrived in an icy, gray, early morning drizzle way before our hotel room was ready, sat and drank coffee from dainty china cups in the hotel restaurant without speaking, and eventually were let into our room. The room paralleled our mood precisely because it was positively arctic, even colder than it was outside, and it didn't warm up, figuratively or literally, until a week later when we were on our way home.

My mother had consulted a travel agent to find an economical trip for us, and the fellow had uncovered some sensational deal in a hotel on the Right Bank, near the Champs-Élysées. To my mind, this was the wrong part of town to stay in, but it was, of course, Mom's trip and her decision. I was only along for the ride.

Seldom in my life have I spent a week so indecently squandered. Because of the endless, raw, bitter cold in our room, we ended up sleeping inside two battered, old fur coats that my mother had packed. Management apologized eloquently and often, but the heat in the room never ran properly.

One night at dinner in a modest bistro across the street, during a salvo of pointless bickering, Mom suddenly got a chicken bone lodged in her throat. One of the waiters immediately switched into crisis command, *thwacking* her back with such force I thought she might land in Stuttgart. Mercifully, she was deboned. Afterward, sipping water to clear her throat, she looked at me slyly. "You were almost rid of me there for a minute. You must be so disappointed," she said. She might even have meant it.

It sleeted almost every day as we trudged around a Paris gaily dressed on every street for the holidays. We plodded to museums, and one afternoon sipped the obligatory hot *chocolat l'Africain* at the Salon de Thé Angelina. It was blissfully thick and sweet and it almost melted us.

We talked, but never said what either of us was thinking, so the friction was always there. Mom never said to me about my father's ruse, "All those years you never believed me." And I never asked, "How could you have been so angry at me when I was the one who had cancer?" Instead we traipsed along, noses dripping, antagonism churning.

On our third day we decided to take a bus trip to visit Versailles, where, in 1682, Louis XIV officially installed the court and government. We were shown through the Royal Apartments, the Hall of Mirrors, and the Queen's Apartment, and it was amazing, but I kept thinking of the Apthorp, expecting doormen Ralph or Pedro to appear around a gilded corner. On the way back to Paris in the frozen dusk, our bus broke down, and it took hours before a replacement was dispatched. On the second bus, as we settled into our seats, I glanced at Mom's profile and felt deflated. She looked so tired and so unhappy.

The night of New Year's Eve, just before sundown, we walked in the murky chill across her favorite bridge, the ornate, opulently appointed Pont Alexandre. Just the sight of those exuberant art nouveau lampposts, the bronze statues of sea nymphs, the cherubs, and golden, winged, rearing horses flanking each side and end always brought a delighted sparkle to her eye.

©Alison Harris

My mother's favorite Parisian bridge, with which she had much in common

This bridge, I remembered, had been built between 1896 and 1900, and was named for Tsar Alexander III. It had been erected as a monument to Russian-French harmony. My favorite fact about it, though, and something I thought of whenever I crossed it, was that the bridge's design had been subject to strict controls, preventing it from obscuring the view of either the Champs-Élysées or Les Invalides. In other words, it had to be good, but not too good. I never met the much revered Rose Styron or the beloved and accomplished late Norris Church Mailer, but oddly enough, I thought of them both that day when standing on the bridge with my mother. The literary lion can be unstintingly proud of his mate, just never eclipsed. The bridge was designed to dazzle and overwhelm, while still taking care not to eclipse or diminish in any way what had been there before it. It was meant to display unparalleled grace and beauty, yet know how to keep its place in the natural order of things *à la française*. No wonder my mother loved it so; after all, she and this bridge had once had a great deal in common.

Later that night, our last in Paris, Mom was wrapped once again in her vintage mink, huddling under the covers of her bed, reading French decorating and fashion magazines. I went out to find us some dinner and eventually brought back a couple of mushy, too-salty sandwiches from a little shop still open nearby. We ate them in stony silence. There was no celebrating, no champagne, and no joyful midnight toast.

In the cab to Orly the next morning, Mom suddenly turned to me and asked: "You really don't think much of me, do you?" and my breathing almost stopped. I instantly wished we were back in our arctic hotel room, shivering, with our noses running, raising a glass of champagne to toast each other at midnight the night before. We should have wished each other love and health and, yes, even joy. What would that have cost us? If I could have, I think at that moment I would have turned the cab around. At that moment I would have done anything to rescue our frosty and fractured little holiday trip.

At the airport, just before we boarded the plane, for half an hour we became the mother and daughter I'd been so missing. "Nobody ever loves you like a mother," Grandma Dottie used to say to me, making it sound almost like a threat. Despite everything, I'd never doubted that that was true, and even hoped to take more trips with her.

The next time I traveled to Paris was a few years later, and it was for another trip orchestrated by Shirley. And in a way she was with me again, but not really, because that time, in accordance with her wishes, I was returning to scatter her ashes.

SHE WAS MEANT TO GROW OLD IN PARIS

My archetypal East Side–West Side story (old-style) is about the Fifth Avenue dowager who admits that yes, she actually had been to the West Side once, "but only to board the Île de France *for Cherbourg, my dear."*

—Peter Salwen, *Upper West Side Story*

My mother was not yet seventy when she became ill and was diagnosed with lung cancer. Her prognosis was profoundly bleak. By the time it was discovered, the cancer had already spread to her brain. One day she was fine, up and about, making plans, and the next, weakened by a pain in her shoulder she wrongly attributed to arthritis, she dragged herself to the doctor, a man whose care she had been in for several years who she actually had to prod to give her a chest X-ray. She'd been a heavy smoker for forty-five years up until quitting eight years prior.

The day after Mom's chest X-ray, the doctor phoned her, and then she phoned me at work. All in that moment the world became a different place, even though I knew little or nothing of lung cancer and its dire implications. I knew that it was grave, but not that in all likelihood it was fatal. My mother knew that. Her years of puffing on a cigarette while on the phone, after a meal, while reading or doing a crossword, when nervous or pleased or tense or distraught, had caught up with her. And when it did, she was like several smokers and recent quitters I have known. When the knock on the door comes, they are not a bit surprised—only that it took so long to arrive. A Sloan-Kettering doctor told my mother several weeks after she was diagnosed that by quitting smoking eight years before, she had actually bought herself eight years.

After Shirley's initial diagnosis, many phone calls were made to schedule consultations and various tests. In no time, we were back yet again at Mt. Sinai Hospital, in the office of an oncologist who was talking to us about Mom's advanced lung cancer and about a Pancoast tumor. We visited lots of doctors over the next few weeks, all of whom told us that things were very bad, and Mom at last settled on receiving treatment at Sloan-Kettering. They too held out virtually no hope for remission, but seemed the best equipped by far to help her make the most of the time she had left.

Within about a week it was determined that she would need brain surgery, lung surgery, chemotherapy, and radiation, and at first she said no to all of it. "Why can't we just go to France? We can spend a few days in Paris, then go to the sea. I can walk in, and just never come out." I honestly had no good answer to that question, but soon she stopped asking it. Not long after her diagnosis, terrible pain began, and with it, the loss of her appetite along with huge amounts of weight. I still had my job but was spending more and more nights at the Apthorp. While it was certainly upsetting to be with her and witness her rapid deterioration, it was far more upsetting to be away from her.

Friends came day after day to visit. My uncle, Mom's younger brother, flew in to see her from Colorado and found her in her bed, reading and smiling, uncharacteristically calm. "Why can't it just stay like this," she asked him, "with me lying here and everyone coming to see me, bringing me beautiful things and telling me how

much they love me? Every day feels like a beautiful birthday party."
He stammered something meant to sound cheering and flew out
the door and over to Zabar's, in search of some British seedless
raspberry preserves he claimed could not be found in Colorado. On
my mother's side of the family, as on my father's, highly emotional
discussions were anathema.

Soon after Mom's diagnosis, a good friend sent me to see a
therapist because I was crying everywhere, all the time: in my office, in elevators, in supermarkets, in taxis. I couldn't stop crying,
and I couldn't anticipate it. This very kind, avuncular fellow put me
on medication immediately, and then we began to discuss the idea
of me leaving my job, selling my East Side apartment, and moving
back to the Apthorp to take care of my mother. Things were bad
now, and would only get worse. I fretted constantly over her.

My therapist, a thoughtful and perceptive man, unbeknownst
to me then, had just gone through a divorce and was waiting to occupy an apartment on the Upper West Side. He needed a place to
live for several months. In my discussions with him about whether
or not to move back to the Apthorp, I indirectly spoke a good deal
about the building, rhapsodizing about the fountains, the limestone
arches, the carpet of tulips in the courtyard, the high ceilings and
elaborate molding—the building's tangible, Old World grandeur.
In the process, I also inadvertently sold him on it, because one day
he told me that he'd taken a room there and would be subletting
for a few months. I was horrified. Mom was far more sanguine
and felt that his moving into the building only meant that she
now had an on-site doctor, day and night, if we ever needed one.
Seeing him in the Apthorp felt strange, but not nearly as strange
as when he moved out and into his new apartment on Riverside
Drive, because, as it turned out, his new apartment was none other
than my grandparents' old apartment, the one where my mother
had grown up.

I called my father the day I received Mom's diagnosis and told
him everything I knew so far, and he was utterly silent. When I was
saying an awkward good-bye and hanging up, he stifled a terrible,

prolonged sigh that went from a low octave to a higher one and ended in "*oy.*"

Mom's frequent stays at Sloan-Kettering and then the interludes in which she'd return home had occasional moments of levity, although I certainly would rather have laughed less and been elsewhere than the hospital. One afternoon, she suddenly began talking about her wardrobe. She'd decided that she hated all her clothes and that nothing fit her now, so she asked me if I'd run across the street to Filene's Basement, a block from the Apthorp, and find her something interesting to wear. It was winter, and she wanted a suit—something tailored and sleek, perhaps with a bit of velvet at the collar or cuffs. She shoved a credit card at me and with great urgency challenged me to go find something right then and bring it back to her immediately.

In Filene's, I found a suit of bottle green, cut simply and grandly, with many tiny buttons and even the requisite velvet enhancements. I raced back to the hospital, eager to show Mom my find. On arriving, I handed her the package, which she eyed suspiciously. Then she looked inside and kind of liked it but wasn't sure.

When she said, "Why don't we ask Oscar what he thinks?" I naturally inquired, "Oscar who?" And when she told me Oscar de la Renta, because he was out in the hallway, I remember feeling greatly alarmed, thinking that she was hallucinating or else that the cancer of her ravaged brain combined with the powerful medications being pumped into her were nudging her into a psychotic state. Imagine my relief and surprise when I went to find a nurse for her and nearly slammed into Oscar de la Renta, apparently there to visit someone in the next room. I retrieved the Filene's shopping bag and somehow managed to show him a little corner of the suit. He liked it. Armed with Oscar's endorsement, my mother loved the suit and, of course, kept it.

Meanwhile, my father was calling me at the Apthorp every night. In the year and a half that my mother was sick, I don't believe he ever missed one. And he was never anything but concerned, extraordinarily tender in his inquiries. To me, he seemed wrapped in a sadness I had not previously seen. I didn't love him more because of it; I had always loved him. But perhaps seeing his reaction to Mom's illness helped me to remember why.

One exception had been the raw, blizzardy night Dad took me to dinner at Etats-Unis, a tiny, sparkling jewel box of a place on the Upper East Side, near where I lived. It was intimate and plush, expensive without being pretentious, with fresh, sophisticated food, and was my favorite restaurant. My friend Tom Rapp was part owner and head chef, and seemed like a quiet, magnificent wizard working behind his compact open counter. His partner, Toshi, turned out soufflés and desserts good enough to make grown-ups weep. Dinner at Etats-Unis never failed to be brilliant, unless your mother was dying and your father was feeling surly, cruel, and ambivalent—then even the best recipes and culinary artistry in the universe couldn't save you. And nothing did.

It was a small, dimly lit room, and upon entering I searched for Dad, who, uncustomarily, hadn't yet arrived, let alone ordered and bolted through part of his dinner prior to my arrival, as was his habit. He arrived about twenty minutes late looking wretched, wearing galoshes and a big woolen coat and a ski cap. He seemed ornery and preoccupied, and after we ordered I excused myself and went to the ladies' room. When I returned, he was drinking a huge tumbler of water in a beautiful amber-colored glass. He seemed unusually thirsty throughout our meal and kept handing the glass to our waiter, who kept silently refilling it.

The first thing Dad said to me that night, even before we'd looked at menus, was that I had to prepare myself for the inevitable, sooner rather than later. Mom would die soon, I'd be evicted from the Apthorp, have no place to live, have no job, and would someday die both broke and alone. From there he segued to a list of all the jobs he'd tried to interest me in for decades, jobs with pensions, with security; jobs with the post office, the city, the MTA. I was exhausted and hungry and felt utterly vulnerable. By then, my life for a full year had been helping to take care of Mom, which meant watching her break down and disappear before my eyes. I had left her for the evening to come out to this? I hadn't necessarily expected comfort—that would have been delusional. Perhaps, though, I had imagined something like kindness from the sorrowful soul who called to inquire about Mom night after night.

Dad's mouth was drawn and his eyes were chilly as he kept swigging that water, detailing the "open coffin or grave" that was my "future." Piece by miserable piece he was laying out my future, and it was dank and cheerless and lonesome and more horrible than even my present, and suddenly listening to him was unbearable. I stood up and ran out crying into the frigid, snowy street with no coat. I crossed the street and walked around the block several times like a zombie, not knowing where I was going or what I was doing. I had no wallet with me and certainly wouldn't get far. In a little while I made my way back to the restaurant and sat down. With my wet hair plastered around my face, I somehow managed to eat a little bit and even to talk. Dad changed the subject and was on to a book he was reading, a trip he was thinking of taking. He didn't ask where I had been or why I had run out into the street like a madwoman; he just ate his dinner and kept drinking that water, thirstier than anyone I had ever seen.

When the meal was over, I told him that I wanted to stay behind a bit to talk to Tom and Toshi, since it was closing time. Eventually, after closing, we sat around and had some coffee, and Tom said: "Your father looks pretty shattered." I had to agree. I said nothing about my snowy perambulation nor about Dad's bitter forecast for me, but only commented to them that his vigorous thirst had rattled me, all those glasses of water, drinking so fast and in such great quantities. "How much water can somebody drink?" I asked. They both looked at each other and started laughing. "Water?" Tom said. "He asked for our best house rum, so that's what we were pouring him."

In the following months, Mom became increasingly ill, but also more outspoken and somehow fearless about what was happening to her. Every day I was astounded by her courage and humor. Then again, some things about her did not change. Her terror of the phone, for instance, never receded. She'd forgone getting an answering machine, because people who leave messages expect to be called back. After a few months of the phone ringing all day and night with well-wishing and inquiring relatives and friends, she relented.

But what actually pushed her over the edge was, unexpectedly, the very busy coffee shop located directly across from the Apthorp on Broadway. It had almost the same phone number as hers with the exception of the last digit, which was only off by one number. This meant that she received sometimes as many as fifty or a hundred calls a day asking what the day's specials might be or else for the name of the soup du jour. It became so excessive, so annoying and nonsensical, that Mom began answering a call by yelling, before the caller had even spoken, "Manhattan clam chowder!" or "Navy bean!" and then would slam down the phone. When one day the call came from her brain surgeon at Sloan-Kettering and she answered by barking, "Bouillabaisse, with garlic croutons!" before smashing the phone back into its cradle, this odd behavior was discreetly brought to her attention at her medical appointment the following day. Only then did she allow me to bring an answering machine into the house. It simplified things, for us as well as many members of the hungry neighborhood masses.

My mother's friends helped her out in varying degrees. Dolores Karl was tireless. She came often and cooked, fetched prescriptions, took my mother to lunch if she was up to it, and went with Mom to buy turbans and a particularly fetching raspberry cloche to wear in winter after her hair had fallen out from chemo and had just begun growing back in thin, wispy, wheat-colored shoots. Dolores ferried Mom to Suarez for a leather pocketbook and took her to Searle for a couple of coats—many of those items were far too rich for her blood, but she bought them mainly so that I would have them later, when she was gone.

Throughout Mom's illness, the Barasches were almost always there. This was the comedy writer, Norman, he of the frozen lamb episode decades before, and his wife, Gloria. Years before, they had moved back to the East from California and were now living in Greenwich, Connecticut. If Mom were having any type of procedure done at Sloan-Kettering, regardless of what ungodly time in the morning I'd arrive, the Barasches would already be there, sitting in the lobby, drinking coffee and waiting with a cup for me. They would stay all day, take me to lunch, to dinner, and drive me home on their way back to Connecticut. The next day they'd do it all over again.

After Mom's chemotherapy and radiation, after thoracic surgery, she was scheduled for stereotactic brain surgery, the first thing about which she seemed truly petrified. The operation was meant to last several hours, and when her surgeon stepped off the elevator with a grim expression after only twenty minutes, the group of us who'd assembled to wait it out naturally assumed the worst.

As it turned out, the doctor had been unable to find the exact spot he'd gone in to operate on, so he'd left in markers and would have to go in again the next day. This was horrendous. She would have to go through all of it, the anesthesia, everything, all over again. She would awaken soon thinking it was all over, and in truth the surgery hadn't yet begun. The surgeon looked at me and at Ted and asked if we wanted to be the ones to tell her about this or if he should do it. We told him that we'd absolutely not deprive him of the honor. Then we went upstairs to stand outside Mom's room with the Barasches to listen to her reaction, which we'd assumed would be startled, angry, and vociferous—and we weren't disappointed.

The doctor broke the news to her in low, consoling doctor's tones, and the next thing we all heard was Mom squealing "You couldn't find *what*? My *brain*?" We went into her room with the Barasches and none of us could stop laughing. It was one of those loony, demented moments. It helped immensely to have Norman and Gloria there. And that my brother, who even on a bad day, and that certainly was one, was probably the most hilarious person I've ever met. It helped, too, that on the way to the hospital the Barasches had picked up a special bottle of Brunello, Mom's favorite wine. When the brain surgeon left, they handed it to her and told her that when she was back home and feeling better, they would all drink it together, and finally she smiled.

That night when I walked into the Apthorp, the phone was ringing. It was Dad, and he'd called the hospital several times about Mom's surgery, but no one had thought to call him. He sounded beside himself. When I told him about the surgeon and how the operation would have to take place again the following day, he said, "Fucking idiot doctor. Poor Mom."

In the very second that Shirley had been diagnosed with cancer, for Dad she'd reverted from being referred to as "your mother" back to "Mom," and thus began Dad's great thaw, the sylallable and signal that all hostilities had ceased.

The actual brain surgery took place the next day, and was thankfully uneventful and by all accounts successful. When I went to see her the following day, her room was filled with nurses, and they were all crowded around her television. Looking at the screen, I saw what was later known as O.J.'s "car chase." Shirley's head, which had been opened twice in as many days, looked raw and had huge jagged stitches crisscrossing it. I was going to have to wash her wound when she got home, and I was frightened about touching her, afraid that I would only add to her considerable pain. I was saved on the first day she came back to the Apthorp by an old family friend, a kind of saint who walks this earth, Irene Towbin, who, having been a nurse many, many years before, approached the task with stolid equanimity, patiently showing me the proper way to do it. From then on, I did it each day without thinking.

Meanwhile, Mom's thoracic surgeon, Indian-educated, was almost as well known for being taciturn as he was for his surgical mastery. Several weeks later, I walked into my mother's room and found him showing her pictures of a vacation he'd taken to Bryce Canyon. From then on, he was positively verbose. I asked her what on earth she'd done to defrost him, and she told me that that morning he had walked in and told her that her robe, a modest pink silk design, was lovely. "I quoted Diana Vreeland and told him, 'Pink is the navy blue of India,'" she told me very matter-of-factly. From then on, he almost always had a kind word, a story, even occasionally a joke.

One morning when Mom was home, in between hospital stays, we somehow got onto the subject of Dr. Bugs, wondering about what had finally become of her and how she'd seemingly vanished, most mysteriously indeed, after my father's Guillain-Barré syndrome. My mother was certain that the gum-chewing love of my father's life had taken one look at him in his hospital bed looking old, enfeebled, and paralyzed, figured out that every last cent of his was going to go into his recovery, and had quite possibly vanished into witness protection, or at least had run as fast and far as she could. Enough time had now gone by so that we could talk about it without emotion, as breezily as any other gossipy tale from which we were detached. But when she told me that before she died she would really like to have the answer to this riddle, I knew at once who I had to call.

I went to the rear of the apartment where I knew she couldn't hear me and looked up Speed Vogel's number in Sag Harbor. Lou Ann answered and went to find Speed. Speed and I had not spoken for some time, and I'm sure he couldn't imagine what I was calling about, but before I had a chance to ask anything, he told me how terribly sorry he was about Mom's illness. And when he told me to please, please give his love to Mom, I knew that he meant it. I explained to him then that Mom and I had been discussing what had become of Dr. Bugs and that my mother badly wanted the answer to this question. Speed then explained to me that Dr. Bugs had been but a small and unimportant phase in Dad's life, and had never been anything my father had seriously considered making permanent.

"Your mother just doesn't get it, does she?" he asked me, baffled. "Shirley doesn't understand that she is the love of Joe's life? That she's the best thing that ever happened to him? He has never not loved Shirley. You have to know that," he told me with real emotion and impressive Vogelian emphasis.

Suddenly I felt impossibly sad. "But what the hell happened to them?" I asked him.

"What happened?" Speed repeated, laughing. "They were *meshuggah!*"

When I hung up, I went into my mother's room and told her what Speed had just said, and to my astonishment, she burst out laughing. "What's so funny?" I asked. "Well, what else is he going to tell you to say to a dying woman? Of course he said that. You're so gullible!" she said. But I'd heard what Speed had said and also the tone in which he'd said it. I believed it was the truth.

A few days later, a letter addressed to Mom came in the mail from Speed, reiterating everything he had said to me on the phone. Mom was dubious, but I believed every word. After she died, I spoke to Speed again and asked him if he had been telling her what he thought she'd wanted to hear. "If that were true, this whole thing," he said, meaning my parents' marriage and the way it had ended, "wouldn't all be such a shame."

After Dad died, I asked Speed one last time. He stuck to his story.

Then, when Speed died, I asked Lou Ann, who said to me: "Read his books. It's all there. Look at the way he wrote about Shirley after the divorce. He always regretted leaving her." I spoke to George Mandel and Per Gedin and they concurred. Now there was no one left to ask, and I came to accept the fact that all the responses had been the same because they had all been true.

One rocky night near the end of Mom's life, I was up late reading in my room when I heard a crash in the front of the house. By then she was wraithlike, all bones and angles with skin stretched over them, and could speak only in a kind of harsh, exhausted whisper. When she fell that night she was unable to get up, even with my assistance and the doorman's, who I immediately rang for. She started to cry, sobbing loudly, in a way I had never heard. She wouldn't let either of us touch her, and seemed to be vibrating with pain. She insisted that I call my brother, Ted. He lived downtown with his girlfriend and it was 4:00 a.m., but they got there quickly and were able to somehow lift her gently but firmly from the floor.

It is the way I see her today. I have tried to substitute healthier, cheerier images of Mom, but they are not what spring to mind in my brain's inexorable slide projector. In it she is forever ghostly; frighteningly thin, with stalks of new baby's hair poking out from her surgically ravaged scalp. People told me that after she died, in time I would again begin to picture her as she was when she was well—pretty, scrappy, robust, and lively. Nevertheless, I still see her as brittle and thin, desolate and in pain, my once sparkling, witty, vivacious mother.

DOTTIE IN THE DARK

As soon as Mom was diagnosed, we made the decision not to tell Grandma Dottie. Apart from the obvious reason, that we rarely told each other anything, my grandmother was already well into her nineties with health concerns and old grudges that kept her warm at night. We thought she'd be stretched too thin, and also, of course, she would undoubtedly think it was happening to her, and in this one instance, at least, my mother wanted to avoid this. As it was, Dottie provided Mom with a regular diet of strife and stress. No matter what my mother did or tried to do, nothing was ever good enough and never would be. If she flew down to spend three weeks with Grandma, it should have been four. If she sent my grandmother a dozen roses, it should have been two dozen. One of Grandma's sneakiest tricks was to answer the phone in a low, pitiful voice, a death whisper really, just in case it was my mother; if it wasn't, she'd talk normally. "Oh, hi!" she'd brighten, without explanation or remorse.

The only snag in our plan to keep Grandma in the dark about Mom's illness was the fact that Grandma was eerily psychic. We'd seen proof of this often. Once in Bridgehampton, the railroad arm that stops cars from crossing the path of oncoming trains was broken, and we crossed the tracks within perhaps two seconds of being decimated. When we got back to the house, the phone was ringing. It was Grandma, from Florida, telling Mom that she'd dreamed of a car wreck at a train crossing the night before and to please be extra careful driving.

When it came to Mom's illness, Grandma's intuition was just as startling. We told her nothing and told no one else who might. Mom managed to phone her regularly and attempted to sound as natural as possible, and yet the morning Mom was to have lung surgery, Grandma was taken to a Florida hospital because she couldn't breathe, and the afternoon that Mom was scheduled for brain surgery, Grandma had the worst headache of her life and again visited the emergency room. And saddest of all, the Sunday morning that my mother died in Sloan-Kettering, the phone rang at Mom's apartment no more than twelve minutes after she'd died. Alone in Florida with what must have been horrific visions, "Mother is gone, isn't she?" she asked, in a strangled little voice that I could almost not recognize. At that point, my brother and I called several of Grandma's surviving brothers, all younger than she, all living near her, and they went over to her apartment with their wives to tell Grandma and, we hoped, to provide her with solace.

Grandma was inconsolable that day, but she was not surprised. That balmy Sunday in June of 1995, which happened to be Father's Day, she got into bed to grieve and vowed never to get out of it again. Eventually she relented, at least at first. She went out to dinner a few times with her brothers and their families, but after that she retired from her social life, the card games, the lunch dates, the shopping. She saw almost no one except members of the family and went almost nowhere, telling people that if my mother couldn't go anyplace anymore, neither would she. From her it was an especially selfless and extravagant gesture, but there was no reason to doubt its sincerity.

AU REVOIR A LA APTHORPIA?

My mother left little to chance regarding her own memorial service. She'd approached it like any other of the Apthorp parties she'd given over the years—she'd made her wishes clear in remarkable detail.

During her illness, my mother had kept lists of lists, files and clippings, menus and phonebooks, reams of photographs of flowers, all of which were to figure into the plans for her final fête. There was never any question about where it was to be held—it would be in her living room—or of the type of food or music, which naturally would be French. This apartment, her third and last at the Apthorp, the one she moved into after the divorce, had a very unusual kind of rounded corner in its living room. It was uncommonly bright, with ornate molding and lots of detail, and had a fireplace with an exquisite mantel. The windows on either side were French, and the whole room, crowded with the sunlight at odd times of the day, and trees, warm colors, and cheerful chintz, looked extremely French. In fact, she'd always referred to it, jokingly, as "the Bois," but I promise you, Mrs. Simpson had nothing on Shirley.

Shirley had always said that when she grew very old, either with or without my father, her plan was to live in Paris, preferably somewhere in the Marais (way before that was de rigueur), but she would be flexible about that. Whenever she spoke of it, I could envision her as one of those tiny, elderly, outspoken Parisiennes, with their chic, short-cropped hair, rough, weathered hands, and a bicycle, the type of woman one spots in all corners of Paris. Of course, I had never seen my mother on a bicycle, but I had no doubt that she could master it when the time came. After all, she'd waited until she was in her sixties to learn to drive a car. (Neither I nor my brother know how.)

One morning soon after she'd gotten sick and I'd already come back to live at the Apthorp to take care of her, she summoned me to her bedside to tell me that she'd come up with the perfect plan. If she couldn't grow old and live in Paris, she could damn well have a funeral service in her apartment that was French.

During her illness, my mother had spoken often about the first time she and my father had seen Paris. It was 1949, during the year they were at Oxford, and their visit to Paris had made an ineradicable impression on them both.

The gloomy, gray winter at St. Catherine's College was so cold that year, my parents had had to sleep nights in all their clothes. At some point, about as broke as they could be, they decided quite spontaneously one Friday that they could wait no longer to see Paris, and so they piled on as many sweaters as could fit underneath their coats for extra warmth and ran for the night train. Hungry, sleepy, but also thrilled, they pulled into the Gare St. Lazare just as the city was rising. Breakfast was good, strong coffee, penny chocolates they'd brought with them, and fresh-peeled oranges, consumed as they sat in wide-eyed wonder near the Opéra. A hotel on the Left Bank had been suggested by a school friend of my father's, and it was the right price and in the right place. They arrived midmorning, and while my father settled into their room for a quick nap, my mother went out exploring the shiny, rain-slicked streets. Returning to the room about an hour later, when my father asked her what she thought of Paris so far, she said she thought that it was marvelous. "Only I never expected the women to all be so dressed up."

According to my mother, an eyebrow of Dad's went up then. "Dressed up, how? This is hardly a fancy neighborhood."

"Well, I know," she told him, but "their hair is all done and they have so much makeup on and are wearing such . . . elaborate outfits, kind of almost like *costumes*," she told him innocently.

Ten minutes later, they poked their heads out the door when they heard some of the clientele coming up the stairs and realized immediately that their quaint little hotel was a busy, humming brothel.

Twenty minutes later, they were resettled into another hotel in a contiguous arrondissement, but returned for almost every meal during that weekend to a place called Les Balkans, on Rue de la Harpe, a bustling, crowded, tourist-mobbed street.

Les Balkans was spacious, colorful, cheap, and noisy, filled with both the French and expatriates. The pitchers of wine, the platters of charred, well-seasoned shish kebab, and towering pyramids of couscous were so delicious and abundant, the bread so warm, crisp, and delicately flavored, and the waiters so tirelessly cheerful, that even though the cuisine wasn't French, for the rest of that trip, it never occurred to my parents to eat anywhere else. Years later, I went with my parents, in the 1960s, and it was still a find. Then, in 2002, I went with my then husband, a dour Dutchman. As we ordered, I spotted a dead fly in the powdered sugar and remembered that not everything was meant to last forever.

Now, Mom had planned her "French" funeral down to the smallest detail. She'd arranged the guest list and even helped me write her obituary, but there was one detail that she had no interest in whatsoever and had left entirely to me: the finding of a rabbi. I couldn't understand why she even wanted one; after all, our family was profoundly unreligious. But to my surprise, during one of our planning sessions, she told me that she did. "Where am I supposed to find one of *those*?" I asked her one night about a week before she died. She laughed. "Look, I'll do everything else, but when it comes to that, you're on your own."

As always, Norman and Gloria Barasch came to the rescue. They gave me the name and number of a rabbi they knew personally and who, according to them, had recently left a large and very loyal congregation in Florida. The way they explained it was that his popularity among his congregation was so great that as a parting gesture, they had presented him and his wife with the almost obscenely generous gift of an endless trip around the world. This meant that they could just keep traveling and traveling, wherever they liked, farther and farther, staying away longer and longer. Unfortunately, the moment I met him the day of my mother's funeral, I instantly wondered if this gift was about generosity or desperation, because these people never wanted him back.

About an hour or so before the service was to start, with friends and family members arriving and taking their seats in the rows of chairs we'd set up in the living room, this rabbi appeared and asked to speak with my brother and me. We went into one of the bedrooms with him and shut the door. This was when he announced to us that he had actually met Mom, had met our whole family, in fact, many years before, at one of the Barasches' pool parties in New Rochelle. "I met you both that day, as children," he told us, his eyes closed, trancelike, yet in no way preparing us for what was to follow. Then he rocked back and forth on his heels and held a bejeweled hand to his chest, as if his heart might attempt to escape. "I can see Shirley Heller as she stood before me on that long-ago day in New Rochelle," his voice blared. "She wore a bathing suit, had a magnificent bust, and a pair of dancer's legs to match." I snuck a peek at my brother, who looked as if he wished the funeral were his own.

"You might want to avoid mentioning that," I told the rabbi gently. Meanwhile, I could just imagine my mother, overseeing all this, rolling her eyes if and when this character mentioned her "bust" and legs, apparently a distinct possibility.

The night before, my father had come over to pay his respects. He brought Aunt Sylvia with him, up from Florida for the funeral. It was an emotional visit. Neither my father nor my aunt had ever been in Mom's apartment. My aunt came in and looked all around as if she was expecting my mother to pop out of some hiding place. The whole place was, as my aunt put it with a sigh, ". . . so Shirley-ish." As we sat talking in the living room, I watched my father's eyes suddenly wander over and fall upon one of the couches with the stolen slipcovers.

My aunt was recalling earlier, happier days, when Dad suddenly interrupted her and, pointing to the couch, asked me: "Is that . . . ?" His voice trailed off. I nodded dumbly. He looked down, smiling to himself, and suppressed a kind of half giggle. Was it my imagination, or did his eyes light up at just that moment with some kind of bemused, proprietary pride in my mother? Was that the millisecond this flicker settled there and then never left?

That day, about eighty people had assembled in the living room—old friends, building friends, my work friends, relatives from all over—and just as the funeral was about to begin, in walked my father. An audible hush rippled through the room. Mouths opened and wineglasses froze midair. Joe Heller? Could it be? In Shirley's apartment, at Shirley's funeral? I had expected him and yet had not expected him. He took a seat in the back, and rows and rows of necks swiveled to gawk at him. It took courage for him to show up that day. But there he was, and there he sat, looking desolate, unhinged, as if he hadn't slept in months.

Then suddenly, that booming rabbinical voice began rumbling, swelling, falling, and droning on and on. I held my breath as he uttered the terrible words, "I can see Shirley Heller as she stood before me on that long-ago day in New Rochelle. Shirley wore a bathing suit." I was certain that her bust and legs were about to be memorialized, but miraculously, perhaps due to my audible gasp from the front row, his diatribe veered sharply away. With his eyes again closed and while rocking on little feet, it was not her bust and legs he extolled, but the fact that she had been a superb mother, wife, friend, and person. The rest of the service went smoothly. Others spoke, including myself; people laughed, wiped tears away with napkins and hankies, ate a French lunch, and drank lots and lots of lovely French wine.

I remember, toward the end of the afternoon, Dad picking up a framed picture of my mother from a round, skirted table in the living room. George Mandel, my friend Sara, and I were standing and talking to Dad when the gabby rabbi zeroed in. With a mouth full of runny Saint-André and an avalanche of cracker crumbs cascading down his summer suit jacket, his rabbinical eyes grew dewy with admiration as he asked my father, overearnestly, "Joe, how *are* you?"

Shirley-chic, in Europe, 1966

Apparently they had met at a wedding somewhere once, prior to his induced circumnavigation of the globe. "And how is your wife?" he inquired of my father amiably, trying to launch a conversation about my stepmother, who that day was at home in East Hampton.

My father looked into the rabbi's eyes without emotion or the vaguest trace of irony and told him, "*Shirley* was my wife." This was reminiscent of a well-trodden wisecrack he and his friends made sometimes, friends who had been married more than once. "I'm married to (*current wife*), but (*first wife*) is my *wife*," went the gag. Was Dad joking now? It didn't seem like it, but I never got to find out. He put Mom's framed photo back down on the table, headed for the front door, and was gone.

GRIEF MIT SCHLAG

The minute Dad heard Mom's diagnosis and prognosis for lung cancer, the anger he had felt for her during the last years began leaking out of him, like air escaping from a balloon. Without it, he was lighter, certainly less prickly, but I also believe that from then on his face revealed an unmistakable patina of sorrow. He seemed diminished. I had never seen him seem defeated by anything, including his own catastrophic illness, but with my mother's death he seemed to age enormously and rapidly, and perhaps more strikingly, not to care.

It was in this state that he abruptly turned around and began to be and act like a father, or what constituted his version of one since he had lost his own so early. His battle with me was suddenly over. It ended just as incomprehensibly as it had begun. The fight, whatever it had been, was finished.

I stayed in my mother's apartment, 5B South, for two years after her death, with her Wedgwood blue-and-white–trimmed living room and stately marble floors, marble baths, and tiny mahogany and paisley fabric-covered den, planting geraniums every Mother's Day in her honor on the minuscule Juliet balconies attached to her living room windows. To me, it was still her apartment, the one she had chosen and made her own. In her place, I would perhaps have picked something else, something far less opulent, but she had needed it to buoy her morale after the divorce, and it was, after all, Shirley's first apartment. Shirley's *only* apartment.

But because she was a rent-stabilized tenant at the Apthorp and
New York law dictates that one must be in residence for a full two
years in order to inherit a lease, and because I had only been there
for a year and a half, in all probability I was not going to be allowed
to stay. In the meantime, I lived there, waiting to see what would
happen. I lived out of boxes and suitcases, not knowing how long I'd
be permitted to stay or where I'd live if I couldn't. I looked for work
in advertising as a copywriter again, but having stepped out of the
business for several years, it seemed to have shriveled. There were
fewer agencies, and those agencies were employing fewer writers.

The first Thanksgiving after Mom's death I badly wanted to be
away, so I went with a friend to see Prague, Vienna, and Budapest,
three places neither of us had ever been, but I never made it to
Budapest.

The much talked about beauty of Prague, I must say, eluded me
completely; then again, it was November. I have always loved gray,
dreary days—they are for me like others' sunshine—but somehow
in Prague, months after Mom died, everything, even Old Town
Square and Prague Castle, just looked and felt wretched, dispirit-
ing. The Charles Bridge was no substitute for Mom and the Pont
Alexandre, even when we weren't getting along.

From sunless, slushy Prague we dragged ourselves to Vienna,
to see the Ringstrasse, visit St. Stephen's Cathedral, a handful of
grand palaces, and Freud's House, at the famous Berggasse 19, and
to drink cup after cup of *kaffee mit schlag*.

I did not chew gum and have never before felt the urge to litter, but there in pristine Vienna, I was seized by a strong wish to
crumple up chewing gum wrappers and drop them in the streets as
we walked, if only to leave behind some tangible sign of human life.

Our last day in Vienna before Budapest, we elected to subject
ourselves to some sort of bus tour that would take us into the Vienna Woods, including one stop we knew nothing about.

It turned out to be, quite possibly, the most terrible and frightening place I have ever seen; a former mine, now with an underground lake, known as Seegrotte, in Hinterbrühl. Hinterbrühl was

the location for part of no less than the Mauthausen concentration camp, which the otherwise garrulous guide stunningly neglected to mention.

A catastrophe in 1912 from a blasting operation in this once active gypsum mine caused a flood of twenty million liters of water, creating Europe's hugest subterranean lake. In World War II, the mine was requisitioned for German military forces, and since its depth, sixty meters below ground, and the fact that it was hidden from sight, offered the greatest possible protection against bombing raids, the national *Heinkel Werke* established an aircraft factory there, where two thousand "workers" were used to build the world's first jet fighter, the "He 162." This was more or less how this bizarre, dark, and sinister underground floating circus was described to us and the rest of the visitors that day while on the boat ride taking us to view the mine: deep inside these caverns, afloat on that green and oily lake, the oddest body of water I had ever seen.

We were shown a chapel once used by miners, a wine cellar, even the stables for working horses, toiling their entire lives in this tomb of darkness. Suddenly I saw it all as it must have been then, blind horses doing their backbreaking work, Jewish slaves living for years underground, without light. Clearly it had been a place of inexpressible horrors, and yet now had been polished, repackaged, and served up as an agreeable, money-making tourist haunt. I felt rage, revulsion, and also claustrophobia, and needed to get away quickly, back to the light and to air, but I was trapped there until the tour guide was ready to float us back across the grease-limned lake and back up to daylight.

When we were at last delivered to street level and had piled back onto the tour bus, on our ride back to the hotel we passed a sign for Heller Candies. I asked our driver if he had ever heard of this company and he nodded. His somber face suddenly glimmered with joyous recognition. "Aah yes, Otto Heller. The Chocolate Jew!" he exclaimed.

Meanwhile, between seeing the grisly Seegrotte and hearing about the Chocolate Jew, I had experienced more than enough of Vienna. Perhaps if I could have lain on Freud's couch that day and spoken to him of these odd and curious things it might have helped, but, of course, his place, too, was now just a honeypot for tourists, closed for business.

My friend went on to Budapest without me, and I flew home to look for work and figure out where I was going to live. The Apthorp being on Broadway, the first thing I saw getting in from the airport, a peculiarly welcoming sight, was litter in the street and overflowing trash bins. Beer cans and soda bottles lolled in the gutters next to hamburger wrappers. Stepping out of the taxi, I nearly planted one foot in an open Styrofoam takeout plate filled with rice, beans, and the detritus of a slithery tangle of picked-clean chicken bones, left there from the night before or perhaps even longer.

My heart soared. It was a glorious sight.

APTHORPIUS EVICTUS?

I came back to New York determined to find a job and resolve the apartment situation, one way or another. I needed badly by then to know where I'd be living, to sign a lease, my *own* lease, wherever that might be. But would it be at the Apthorp?

In the years since I'd moved back there with my mother, after eighteen years spent on the Upper East Side, I had fallen once again under the almost supernatural spell of the place. The Apthorp had lured a remarkable mix of tenants once: Nora Ephron and Nicholas Pileggi lived there. So did Cyndi Lauper, Rosie O'Donnell, Steven Kroft, Jennet Conant, Conan O'Brien, Boaty Boatwright, and Al Pacino. These were people who might conceivably live anywhere, and yet at various points had chosen the Apthorp. Why would I have wanted to live anywhere else?

When my mother had swapped apartments, her verbal contract with the building management at the time had explicitly stated that if she predeceased her lease, I would inherit her rent-stabilized apartment. But a verbal contract, as Sam Goldwyn so craftily put it, isn't worth the paper it's written on, and this one was worth even less. I had already depleted my savings fighting to try to keep Apartment 5B South, paying for lawyers and depositions, but I began to see that this campaign was, for me, largely sentimental. It was about Mom and hanging on to a piece of what had been. Meanwhile, the business reality for the Apthorp was that with me out of that apart-

ment and with just a little work done, the rent might well shoot up
to ten times what I was paying. Clearly I was going to have to leave.
The only question was, where was I going?

A solution, one far better than I'd hoped for, arrived on the
wings of one Barbara Ross, longtime Apthorp building manager.
She knew that soon I would have to vacate the apartment, and she
had always been fond of my mother. It was Ms. Ross's idea to show
me alternate apartments, also rent-stabilized, and my gratitude was
immense. I told my father about Ms. Ross's plan to put me into
another Apthorp apartment and he seemed suspicious about the
building management's motives, but advised me to take a look at
whatever was going to be shown, and even offered to come with me
if I wanted another set of eyes.

Ms. Ross and I began to tour available apartments. Several
were dark layouts the size of a broom closet, without room for the
brooms. I could hardly afford to be picky, though, and just as I
began adjusting to the concept of closet living, Ms. Ross rang me
on the housephone one morning and asked if I could meet her in
Apartment 6LE. It was back on the other side of the building, in
the wing with our very first apartment, where Dad had stashed me
up in a closet to tease Mom, where Ted and I shared a bedroom and
had gone to sleep at night by the light of a stagecoach lamp. I met
Ms. Ross at the elevator, and with her key she let us both into the
apartment I was to consider. It was half of a larger apartment that
had long ago been split in two.

Walking inside, it instantly felt perfect. It was remarkably comfortable, like some cozy country house up in the sky. The space was
empty and the rooms felt enormous, and were filled with the mold-
ings, touches, and details that were the hallmarks of the Apthorp.
The living room had a high ceiling with coffering and beams. The
dining area had built-in leather banquettes with cherry-wood stor-
age boxes beneath them. Most rooms had a cherry-wood door, and
the bedroom door had glass inside it with a curtain on rods, *très,
très* European. There was also a washer-dryer hidden away in the
recently renovated kitchen. The beautiful Old World tiled bath-

room had a Speakman showerhead. I was in rent-stabilized paradise. I almost broke down before Ms. Ross, but managed to hold it together, telling her simply that I would take it, that it would be fine. We agreed on a moving date several weeks ahead, and I began the arduous task of clearing up and cleaning out Mom's apartment, forty-plus years of life spent at the Apthorp, with closets galore and every one of them crammed within an inch of its life, ready to award a concussion to anyone who dared open a door.

As I prepared to move, it soon became clear that those prized slipcovers, the ones Mom had lifted from East Hampton to the Apthorp, amazingly, still had some traveling ahead of them. They had not yet reached their final resting place.

Unbeknownst to me, though, the move—within the same building—was to be quite a costly and complicated enterprise. The building policy was strict: furniture could not simply be moved across the courtyard. Tenants moved within the building all the time in those days, and although the process could have been executed simply, instead it took on the complexity of an intricate operation. Everything had to be transported through the basement, at the time an elaborate and nefariously devised, poorly lit labyrinth of dark hallways, secret rooms, and hidden stairwells that ran the building's full perimeter, an entire city block. It seemed to me then, as it does today, that this Apthorpian law was hammered out by a conspiracy of greedy movers, who saw that a fortune could be made just by moving from Building A to Building C, involving forty-two people lost in the basement's twisting mazes and circuitous subterranean corridors for weeks as the meter ticked ever upward.

My move across the courtyard with my mother's things and my own, plus all of the contents of her Bridgehampton house that had been brought there, was so complicated and ridiculously costly that I felt like I was masterminding and executing a war. In the end, I gave away or sold many of Mom's furnishings, but because my father and his wife had just rented an apartment nearby at Lincoln Center, and because he still prized my mother's taste and it saved him the cost and trouble of confronting any decorating dilemmas

or disappointments in his new place, he asked me if he might possibly purchase some of the things himself, including those still-
splendid slipcovers, now a bargain for him. I hesitated. What would
Mom want? Would it be disloyal of me to let him have them? Was
this really any different than her mother's pot roast recipe, which he
still wheedled and mewled for at regular intervals?

I called my grandmother in Florida and asked what she thought.
Without a moment's hesitation she issued her verdict: "Why would
it be 'disloyal' to Mother? Are you kidding? He bought all of this
the first time. Now he's buying it all back. She'd think it was funny.
He's paying for it all twice. Sell it to him and charge him plenty."

Yet again, a kind of warped *Catch-22* logic was at work. The
Apthorp had been inextricably linked to my parents' marriage,
and the thread had been strong and sure, interlaced with complete
logic, and yet also total and absolute nuttiness. It was a thread that
wound across and underneath the courtyard and stretched out to
East Hampton and now all the way to Florida and back, weaving
logic with a dash of Dottie Held's classic vengeful lunacy.

My father got the slipcovers back and some furniture, elect-
ing to pay for my move, which was a fortune. But they were not a
"bargain," since as my grandmother had pointed out, he had already
bought them once.

It was a deal about which Milo Minderbinder himself, I
guessed, might have been inordinately proud.

ASHES TO ASHES, DUST TO DUSTBUSTER

When it came to dying, a subject Dad wrote about as much as he wrote about anything, he always said in regard to being buried that if he was going to buy real estate, he wanted to be around to enjoy it—and, of course, harvest the rewards of reselling it. Mom felt the same way. At least they agreed on something. Perhaps later, he had changed his mind about this, though.

The time had come to deposit Shirley's ashes off the Pont Alexandre. This had been her wish, and now that I was leaving her apartment and moving back across the courtyard, the time felt right. For this deed, I enlisted the company of my friend Fred. Fred and I decided to go during the summer and to combine the visit to Paris with a few days in Amsterdam, a place that would figure prominently in my life just a few years later.

The last six months that Mom was alive, we'd had many discussions about her ashes, and there was never a second's hesitation about where this scattering should take place, but she was very concerned from the first, waving a finger at me, that I do the deed at night, under cover of darkness—otherwise she worried that I might be arrested. From then on, whenever this subject arose, and she mentioned it frequently, I reassured her that living out my days in a French *geôl* was not a secret wish. Whenever she was in Sloan-Kettering and I left her room at night, she'd say to me, her eyes refulgent: "Remember, do it at night. Paris has to be *dark.*"

The night before I left, I took the metal canister holding my mother's ashes down from a shelf in a hall closet and tried to open it. I had chosen a large satin hosiery bag of hers, which she had kept since her honeymoon, and I felt it would be the ideal vessel for the ashes. My plan was to also include a brick taken from her garden in Bridgehampton, the place my brother and I had sold after Mom's death. All together, I felt it would make a fine metaphorical package to drop into a foreign body of water. First, though, I had to pry open the sealed canister, and try as I might—with can openers, hammers, pliers, screwdrivers—it couldn't be done. I sat in Mom's small mahogany den and attacked her last refuge from all angles.

Finally, a butcher knife managed to nudge the seemingly welded top away from its appointed place. Then all at once, as the whole thing opened, it went flying across the room, where much of its contents spilled across my mother's rug. I stared in horror, mad with worry, knowing how dim the chances of recovering most of what had escaped were. I tried sweeping it a bit, but that only ground the ashes further into the rug.

Not knowing what to do, how to remedy this disaster, I called Dad in East Hampton. "Do you have one of those small cleaning appliance things?" he asked right away. "One of those minivacuums?" I was astonished that he'd even heard of such things. I told him yes, I had one.

"Try picking it all up that way and then taking out the removable part and emptying the ashes." I thanked him for his clear thinking, and just as I was hanging up he muttered, sadly: "So, she's going back to Paris, eh?" his voice nearly cracking. "It was Mom's favorite place," he murmured dreamily. Not "your mother" any longer, but more "*my Shirley.*"

Moments later I was Dustbusting my mother from the rug, then emptying out the cylinder and pouring what was inside into her hosiery bag, the bag that had begun its journey with her all the way back in 1945 and was now fated to land in Paris, of all places, at the cold bottom of a river. At night.

Fred and I arrived in Paris. On the appointed night, I placed the ashes and the Bridgehampton brick into a Cartier shopping bag I'd found in the lobby of our hotel. As the sun was setting, we dressed up and started out with a drink back at the old and venerable Bar Voltaire. From there we took a taxi to my favorite Parisian restaurant, Le Pré Catelan, hidden deep within the forest of the Bois de Boulogne, an imposing place with tall mirrors, Grecian columns, and plush, moss-green banquettes. I felt that it would be appropriately festive and suitably grand, but halfway there, Fred realized that we'd left the bag with the ashes and the brick back at the Voltaire, beneath our outdoor table, so we went tearing back to retrieve it. As we approached, the manager, looking frantic, ran out into the street and toward us with the forgotten shopping bag, thinking we had left behind some costly, much-coveted treasures bought at the Place Vendôme.

With the bag back in our hands, we ate a fine, festive supper, toasted Shirley, even toasted Joe, and then, when it was almost midnight, we went to the Pont Alexandre to at last perform the ritual.

Because of the lanes of traffic on the bridge, it is impossible to look out from both sides at once, both up- and downriver, and this presented a bit of a problem, since boats were passing by underneath every few minutes. I had a sudden vision of President Chirac cruising by at just that moment in an official gilded *bateau*, and of having the ashes and garden brick come crashing through the roof of his boat. Ultimately, Fred stood at one side of the bridge, scanning for traffic underneath, and I stood at the other. The wind was blowing and I couldn't really hear what Fred was yelling across to me, but at some moment he nodded and I hurled the satin bag into the river and saw it graze the water's surface and sink. We stood there for a while, looking out at Paris. I felt an overwhelming sense of loss for my mother, but also relief at having finally completed this task.

Right then, right there, while still on the bridge, I thought of my father and of his voice, so small and sad the night before I'd left. I felt great sorrow for both my parents and for the bitter implosion of their marriage, the full weight, force, meaning, and consequences of them having been, in Speed Vogel's word, *"meshuggah."*

On the train ride to Amsterdam the next day, as we hit the out-skirts of overcast Paris in a car filled with the smell of strong coffee and heavy with tobacco, I forgot about Dad and felt only a sense of rightness about Shirley.

But by the end of the trip, wonder and worry had already set in, about myself.

Mom was at last where she wanted to be. What about me?

PART 4

Apartment 6LE

And then there was one

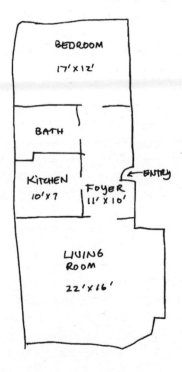

1997—Present

"NO APARTMENT'S TOO GOOD FOR MY LITTLE GIRL."

It took a while for Dad to come to see my new place. When I'd moved to 6LE, back in the A wing where my family had started out, he took his time.

By then he had an apartment near Lincoln Center, and we would meet somewhere in between his pied-à-terre and the Apthorp. Several times I asked him to come and see the apartment, but he made excuses, generally saying that he was too busy. When he finally came and saw it, it was suddenly *his* idea, and I could sense that his curiosity had finally gotten the best of him.

His reluctance made sense. When I was growing up, I think no one was ever more smitten with the Apthorp than my father. To my mind, he really didn't care which apartment we lived in or how big it was—he was happy as long as he had a separate place where he could disappear and write. For the kid from Coney Island and World War II, coming home from work to this grand, imposing place must have felt extraordinary every day. Dad felt lucky to live here and that never changed. Until he left. Then, in true Hellerian style, he created an impermeable boundary between himself and the building. *It* was now the one getting his silent treatment, being shunned.

When he finally came over to see my apartment, he seemed

still—or again—in awe of the place, like a devout believer revisiting a forgotten cathedral. I took along my dog and met him downstairs in the courtyard, and he looked around with something like reverence, taking it all in. He bantered with the doorman, who remembered him from when he'd lived here. He walked a step or two ahead of me and turned, seemingly automatically, as if to enter Building A, the one with our huge apartment where we used to live, babbling all the while.

I steered him back across the courtyard, brought him upstairs, and showed him around. He stared out one of the living room windows, across Broadway to the coffee shop, the one with the nearly identical phone number as Mom's.

As Dad surveyed my living room for the first time, he eyed me quizzically and asked: "How come *you* get to live in this apartment? The rooms in my apartment are like tiny boxes." I had to laugh. I also had to say to him: "Your apartment is fine. And you have a house in East Hampton. What is this, a contest? Do you begrudge me this apartment?"

He rolled the possibility carefully over in his mind and then nodded. I laughed again because what he'd said was so funny, so true, and because this was vintage Joe. I couldn't imagine it coming from anyone else's father. It was a preposterous response to an equally preposterous question. If he had said "No apartment's too good for my little girl," I would have assumed he was febrile, in the grip of delirium, in dire need of a visit to the nearest ER.

Quite possibly, beneath Dad's ambivalent façade, at that moment he was thinking that if he had never left Mom he would still be living in our big, grand apartment, 10C. But, he queried, "What does this face—Broadway?" acting like a stranger adrift in exotic territory. I nodded. He paused, and then said softly: "I *do* begrudge you," perhaps realizing for the first time himself that it was true.

I was astonished by this rare nugget of candor. He wasn't joking or trying to be funny. He was telling the truth. This was Dad. Blunt, snarling, and hilarious.

In 1994 a letter appeared in *New York* magazine from someone named Melvin J. Grayson, from Edison, New Jersey. It referred to a laudatory article about Dad that had been written by David Streitfeld and demonstrated how my father's "wit" and asperity were not only reserved for family and friends:

> Those readers wondering who's right—David Streitfeld, author of "Catch-23"/Books, September 12, who said that Joseph Heller is "a nice guy," or Barbara Gelb, who described Heller's unpleasantness—may be interested in my three brief encounters with Heller in the early sixties. For several months, just before *Catch-22* was published, we occupied adjoining offices in the promotion department of *Look* magazine. The day he arrived, I went to welcome him aboard. "Hi," I said, "I'm Mel Grayson." He was seated at his desk with his back to me, gazing out the window. "Come back later," he said without turning around. "I'm busy." Our second meeting came two weeks later as we passed each other in a hallway. "You have dandruff," he informed me. My third and last contact with Joe Heller occurred on a Fifth Avenue street corner several months after *Catch-22* came out. He had left *Look*. "Have you seen the reviews for *Catch-22*?" he asked me. "I'll bet you wish you could write like that."
>
> David Streitfeld was correct. Joseph Heller is one absolutely [sic] sweetheart of a man.

I found this letter both amusing and peculiar. Amusing, because Dad was only being Dad. And peculiar because who had ever written about Dad as sensitively and with more love, insight, and compassion than Barbara Gelb? When young writers or foreign writers inquired about Dad, he'd always suggest that they read Barbara's *New York Times Magazine* piece. He referred to her as "my biographer."

Of course, Melvin was subjected to the full Joe Heller treatment, three times, in fact. This was Dad, funny yet not funny, humorous and diverting to witness, so long as the arrow wasn't aimed in your direction.

Yes, he begrudged me my new Apthorp apartment. But I felt that this was only his way of saying how much he missed living here. I could well understand that and did not begrudge him his begrudgement.

The next time he came over was after we'd just had lunch and I was leaving that night for Amsterdam to do research for a possible, hopefully humorous book on van Gogh. Dad and I talked over my idea in my apartment, and he spared nothing in telling me what he thought: it was ridiculous, impossible to pull off, and that if it was a truly intriguing concept, someone would already have done it. I stared at him. "But that would mean that nothing original is ever worthwhile. What about the whole 'concept' of *Catch-22*?" I asked him.

"That's different," he explained. "That was *good*."

Just then my lakeland terrier, Thistle, came in and took a running leap onto Dad's lap. She began licking his chin, and Dad petted her head, looked into her face, and said to me, "You know, your dog has a very cute face," as if that had never occurred to me before.

Then out of nowhere he asked me if I was afraid to fly, and I said no. At least, I never was until and unless someone asked if I was; then I was petrified.

Thistle jumped off his lap and started chasing a tennis ball around the coffee table, growling and barking at it as Dad and I sat on the couch. I had a thought and put it to him. "If anything ever happens to me, would you take care of Thistle?"

His "no" was immediate. "From what you've told me," he said smoothly, "she's not that well behaved. I don't need extra problems."

This was priceless. What father would say something so injudicious to a fretting daughter about to take to the skies? "Of course. Don't worry," I imagine some fathers might have said. "Stop being silly and morbid. Go. Have a good trip. Nothing's going to happen to you." Somehow, the stark nonchalance of his truthfulness struck me, again, as riotously funny. Dad's oblivion toward sparing my feelings suddenly appeared ludicrous in its predictability.

The mellower, postdivorce Joe Heller may have been kinder, but he was nonetheless still Joe Heller.

His attentions, solicitude, or occasional generous gestures had always felt haphazard to me. After one operation I had to have, he insisted on coming into Manhattan from East Hampton for my follow-up medical appointment. It was a cold, blustery winter's day, snow was in the air, and I told him that coming in wasn't necessary, but he got on that Jitney anyway and picked me up at the Apthorp. We took buses to Ninety-sixth and Fifth. When we left, it was dark out. "Get healthy so I don't have to do this anymore," he said simply, as we bent together against the whipping wind, and he headed for the Jitney, back to East Hampton.

One year, when I wasn't working and it was almost Christmas, he asked me, in the Apthorp lobby, just what I planned to do about tipping the Apthorp staff—the super, the subsuper, the doormen, elevator men, and porters, a list that some years has exceeded fifty. "What are you going to do? What if you need something done in your apartment or there's some problem in the building and you need help this year?" I hadn't a clue about what I'd do for Christmas tipping; I hadn't thought about it yet, as it was perhaps not at the head of the list of problems that had resulted in my unemployed status, but before I could reply, he was suddenly peeling off hundred-dollar bills from his wallet and handing them to me, asking, after ten of them, "Is this enough?" And then twenty. "Is *this*?" He kept going way, way after I'd told him to stop, that it was far too much.

When he left to go home that day, he stopped and said good-bye to the doorman, who told me about it later, and who, of course, had no idea whatsoever what Dad had been referring to when he'd said jauntily: "Have a merry Christmas. And don't ever expect me to do this again."

THE WOMAN WITH A GUILLOTINE ON SOUTH OCEAN DRIVE

Er zol vaksen vi a tsibeleh, mit dem kop in drerd!
—Famous Yiddish curse: "He should
grow like an onion, with his head in
the ground!"

Grandma Dottie's absolute finest hour was one that my mother did not live to see. Grandma outlived Mom by almost three years, but much of her inimitable *joie de vivre* evaporated with her daughter's death. Still, Grandma's last real hurrah, as far as I was concerned, took shape on one of my last trips to visit her in Florida, years after Mom was gone.

I hadn't seen Grandma for several months. It was August, and the air in Hollywood, Florida, was damp and smothering.

Coming in from the airport, I rang Grandma's doorbell and let myself in with my key. Walking down her long, narrow entryway, I scanned her massive collection of framed family photos on both sides of me, floor to ceiling, all hung in neat, perfect rows, with almost no space in between for them to breathe. Right away I knew that something was different, just not yet what; then I suddenly realized that every photograph containing my father, her ex–son-in-law, had been cut apart. And that in each one, instead of a head or a face, in its place was now stuck a cotton ball. I knew that following my mother's death, Dad and Grandma had never spoken again, but I had evidently underestimated the poison she still held for him in her heart.

I looked up and down the extended hallway. Here was my father, again and again, him but not him, faceless, headless. With a glob of cotton mashed up and flattened against the glass, pinned beneath the frame, all up and down the entire length of the hallway. As far as I could see, there were cotton heads posed in assorted family tableaux, sometimes jauntily, sometimes somberly: my father in tuxedos, ski clothes, pajamas, on horseback, at the beach, all headless. Standing by a baby carriage or a playpen, on skates, swimming, eating a hot dog at Coney Island, each with that same outrageous, ghoulish, cylindrical puff of cotton poking through its precisely cut hole. Taking it all in, I half expected to see blood from all the decapitations spurting along the white stucco walls.

I pictured my ever-resourceful grandmother devising this plan and then sitting down to actually implement it. I imagined this frail, elderly darling, exhilarated by her own diabolical inspiration and artistry, sitting at the desk in her living room, snipping merrily away. Or perhaps parked on one of her overstuffed couches, surrounded by all the frames and photographs, lustily carving and slicing them to pieces with her scissors. Maybe she'd used her small, dainty, snake-shaped embroidery scissors, fake gold with jeweled eyes, carefully peeling away each photograph from its frame, performing its surgery, and then gaily replacing it, guiding and pressing it back into its frame, up against the glass. And then, when they had all had their decapitations, she had rehung them all on the wall, each one in its former, proper, and appointed place.

I could just see her stuffing the cotton balls into the gaping holes and then smooshing on the glass and the frame so that the cotton was flattened, spreading outward when pressed, like the petals of some bloated, showy underwater flower.

Realizing all this, surrounded by the two sides of this gallery, I at first froze, thrilled at just the sheer invention of it. Snip, snip, and away fell thirty-plus years of my mother's life.

I walked through this gruesome spectacle, this Hallowed Hall of the Headless, into the bright midday sunlight filling her sprawling, oceanfront living room and found the Mad Cutter sitting there, thumbing through a magazine sweetly, quietly. She was happy to see me, and when she looked up at me and I hugged her hello, I gazed into her eyes, half expecting to see the purplish, bloodshot eyes of a lunatic, to hear the unhinged, violent ranting of a crazed slasher, but she was just Grandma. She was ninety-four, my father had hurt and disappointed her very badly, and there would not be enough time fanning out ahead of her to be able to forgive. She had merely found her own way to live with it. I thought suddenly of the surely tall heap of Dad's faces piling up as she did her gashing and

My parents in the south of France, 1949, as Dottie Held chose to see them

Courtesy of the author

chopping, of his various expressions and the evolving styles of his hair: slicked back with Vitalis for his wedding to Mom, long, white, and a bit wild in recent years. You could spot him a block away. And I knew I would never tell him about this, these beheadings. That would be too cruel.

As for Grandma, when you live in a dream, apparently all it takes to reestablish order in your universe is a pair of scissors and a few bags of cotton puffs from Publix. To her, it was the same as trimming an uneven privet or mowing a sloppy lawn.

All was once again right with the world.

THEY JUST DANCED

I believe in plenty of optimism and white paint.
—Elsie de Wolfe

All through the 1980s and early nineties, whenever I'd gone down to visit Dottie, my single greatest fear was always getting trapped in the elevator with one of her neighbors who knew me. Grandma's bragging and lying, it seemed, were everywhere.

"So I hear you became a lawyer?" a neighbor might say to me conspiratorially, laying a ring-laden paw like a talon on my forearm in the back elevator leading down to the building pool. "And you're working for the district attorney?" Or perhaps it was, "I heard that you just graduated from med school and are taking over the neurology department at Columbia-Presbyterian. What a good girl! Your grandmother is so proud."

Lawyer, doctor, chief. I never knew from one elevator ride to the next at Galahad Court what great coup I pulled off, what stratum of which profession I'd ascended to, because Grandma never prepared me for any of it. From the second I entered that elevator, my best bet was to just begin nodding to whoever was on it. There always seemed to be someone riding up or down, someone who knew about me and was ready to congratulate me for something I hadn't done, praise me for being someone I'd never be. There was no end to the fantasies propagated, the degrees I'd amassed. One time, in the mid 1980s, I remember my brother being dragged into the act. It was when, on that same aforementioned, accursed elevator, a neighbor of Grandma's had leaned into my face and said: "*Mazel tov!* Your brother now runs *The New York Times?* What a mitzvah!" According to my Grandma's fairy tales, her two oldest grandchildren now single-handedly ran New York's biggest newspaper *and* both the legal and medical communities.

But I also had a second cousin, Marcia, younger than I, living in Chicago. She was from a moneyed branch of Grandma's family and had lost her own grandmother at a young age, so had essentially adopted Dottie, even called her "Grandma." Marcia was like my grandmother's crack pipe. Whenever Grandma needed anything, and as we've seen, Grandma needed a great deal, she would ask Marcia. Luckily, Marcia loved to please Grandma and would cheerfully dispatch silk bed jackets, books, fancy magazine subscriptions, lipsticks, whole catered seders—whatever Grandma requested soon arrived. Marcia would also send Grandma extravagant floral arrangements for holidays. Of course, once trapped in that elevator, I was constantly awarded credit for things I hadn't sent, gestures I hadn't made. More than once, on that same elevator, someone had said to me: "*Oy*, those flowers you sent Dottie for *yontif!* Gorgeous!" Poor Marcia, who was anything but, racked up the bills in Chicago but reaped none of the credit. Not that these flowers were ever up to Dottie's standards. Regardless of what they looked like, what shape the flowers were in when they arrived, she'd still immediately call the florist and complain—"These flowers are *dead!*"—even if they were fresh. Then the florist would deliver a newer, second arrangement, and, of course, never retrieve the first. And in this fashion, Grandma managed to double the deliveries. Marcia was such a steady customer, what could the florist do?

At one point when my mother was sick and we were inventing excuses for Grandma for why neither of us could come down to Florida to visit, my mother's brother, by then into his sixties, thought that visiting Grandma for a few days from Colorado might be a decent thing to do, even if he loathed Florida and had never been a great fan of Grandma's.

During the daytime while he was visiting, he would humor her with conversation, but had not much patience, and his lifelong aversion to her inevitably rose to the surface by the end of each day.

In her apartment at the Galahad Court, on South Ocean Drive, two bedrooms stood at opposite ends of the apartment, and, since she was in her nineties and unwell, she would ask him to please keep his door open in case she needed to summon him for anything. By then she had a companion staying in the apartment with her day and night, thanks to her generous, adoring brothers, but if a family member was visiting they would take over. To Grandma's great consternation, my uncle insisted on closing the door to his room in the evenings, and quite late one night, his last there and his last while she was alive, as he lay in his room reading, the phone rang on the desk. Grandma had had enough. It was the Ft. Lauderdale operator.

"Your mother would like you to keep the door to your room open," she admonished this grown man, who had been born when Calvin Coolidge was president. He was so disconcerted by this call and the woman's disapproving tone, he got up, opened his door, and left it open. Grandma was a magician. Who else could open a door without being anywhere near it?

The last time I went to see her, she had pretty much run out of steam. I could tell that living had become entirely too much trouble. The returns were diminishing, and she was in no mood to linger. She seemed very small in her bed at home, and spoke very slowly. I think she sensed that this was our final good-bye, my last morning there, and told me, ten minutes before I was due to leave for the airport, that there was something she wanted me to know, that it was time. I pulled up a chair and sat beside her bed.

She then explained to me, speaking faster and louder than I was accustomed to hearing her, that she had never loved Grandpa, that the marriage had been a mistake, and she told me the name of the man who had been the love of her life, a name I'd never heard. She explained that he had been a colleague of Grandpa's in the garment district and that he and his wife had been friends of my grandparents' for many, many years. "Grandpa knew all about it, and his wife knew, too," she told me. "It was okay with *everybody*," she said, waving away any doubts I might have had.

When she'd been young and beautiful, with two small children, she'd apparently leave my grandfather and go off on cruises, usually to Cuba, with this man. They would play cards, drink watery rum and Cokes, and dance all night. She began telling me about him, and the trips they'd taken and fine times they'd had. He had lived with his family in a fabulous apartment in the El Dorado, on Central Park West (where Maurice Mann, a current owner of the Apthorp, has an apartment), and had been very rich, sophisticated, and ambitious. The implication was clearly that he had been everything my darling grandfather had not been.

She held up an admonishing finger to me then, as if just realizing the full import of all she had now revealed. "For thirty-five years, we just danced!" she said to me then, as if to shake me off her twisted path. I checked my watch. I had a plane to catch, but would take a later one. There would be other planes, but not other Grandmas.

She told me then all about the romance, and that she and this man had finally drifted apart and hadn't spoken for more than thirty years, but that a few years earlier, he had written to her out of the blue, saying that his wife had died and he wanted to see her. Grandma never answered. When I asked her why, she said: "It was too late. He remembered me as a real doll, skinny like a toothpick. Look at me! These aren't even my real teeth!" she announced, pointing at her mouth. "Besides, who wants to end up taking care of an old man? And who the hell even remembers how to . . . dance?"

About a month later, the last time Dottie was in the hospital, Marcia was down in Florida, taking good care of Grandma as always, and was arranging to take her back to the apartment on South Ocean Drive. Grandma wanted to die at home.

Marcia called me from the hospital while they were waiting for an ambulance to fetch them.

"She goes in and out," Marcia whispered. "A little while ago she looked at me and asked, 'What kind of a lousy Chinese restaurant *is* this, anyway?'"

Then I heard Marcia tell Grandma, who by then no longer got dressed or left the apartment unless it was to go to the hospital, "Just calm down. The ambulance will be here for us soon. You'll be home by four, I promise."

"*Four?* By then the whole day is shot," she groaned, and it was the last thing I ever heard her say.

Last year, I had occasion to get back in touch with my second cousin Audrey, who lives in Florida. Audrey was my mother's favorite cousin, also had red hair, was legendary at family meals for being able to load a dishwasher so fast she'd practically earn a speeding ticket, was and is clever and kind and bountifully compassionate. Audrey was the one who dubbed Grandma Mrs. van Upsnoot, because of her carefree overspending and occasionally winsome pretentiousness. I asked her about Grandma's rich boyfriend of yesteryear. Was he a hallucination or had he been real? Who ever knew with Dottie?

She told me that he had been for real, all right, and that the whole family had known about it. "It was a great love affair," Audrey told me. "And he gave her an allowance," she added. "Where do you think she got all her jewelry? The whole thing was a huge family scandal. But your parents never knew about it."

It was all just too much for the mind to grasp—at least *my* mind—at that moment. Grandma? In love? The idea that Grandma had liked, let alone loved, any man on this earth who wasn't a relative was unimaginable.

Then again, this was Grandma. They just danced.

"IK HOU VAN JE" MEANS
"I LOVE YOU" IN DUTCH

Love comes, at least for me, when I least expect it—and I never expect it. When in 1999 I met the man who was to become my husband, I was looking for a job, not a love affair. I did not find work. Instead I found the *grande amore*, the kind of love that changes your life overnight, where things go from black and white to vibrant color.

Although Dad had tried quashing my idea to write a book about van Gogh's life in a comic way, I decided to try to go to Amsterdam for a year anyway to delve into van Gogh research, and meantime find work at an advertising agency there, writing ads in English. I wrote to every Dutch agency I could find and began to dream about subletting 6LE, packing up Thistle, and trading Riverside Park for Vondelpark. I imagined myself taking the Van Baerlestraat tram and spending days digging around the Van Gogh Museum. I heard back from several agencies, but one letter stood out and made me laugh out loud. It was from an art director, skydiver, and artist, and soon we began to correspond. One Saturday afternoon he called me from his ex-girlfriend's house, where he was spending the day with their teenage son. They were waiting for one of the ex's dogs, a bearded collie, to give birth to puppies. We talked for four hours, and then again the next day and the next. We e-mailed and talked every day. A few weeks later, he suggested that he might visit New York. We were both nervous about the prospect of meeting, but the visit was terrific. As a gift, he brought me a finely carved wooden walking stick. "If we're going to grow old together, we're going to need a couple of these," he told me.

By his second visit, about a month later, impulsively or not, we were talking about spending the rest of our lives together; it was just a question of how and where.

His first reaction to the Apthorp troubled me, though. He'd walked by both the Ansonia and the Dakota and decided that in comparison, the Apthorp was but "a slab." I imagined that wherever he was living in Amsterdam must be magnificent. But when I first visited him there, I found him living on perhaps the only dreary block of apartments in the city. His was a second floor apartment in a building dating from the late 1890s, built as temporary housing for industrial workers. His building was so moist and clammy that, climbing the steep, narrow steps to his apartment, sometimes we saw mushrooms growing out of them. Of course Amsterdam is famous for, among other things, its mushrooms, but these would never have made it into any Dutch agricultural catalog.

My soon-to-be husband's son was a beautiful kid, witty and mischievous, a product of the Dutchman's fifteen-year alliance with an actress. Big, blonde, self-assured, and still very present, she was every bit what the comic Richard Lewis would refer to as the "ex-girlfriend from hell." Still, I loved Amsterdam, and he loved New York City. And we loved each other. Why not get married? What could possibly go wrong? Neither of us had significant money or savings, owned property or cars, and we wouldn't be having any children. What was there to lose?

Yes it was an imprudent, reckless, imbecilic idea. Getting married to someone I barely knew was certainly a wild card—I wasn't completely oblivious—but I felt I had nothing to lose by playing it.

Soon after we made this decision, the Dutchman proposed that we have a prenuptial agreement, and I was agreeable. My friend

Sara's cousin, Paul, was an attorney, and said he'd handle it for us. He told me that he'd need to speak to Dad. I called Dad and told him that I was getting married and asked him if it was all right for Paul to contact him. He seemed anxious to meet the Dutchman, so a dinner date was arranged.

On a Friday night soon afterward, the Dutchman and I had dinner with my father and brother at the late, great Café des Artistes. Dad left his derision home. He kept calling the Dutchman "the *shaygetz*" (meaning non-Jewish man) and the *shaygetz* kept laughing, delighted that Dad had so quickly granted him a nickname, although completely unaware of what it meant. The restaurant was crowded and customarily noisy. We were sitting in a booth in the back, opposite the bar. At some point we saw Governor George Pataki and Al D'Amato come in and walk past us. We all commiserated about them, grumbling.

Toward the end of the meal, after my brother left, Dad suddenly began talking about my mother. His reminiscences were loving, wistful, and expressed with a gentleness I hadn't witnessed since Mom's funeral. All in all, it was an astonishingly tender moment for a man so characteristically unsentimental. He spoke for a while about how and when they had met and fallen in love, and then about their first years together. "Our love was supposed to last a lifetime," he said dreamily, "just as yours seems to be," he told the Dutchman and me. In some remarkable way, this master of circular logic seemed to have come full circle himself.

As we were getting ready to leave, a young, smart-looking woman in a cornflower blue silk suit walked past our booth on her way out, spotted Dad, and made her way back. "My God, I love your books!" she said to him above the raucous noise. He cupped an ear and said to her, "I can't hear you. What did you say?" The woman said it again, raising her voice to nearly a shout. Again, Dad said: "I can't hear you!" By about the fourth time she'd screeched her praise at him, she finally caught on to the fact that he'd actually heard her all along, he'd just wanted her to keep repeating it. After she left,

we walked out into the chilly late-night air. We were going to drop
Dad off at his building near Lincoln Center before heading back to
the Apthorp. Dad sat in the front with the driver and I sat behind
him, just behind the black woolen hat he had pulled way down over
most of his head. At his building he said good night and got out
slowly, haltingly. We were still parked there when he turned around
to stop and wave in his sheepskin coat, originally Per Gedin's, smiling sweetly before disappearing inside.

Two months later, he was dead.

"LIKE THOSE DIVERS
WHO LEAP OFF A CLIFF
IN ACAPULCO"

The Dutchman and I planned to get married alone at a tiny light-house on the beach in Nantucket during Thanksgiving week. And since the wedding ceremony would be guestless, my friends planned a party for us that would be held a few days before we were to leave. The site chosen was a Chelsea loft, and the time would be a Sunday afternoon. Comrades old and new would be there, as well as old and young. My brother was coming, the Barasches, old cronies of my mother's, June Ferrin and Penny Miller, who baked a beautiful wedding cake with a lighthouse on top. My soon-to-be stepson flew in for the occasion, as did a couple of the Dutchman's friends from the Netherlands. We envisioned a happy afternoon.

Dad had shown some concern about my impending marriage. He let me know he thought it irresponsible of us to be rushing into it—that we should take more time and get to know each other better. Nonetheless, I invited Dad to the party, and on the phone while we discussed his coming in from East Hampton I mentioned that I thought his wife would probably find my friends and this party extremely dull. I tried to be casual, nonaccusatory, tactful. Right or wrong regarding the issue of her attendance, I had made up my mind that it would be best for her not to come, and I'd believed I'd been sensitive to my father by indirectly making my wishes known. Dad's annoyed response was emitted with a snarl: "Look, I don't care *who's* there and who isn't, but you're creating a potential problem for me, and now I probably won't come." Looking back, the decision I'd made was questionable. This was family, after all.

Over the next few days, Dad became irate. It had little or nothing to do with parties or people in lime green sweaters. I was defying his desire to slow everything down. Moreover, I think he was upset because I was ignoring his basic conception of who I was by planning a life with someone. He may never have imagined that. Dad interpreted my intentions as defiant. I was only doing what felt right, but still, it was certainly uncharacteristically *optimistic* of me, and not in the natural Helleristic order of things. Something was happening indeed to that miserable, morose teenage girl in *Something Happened*, something unforeseen. What would become of, then, the "the open coffin or grave" that my father had imagined for my future?

I can well understand that Dad felt ineffectual and ignored by my decision to marry someone I'd known only a short time. Then, too, perhaps he was having his own difficulties when this all bubbled up around him.

For some time, Dad's friends and even I had sensed that he'd been more restless and irritable than usual. He also seemed terribly tired.

All of this, my ultimate disobedience intermingled with Dad's own "*mishigas*," became the backdrop for his next prolonged silence. He did not attend our party after all, and did not call when I got married, though there was a rather fanciful write-up in the Sunday *New York Times* about my wedding, which I later heard he'd apparently waved around proudly, showing it off to his friends.

The wedding in Nantucket took place on the beach, at dusk, at the lighthouse at Brant Point. The woman who married us, the Nantucket town and county clerk, Catherine Flanagan Stover, still a friend, was yet another peppy redhead who appeared ready for anything and gave it her all. Somehow we were able to hear her over the gusty breeze and savagely rolling waves. Following the ceremony, we had dinner at my old favorite, Le Languedoc.

A year or two later, when my marriage to Pieter van Pan flamed out and fell apart, Catherine, always philosophical, had this to say about us:

> Well, I definitely felt at the time I married you that you two were an unlikely alliance. I would never have matched you up if I had had to choose one from column A to match one from column B.

She then went on to quote none other than the mighty Cher, saying: "The trouble with some women is that they get all excited about nothing—and then marry him."

The writer Nat Russo, who with his wife, Barbara, was on Nantucket for Thanksgiving, were old friends of mine, and they'd met us after the wedding ceremony at the Rose & Crown Pub, on Water Street, for a glass of champagne. Recently, when asked what he thought of our marriage at the time, Nat wrote this to me:

> What I felt at the time was that Erica and her boyfriend were story-book romantics to pick a lighthouse on Nantucket to take their vows—what you'd expect from two people who fell in love e-mailing each other across the Atlantic. Having champagne with them on their wedding night and dinner on another night, I thought they were sweet, but to me, a bit like those divers who leap off a cliff in Acapulco.

As it turned out, after getting married, my husband and I still didn't know each other very well, and even during the moments that we seemed to, we often didn't read each other accurately. For example, he had a great enthusiasm for cars, excellent old British ones, and several times he compared me to a Facel Vega HK500. It's probably not a good sign when you have to go running to Google to look up a car to see what your husband thinks of you. And when he told me a year later that being married to me was like climbing the Stelvio and Google informed me that the Stelvio was one of the steepest climbs in the world, with no less than forty-eight hairpin turns, I knew we were in trouble.

Meanwhile, during the first months of marriage, there'd been only silence from Dad. Based on our volatile history, his cycle of silence, and then the often sudden reacceptance of me that would abruptly end when some hand had reached some number on a clock that only Dad could read, I naturally assumed that eventually we would be friends again, that it was only a matter of time.

Some time later, Paul, the lawyer who'd handled my prenuptial agreement, told me what had happened the day he'd phoned Dad. Paul explained to my father that his primary aim with regard to me was protecting any assets Dad might later bequeath to me, and he asked not for any numbers, but only for the *way* that he was planning to leave me money, if he in fact was. Dad told Paul that even as my attorney, the answer to this question was none of his business. Anyway, Dad added, "What makes you think I give a shit about what happens to my money when I'm gone?" Anyone who knew Dad would know that this comment was anything but malicious or insensitive, regardless of how it sounds. The truth is, it wasn't even about *me*. I know that, because then Dad repeated his oft-delivered line to Paul: "Anyway, I'm not planning on dying."

To Christopher Buckley, with whom Dad shared a lively, affectionate friendship, much, much later I put the question I didn't dare ask many: "Would Dad and I ever have spoken again if he'd lived?" "Oh, honey! Of course!" was his answer. And I believed him.

Then, in the early hours of December 12, 1999, the notion of Dad having the "last word" suddenly took on an altogether new meaning.

THE BEST CHINESE DUMPLINGS IN L.A.?

"I'm here at the hospital with your dad," the voice began. It was early on the morning of December 13th and my father's wife was in circumlocution, attempting to explain to me that she and Dad were at Southampton Hospital. She was never one for getting to the point of a story quickly and was apparently not going to start now, even when the issue was literally life or death.

She wove a long tale in extravagant detail, going on and on about their evening, and then at long last, her recitation came to a halt. That was when she then uttered the nearly incomprehensible words: "And he didn't make it."

"He didn't make *what?*" I actually asked. Only then did she tell me that Dad had died. She said she'd call me later that day with the details about his funeral, which would be held in East Hampton.

My husband flew in that night from Amsterdam, and the next day, a raw December day with air that felt like ice, we made our way out to Long Island with my parents' good friend Irene Towbin. Gloria and Norman Barasch joined us at Irene's house, and we all stayed over in preparation for Dad's funeral the following morning.

After breakfast but before we'd left to go into town for the funeral, my husband and I were up in our room when I started shivering. I looked out the window at the churning winter waves

and just completely broke down. If it's true, as certain friends far
more spiritual than I have said, that people are sometimes brought
into our lives for a singular purpose, I understood then that meeting my husband had perhaps been for this purpose, this occasion.
I cried that day as I had not cried since losing my mother, in loud,
visceral, convulsive sobs. That my husband was there that day to
calmly tether me to him, quietly and without fuss, is something I'll
always be grateful for.

But then, *"oy vey!"* I heard from the *shaygetz* when we'd reached
Guild Hall, entered the East Hampton auditorium, and immediately spotted Dad's casket. It stood at the front of the room, and
ceremoniously draped over it was an American flag. Since it had
always been my understanding that Dad never wanted a burial, the
casket threw me, and the sight of Old Glory seemed even more jar-
ringly incompatible with the person inside.

I was quickly herded into a front row between my aunt Sylvia and
Dad's wife. Meanwhile, my husband was moved to the back by somebody, I know not who or why, to a rear row of the auditorium. My
brother and his now wife were also seated way in the back. I looked
around and saw lots of familiar—and unfamiliar—faces, all marked
with different degrees of sorrow and disbelief. Keenly felt was the
absence of Dad's very dear friends Dolores and Fred Karl. To make a
terrible occasion worse, I learned then that Fred had had a heart at-
tack after picking up the phone and hearing that Dad was dead. His
doctors said that the shock had almost definitely brought it on. It was
imminent, yes, but might not have happened for some time.

The service began. Holding forth was a rabbi who looked to
be on the brink of adolescence. He was not at all bombastic and
seemed to have good intentions, but he did make one important
mistake.

The tributes began. A cousin, transplanted from New York to
L.A., spoke lovingly of Dad and ended his requiem by plugging
the dumplings at his Chinese restaurant in California. Next, he and
Speed Vogel stood up and read seemingly random selections from
Catch-22.

From time to time I peered over at the flag-draped coffin, and for the life of me could not believe that any part of the person who'd been my father could possibly be beneath its lid. It was too preposterous. "What would Dad think of this?" I found myself wondering again and again as the event progressed.

Next, the boyish rabbi stood and began summing up Dad's life, with the help of some genuinely touching anecdotes provided to him by my aunt Sylvia and Speed. Then followed a moving recitation of all of the roles Dad had performed so richly and admirably in his life. Dad had been, the rabbi intoned, a wonderful husband, brother, friend, son-in-law, author, an inspiration to young writers everywhere. The list covered much, but carefully, and obviously deliberately, omitted any mention of the fact that Dad had been a parent.

At the event's conclusion, everyone poured out onto the street. Somberly, most people got into cars and headed for the Cedar Lawn Cemetery, on Cooper Lane, for the interment. But my husband and I did not. I felt no need to participate in all of the choreographed "pageantry," to use a favorite word of Dad's, since to my mind it had nothing to do with him.

George Mandel later wrote to me:

> At the behest of the attending rabbi secular Joe would not
> have bothered with, as his nearest of kin, I ritually shoveled
> dirt into the grave he would not have bothered with, and
> then had to distance myself in case of sobs at my age.

Instead of attending the burial, my husband and I took one of Irene Towbin's cars and drove around. I showed him all the places out there that had been important to me—Mom's house in the Bridgehampton potato fields, the house we'd rented long ago in Amagansett, near the beach. When the tour was finished, we went, for the last time ever, to Dad's house, where everyone was congregating post-cemetery. My husband was excited by having a moment's conversation with Mel Brooks, but I had other thoughts.

Norman Barasch was still perturbed that Dad's kids hadn't been mentioned in the eulogy. When my husband joined us again, the three of us went to where the rabbi was standing. I introduced myself. His eyes became moist immediately. "Excuse me, but I won't ever be able to sleep again if I don't ask you this question," I started. He knew exactly what was coming, and looked possibly even more wretched at that moment than I felt. The next second, Norman piped in: "How the hell do you not mention someone's kids in a eulogy when they're sitting right in front of you?" The *shaygetz* also spoke up, asking, "What kind of rabbi *are* you?"

A tear began to roll down the rebbe's flustered cheeks. He explained that prior to the service, he'd been informed that Dad had been estranged from his children and that they had not spoken to or seen him "for many years." And that we would not, in fact, be in attendance that day. Having realized his error, the rabbi apologized so tenderly and emotionally that all three of us wound up consoling *him*. We stayed for a few more minutes, then left with the Barasches.

As for the Cedar Lawn Cemetery, Dad is gone over ten years and now both he and Fred Karl are buried there. Fred died in 2004 of kidney disease, and the two friends are separated by about five or six graves. Dolores continues to plant seasonal flowers for Fred and leave potted plants for Dad.

A few years after my parents divorced, Dad, seeming at least momentarily contrite, had asked Fred: "Does Dolores still blame me for the divorce?" Fred, who knew his wife maybe better than anyone should ever know anyone, answered: "You'll have to ask her." Which, of course, Dad never did, perhaps because he already knew the answer.

Throughout their friendship, which spanned many decades, he frequently deferred to Dolores in ways he generally did not with women. Barbara Gelb was another female friend who always spoke up and gave him her honest opinions. He listened to her, genuinely interested, without snapping, without sarcasm, without much rebuttal at all—which was practically unheard of.

Since Dad's death, there have been several poignant tributes. A memorial service was held for him the June after his death at the Society for Ethical Culture, a dignified occasion with many speakers including Mike Nichols, Robert Gottlieb, Christopher Buckley, George Mandel, and Fred Karl. George Mandel, my father's oldest friend from Coney Island, referred to Dad's "merry heart of mischief." George has reminded me about many things—Dad stashing me up in the closet as a trick for my mother, the Apthorp pizza tolls, and more. That George was wounded in the Battle of the Bulge and had had a steel plate put in his head was a subject of endless jokes for my father and George's friends, all of whom teased him unstintingly, saying that the tin in his head had made him crazier than all of them combined and that they would all surely outlive him. The stinging irony now is that, like the sound of one hand clapping, he is the only one left to remember any of this firsthand. Luckily for me, his steel plate is like a steel trap.

Another tribute to Dad is a plaque in his name that is placed on the ground next to a towering beech tree outside the East Hampton Library. The library had been a source of great enjoyment and help to him in the writing of his last books.

As for my own tributes, I have several. When I wish to pay

East Hampton Library plaque

©East Hampton Library

true honor to the old man, for instance, I go to Nathan's in Coney Island and have a hot dog, an homage I have no doubt he would understand and appreciate.

In the end, I think he would even have understood my marriage, which ended as tempestuously as it began. It was an adventure. I took a shot. I loved someone more than I ever had and it felt right.

I still love Amsterdam, and the Dutchman still loves New York. Nothing else about us, however, was meant to last.

Yet again Joe Heller was right, but wrong about me. My marriage wasn't "meant to last a lifetime" any more than his was, but I have never regretted taking the chance.

AMIS TO IMUS,
FIRST AND LASTING IMPRESSIONS

*Yes, I should have left all of the interesting people
and stories out of the book.*

        —Christopher Hitchens's deadpan
        response to a charge of relentless
        name-dropping in his memoir,
        Hitch-22, New York Public Library,
        June 2010

By the time I reached Martin Amis at his home in London recently
and spoke with him, I had already called five times and spoken to
a very engaging and patient woman, who kept asking me to ring
back the next day. When we finally connected, it had taken six days
and four hours for me to build up sufficient courage. I'm not sure
what exactly had fired my intimidation. His relentlessly brilliant
books? The fact that Dad had told me many years ago that unless
I could be a "Martin Amis," I shouldn't ever bother to try to write?
(Anyway, is there such a thing as "a" Martin Amis? To me, there is
only *the*.) I had also recently read in *Hitch-22*, by his old pal Chris-

topher Hitchens, about Amis's razor-sharp ear for correct grammar and precise verbiage. He was a stickler, apparently, for the distinction between the words "each" and "both," and, as I sat there the morning I was to finally speak to him, with my voice shaking and my sweaty, quivering hand taking notes, I resolved silently to try to avoid using both when speaking to him. Or each.

As it turned out, he couldn't have been nicer or more helpful. To my great surprise and relief, he was willing and even eager to discuss Dad, to recount the times they'd met, and had given the subject some serious thought, for which I was extremely grateful.

> I was 26 or 27 when *Something Happened* came out and I interviewed him for *The New Republic*. I went to meet Joe and to interview him in his hotel room at the Inn on the Park, Hyde Park Corner. He'd been doing interviews all day and was polite but weary, wanting to get on with it. I was trembling with nerves, as young authors sometimes have done with me. We sat down, and in a quavering voice I began the interview, asking him about *Something Happened*. All day long people had been asking him about *Catch-22*. He immediately ordered a vodka and everything changed. A few weeks later he wrote me a note, and it said: "Thanks for the interview. It gave me an articulate style that I know I don't possess except on the page."

Their next meeting was in New York, when Amis interviewed Dad for *Good as Gold* (1979).

> For that interview, I quoted some of the book's funny bits back to him. Writers like that. At some point the tape ran out and Joe was exasperated. "How do you run out of tape?" he wanted to know. "New York has so much tape!"

Three or four years later, Dad and Amis had dinner together in Oxford.

He was very funny. Somehow we got on to the subject of Joe's hair. He was very proud of his hair. He looked at me at one point, impressed, and told me: "*You've* still got quite a lot."

Joe was a good-looking guy, and my impression was that he loved to eat, drink, and have a good time.

Ian McEwan remembers a night in Oxford, too. He actually remembers Amis being there, but Amis thinks not.

McEwan sent me this page, which I've not touched. (Come on, now. *I'm* going to edit Ian McEwan?)

I met Joe Heller only once, one evening in the early nineties. We were in a cottage a few miles outside Oxford. Our hosts were Redmond O'Hanlon, the travel writer, and his wife, Belinda, the dress designer. They'd invited a few friends to dinner to meet the great man. We'd been indignant to learn that he'd been in Oxford eight weeks without our knowing. But a writer-in-residence was not a common item in British universities in those days, especially in Oxford. And when a college—St. Catherine's, in this case—did get its hands on a writer, it guarded him jealously, like a state secret. Heller was due to go back to the States in a day or two. We were admirers and we knew his work: Martin Amis; the poets Craig Raine and James Fenton; Raine's wife, Li Raine, the Shakespeare scholar; and the philospher Galen Strawson.

The O'Hanlons had ordered in a huge side of beef. Early in the evening domestic disaster struck—the oven failed. So a Thai restaurant in a nearby village brought 'round a complete meal in dozens of tinfoil cartons. There was a lot of wine on the table. Heller sat at the head. He was genial, generous, he asked questions. There was a lot of literary gossip, scabrous stories, opinions, laughter—the usual thing. At some point we stopped eating and went on drinking, and then we had drunk enough to start celebrating Heller without restraint. We talked—almost as if among ourselves—of our favourite

passages in *Something Happened, Good as Gold, Catch-22.*
Martin had some sentences by heart. Joe Heller was beaming, he was delighted. Who wouldn't be? We were a younger
generation and we were giving good face. And all the time
Heller kept pointing down the table for more of the cold,
half-empty cartons of prawns, chicken, rice, and vegetables
to be passed along. These boxes piled up by his plate, three or
four little tottering towers. Finally there was nothing left and
he was done, and he sat back and said something like, This
is amazing. You're all old friends. You know each other so
well. I'm in a literary milieu! There's nothing like this in the
States. He said he'd felt rather isolated in Oxford. He went
on to lament the way American writers of his generation
were hundreds of miles apart in their campus English de-
partments. The jollity of the evening was beginning to fade.
We said we were sorry that we hadn't known he was around
and we hadn't seen more of him. The evening broke up in
the O'Hanlons' driveway, with affectionate hugs of our new
friend, our senior, and promises to meet up soon, in England
or the States. My guess is that none of us ever saw him again.

Salman Rushdie, also marvelously helpful, sent me this:

Years ago, in London, I heard Joe speak about his work
at, I think, the Institute of Contemporary Arts, and even
though his accent plus the effects of his illness made him
pretty hard to understand, he was fascinating. I was impressed by his refusal to speak theoretically about his books:
he spoke always and only in terms of character and event.
And he said a thing I never forgot: that often books started
for him with a sentence, which he knew contained many
other sentences. "In the office in which I work there are six
people of whom I am afraid," "I get the willies when I see
closed doors," and of course the famous opening of *Catch-
22* were examples he gave. I've had this experience, too;

both *Midnight's Children* and *Haroun and the Sea of Stories* began with sentences. I was happy to hear that Joe's great books had been born in the same way.

Dad also had great fondness for the Christophers, Buckley and Hitchens, and although not much has been divulged, my impression is that spending time with one or both involved plenty of drinking and an abundance of penetrating discussion and laughter. Hitchens dedicated his book *The Trial of Henry Kissinger* to Dad, and speaks of him with devotion. The title of Hitchens's memoir, *Hitch-22*, was also, in part, a nod to the old man.

And Christopher Buckley, who wrote the flawless, loving, and incomparably restrained *Losing Mum and Pup*—which surely humbled every memoirist or potential memoirist, including this one—has written about Dad, too. On December 12, 2009, the tenth anniversary of Dad's death, an op-ed piece by Buckley was published in *The New York Times*. It was called *Catch-2009*, and in it he wrote:

The death of any friend leaves a hole. In this case, a succession of holes, for I've often found myself wondering over the last 10 years, "What would Joe have made of this?" Having died just before the start of a tumultuous—to say the least—decade, the author of a landmark 20th-century satire missed, or perhaps another way to put it, avoided:

the Florida recount

9/11

weapons of mass destruction

Saddam Hussein's hanging, available on cellphone and YouTube

Dick Cheney shooting his lawyer

Hurricane Katrina

John Kerry, war hero, being depicted as a Swift-boating
    wimp

Lady Gaga

A.I.G. bonuses

Bernard Madoff

the election of Barack Obama

Glenn Beck

the "controversy" over Barack Obama's birth certificate

Sarah Palin, best-selling author

I'd love to have heard his take on all this over our ritual
martinis. Joe was not a manufacturer of bons mots. *Au con-
traire*—as he himself would have gleefully put it. His conversation was nonornamental. He did not strive to be witty
or to dazzle. He was amused but mostly repelled by professional talking heads, those conveyor belts of forced insight.

But behind the warm smile, he had a switchblade-
sharp mind, and his fraud detector (what Hemingway
called, in somewhat saltier terms, the writer's most indis-
pensable tool) was as fine-tuned as a Predator drone. He
could spot phoniness at a thousand yards and destroy it
with a single Hellfire-missile glance.

For all that, he was playful and avuncular. He provided
one of my books with a blurb. The subsequent *Publishers
Weekly* review was decidedly mixed. I faxed it to him with a
sigh. He drew lines through the decidedly mixed portions
and wrote at the bottom, "Now it's a total rave."

Dad and Buckley shared a particularly spirited and devoted friendship. One element of that was an endless Ping-Pong of hundreds of
wry, witty faxes that flew back and forth between them.

Two other favorites of Dad's, apart from the old guard, were Kinky Friedman and Don Imus. Kinky once asked Dad, in a self-described "Barbara Walters question," if Dad was happy. "What do you take me for?" Dad answered. "Idiots are happy."

"Joe took his work seriously but not himself seriously," said Kinky. The friendship grew, and Kinky and his band played once at a party for Dad, and this was followed by some late nights that they spent together, in the company of Don Imus, downtown at the Lone Star Café.

I wrote to Imus to see whether he had any reminiscences about those nights, but what came back was: "Unfortunately, what happened at the Lone Star stays at the Lone Star." I can't really say I blame him.

Kinky, a prolific, masterful writer himself of books and songs, was a bit more forthcoming, and since he'd written about Dad before, probably felt comfortable discussing him. We had a few especially lovely chats. During one he told me that there were many writers who were ". . . important, financially and otherwise, to their agents and publishers. But they're not 'significant.' There's a huge difference between being important and being significant. Joe was significant." He also said that he felt as if *Catch-22* had been written in the stars. "It seemed effortless, as if it had all come forth in one fluid rush." Kinky told me that Dad's favorite song of his had been "They Ain't Makin' Jews Like Jesus Anymore."

They ain't makin' guys like Buckley, Hitchens, Kinky, Imus, or Dad anymore, either.

TEA, SYMPATHY, AND JUST A LITTLE BIT OF A LAWSUIT

> *The true function of a writer is to produce a masterpiece, and no other task is of any consequence.*
>
> —Cyril Connolly

"Who says you have to know everything?" I can almost hear my father asking, ever the shrewd Talmudic quizmaster, if he were to learn how much about him still baffles me.

How and where do you begin to make sense of a writer who worshiped Dickens and T. S. Eliot, loved the crackling dialogue and ingenious characters and situations (who wouldn't?) of Jimmy McGovern's British *Cracker* series (in which he was mentioned), but also thought *My Cousin Vinny* was pretty much the most hilarious film ever made?

And how was it that an author with such fluid, majestic command of the language couldn't write a note, at least to me, that wasn't stilted, employing the maximum amount of words? "Meet me at the Chinese restaurant across the street" could take 187 lines and read as if written by Anthony Trollope or Thomas Hardy. Oh why, prayeth?

Putting the pieces together, knitting together the bones, when everything you see is a paradox and everything you feel is a contradiction, can be fearsome. After I wrote a novel in 1990, just as it was about to be published and prior to his reading it, Dad advised me that really, one should always throw one's first book away because it was never worth reading. I was halfway across town, on the crosstown bus and nearly home, by the time I had my idiot's epiphany: *Catch-22* had been his first book.

But by far one of the most perplexing enigmas ever, at least to me, something that makes truly no sense, even in the land of the cultivated absurd, involves both my parents, a successful Broadway play, lawyers, and a restaurant in the Village, a riddle that, to this day, has me stymied. And as for explanations, I cannot command any.

When Dad's play *We Bombed in New Haven* hit Broadway in 1968, after a production at the Yale Repertory Theatre under the auspices of the eminent Robert Brustein, audiences and critics alike assumed that this was Dad's first attempt at writing a play. There was no reason to think otherwise and he never corrected them, but apparently this may not have been the case.

After Dad's death, his biographer, Tracy Daugherty, author of *Just One Catch*, and I, pretty much concurrently and through old family friends, discovered that there had indeed been an earlier treatment for a play—or perhaps it was a screenplay—or perhaps it was both. According to Bob Mason, who was writing at the time with Dad (when they were both teachers at Penn State), over Christmas break in 1951, Dad had met some Hollywood producer at a New York City party who was in search of scripts about adolescents. Dad and Bob wrote something and submitted it to Phyllis Stohl, a theatrical agent who happened to be married to the playwright Robert Anderson. Stohl sent it on to Otto Preminger. Bob and Dad met Preminger for drinks one night at the St. Regis, and Bob remembers Preminger saying to them: "I want to make this a

play and then go on from there to a movie." Clearly he loved what
they'd done. They waited afterward, for weeks and then months, to
see what the next step would be, but word never came.

Then *Tea and Sympathy*, the Broadway play directed by Elia
Kazan, opened at the Ethel Barrymore Theatre on September 30,
1953, and ran for 712 performances. Deborah Kerr, the elegant
siren, fresh from her burst of fame in *From Here to Eternity*, starred,
along with John Kerr and Leif Erickson.

Not much more is known about Dad and Bob's script except
that the lawyer they subsequently hired was Rudolph Halley, who
later became a New York political hotshot, and the fact that when
they sued Stohl and Anderson, it was not for plagiarism, but for
"breach of fiduciary relationship." They dropped the suit after it was
learned that Stohl was sick. (She died of cancer in 1956.)

That my father wrote a script with a friend and colleague,
hoped to get it produced, and then had those hopes evaporate does
not by itself make this a riveting dollop of Joe Heller trivia.

Not even the fact that Daugherty and I both happened to
stumble upon all of this so serendipitously: I had mentioned it to
him in an e-mail, and he somehow turned up an untitled note in
the *Philadelphia Inquirer*, on November 16, 1954, written by the
popular newspaper columnist Leonard Lyons:

> Robert Anderson, author of *Tea and Sympathy*, and his
> agent-wife, are being sued by Bob Mason and Joe Heller,
> former teachers at the Univ. of Pa. [sic]. They don't claim
> plagiarism, but a "breach of fiduciary relationship."

Following that, I combed the Internet like a beast possessed, and
succeeded somehow in tracking down the right Bob Mason, in a
country suddenly teeming with them. I had hoped very much that
now, almost sixty years later, he would still be with us, and he was. I
found him and spoke with him and his wife, Abby, who confirmed
everything about the script they'd written and the trial, and separately they also spoke to Daugherty. Bob said that he still had the

court transcripts somewhere and would try to track them down, but that never happened.

No answer came, either, about the biggest question in my mind, why neither Dad nor Mom had ever mentioned anything about any of this to me or to my brother, let alone to any interviewer whenever Dad was asked about writing either for the theater or for movies. In fact, no one except very close friends of my parents seemed to know about it, and when *We Bombed* opened and closed after seventy-two performances, the *Tea and Sympathy* script and trial had still never been mentioned. But this story has yet another wrinkle.

When I found out about this after Dad's death, I thought back to the several times he and I had eaten at Tea & Sympathy, a British restaurant on Greenwich Avenue. He'd never mentioned the play he'd written that either inspired or did not inspire the play of the same name, which brought him and his cowriter friend to court. My mother and I had spent time at that restaurant, too, and yet it had never come up. She had never said: "The name of this restaurant reminds me of something Dad wrote." Nothing.

Had Dad been so bitterly disappointed by the experience? Did it hurt too much to recall? Was it a taboo subject, too fraught with disappointment? Bob and Abby Mason had no answer to my question. Why had it never come up, I pressed in one of my calls to them last year, even when he and I had gone to a restaurant called Tea & Sympathy? They couldn't imagine. To them, too, it didn't add up. "Joe seemed fine afterward," they said of the whole court case and experience. Dolores Karl told me that she and Fred and my parents would joke about it often.

At the very end of *Tea and Sympathy*, the much-quoted line is so freighted with schmaltz you can almost swear you've seen chicken feathers flying: "Years from now, when you talk about this—and you will—be kind."

Still, for some reason I'll never know, my parents chose to take a different route entirely regarding this matter. They chose to never talk about it at all.

WHISTLING PAST A GRAVEYARD FILLED WITH POT ROAST?

Wind goes from farm to farm in wave on wave,
But carries no cry of what is hoped to be.
There may be little or much beyond the grave,
But the strong are saying nothing until they see.
—Robert Frost,
"The Strong Are Saying Nothing"

I can swim but am not a strong swimmer, so when it comes to wallowing in regrets, sloshing around in them like an olive in a martini, I am careful. One can drown in regrets over wasted opportunities and roads not taken, searing, desperately painful stories your mother has told you that you chose not to believe, a recipe for pot roast that your father repeatedly pleaded for and was denied by you.

Have I any regrets? Should I, for instance, have given Dad Grandma's much-vaunted pot roast recipe? Of course. I have come to realize by now that in all likelihood it would probably never have tasted quite the way he remembered it anyway, when my mother or grandmother had cooked and served it to him, but what would relinquishing it have cost me? A recipe is only words on a page. I believe what he missed so much ran far deeper than a few shakes of paprika or a couple of sprigs of dill.

My father was tone-deaf in most ways, except when it came to whistling past a graveyard. Then his pitch was perfect.

The truth was generally that the more he boasted about something, the less sure of it he actually was. Unless it was his hair. (Just ask Martin Amis.)

"I have much to be pleased with, including myself, and I am. I have wanted to succeed and I have," he begins, a far from modest wrap-up to his memoir published the year before his death, in 1998, *Now and Then: From Coney Island to Here: A Memoir*. After that, he lists the many things he has to be proud of about himself and his life, among them the "sterling digestive system that almost never lets me down," that he is in "reasonably good health," and a clever laundry list of other enviable, impressive statements any person would feel fortunate to make. If only they had all been true.

Most were; I just don't believe that *all* were. As I've said, when he blustered and thundered loudest, he was typically on the shakiest ground.

Then again, when it comes to the entire subject of *Catch-22*, you may as well know, I know perhaps less than anyone, because it's a book I've still never read.

THE ELEPHANT IN THE ROOM IS FIFTY YEARS OLD AND 464 PAGES LONG

So there it is, then, the long-held confession. Allow me to explain.

Catch-22 was first published, remember, in 1961, when I was nine. So give me, say, ten years amnesty. At nineteen, I was reading a great deal. But Heller? *Catch-22*? Well, no. To begin with, it was a World War II book. I never read *Mila 18, From Here to Eternity, The Thin Red Line, The Young Lions,* or *Battle Cry*. I'm not especially proud of these gaping breaches in my reading repertoire, but there you have it.

Reading *Catch-22* was never something I was determined *not* to do, but all at once, the years piled up into the better part of a lifetime. Before I knew it, I'd fashioned a nonreading *Catch-22* existence. All of a sudden I turned around and realized "I haven't gotten around to it yet" had forfeited its verisimilitude, although I wasn't exactly sure what had changed.

I do know that not reading *Catch-22* has never been an act of defiance or vengeance, rebellion, or even laziness. To be fair, I have tried reading it perhaps a hundred times, always with the purest intentions, eager to see what all the pachydermal fuss has been about. I use that word most deliberately, because somewhere along the way, *Catch-22* changed from being the elephant in the room to being the room itself.

Norman Barasch, that old family friend, has counseled me many times: "Get past the beginning. It's a lot of men's names and ranks. Don't let that throw you." It does. I start reading, I see all the names, and suddenly I have flies in my eyes. Oceans pound between my ears. My brain turns to soup. "And seeing the movie doesn't count," Norman adds. "Read the goddamned book."

Last year I happened to ask my brother if he'd ever read *Catch-22*, since it was not something I could ever recall our having discussed. He told me that he had and said, "Really, it's not bad. You should read it."

Per Gedin, upon learning that I'd never read it, said to me last year, "You know, I am almost jealous of you for having that experience ahead of you. I wish I could read *Catch-22* for the first time." His exuberance was touching and intriguing. I sat down then and there to give it another chance.

It had to be done, after all. Here I was, writing a book with the word "Yossarian" in the title. I had to know who and what that was. It wasn't Alan Arkin.

I devised a plan: five pages a day. I would take them like medicine and hopefully the taste would improve along the way, but again, as with every previous attempt, I found myself lingering on a single page for hours, or one eye began twitching or the other throbbing. Or the phone rang. Or the dog needed walking, my cheeses alphabetizing. I even bought it on tape, thinking I would just chain myself to a chair and be force-fed, listen passively. Nothing would interrupt or deter me. It didn't work.

To be fair, when I was given my own inscribed copy in 1961 by Dad, somewhere deep within the lines of that inscription I read a kind of open-ended reprieve, giving me ten or fifteen years or more to get around to reading it, to facing the music. But as we have seen, my math skills are dreadful. (Not for nothing was I nearly exiled to Mississippi to learn how to grow corn.) Could it be that I've just gotten the math wrong?

Not likely. As the time has changed, so has my reading *Catch-22* fantasy.

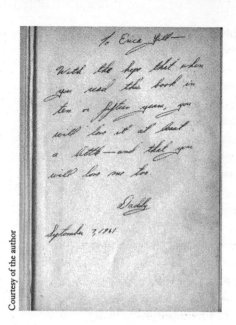

The seedling of a reprieve?

At first, I planned to read it when in college, and when I finished, I'd say to Dad, "Not bad." To which I imagined him replying: "Do you really think I need you to tell me that?" I didn't read it.

Or else I'd read it later on, once I was working, starting to write. We would sit together at the Apthorp, I imagined, and I would point out to him all the parts I found funniest. "You picked the wrong parts," he'd say. "Other parts are much better." In this fantasy, my mother is somehow there with him, in the background, about to serve pot roast. I can almost smell the kitchen, redolent with dill. Still, I didn't read it.

Then I began to think that I would read *Catch-22* when Dad was very, very old. It would be poignant, bittersweet. But he never lived to be very, very old, and now, when I read it, I can't ever tell him what I think. And he can never tell me what he thinks about what I think. If I told him, for instance, that I thought it was a work of pure genius, he could have said: "No shit," unimpressed, having heard nothing he hadn't known himself all along. But Dad being

Dad, he also could just as likely have asked me, curious, leaning back in his chair, "You think so?"

There is a method to all of this, you see, to the kaleidoscope of ever-changing excuses I summon for my *Catch-22* profligacy, although they may well hold less water than the Apthorp tulips after the underground sprinklers had been shut off for a year.

So, am I crazy for not having read *Catch-22*? And if not having read it doesn't mean I'm crazy, does that mean I'd be crazy to read it now?

If I do read it now, the great mystery can never again be mysterious. I have read all of Dad's other books. After *Catch-22*, there can be no more treasure unearthed, ever.

Just the way Dad always answered the question of why he'd never again written anything as great as *Catch-22* with "Who has?" my answer to the same question, as well as many contiguous ones concerning him, has always been "Who knows?"—an answer I find I am oddly and mystifyingly still reluctant to part with.

CODA
ALL IS FORGIVEN:
THE RECIPE FOR DOTTIE HELD'S $10,000 POT ROAST

1. Buy first-cut brisket, about 5 lbs., enough for 10 people.
2. Put into big pot with some butter and brown on high flame on all sides. Start with the fat side down.
3. Preheat oven to 350 degrees. Then slice 2 large onions and place them around the brisket. Put in 2 small cans of tomato sauce and 2 cans of water.
4. Season the meat with salt and plenty of garlic powder and a bunch of dill. You can also pour in about 2 tbsp. ketchup and 2 tbsp. chili sauce. Then top the meat with plenty of paprika powder.
5. Put meat into the oven for 2 or 2½ hours COVERED. Then take it out and "leave" it to cool for about 10 minutes, then slice it.
6. Put back into the oven, covered again, until tender, about another hour or more.

Serve with potatoes, sour pickles, and dark bread. If you're smart, make it a day or more ahead of serving.

ACKNOWLEDGMENTS

My unequivocal thanks to everyone here who helped to fit the puzzle together and keep the engine running. It's appallingly corny but true: I can never thank you enough.

A special thank-you to Henry Dunow, my agent. I don't know how *anyone* writes a book without Henry.

My apologies for the alphabetic listing below, but evaluating each of your contributions in a more deserving fashion would take longer than it took me to write the book. I hope you'll understand.

Thank you, then, to William Adler, Martin Amis, Norman Barasch, Lynn Barber, Betsey Biscone, Guy Blumberg, Ronald Blumer, Christopher Buckley, Audrey Chestney, Peter Chestney, Charles Citrin, Leslie Citron, Nancy Crampton, Tracy Daugherty, David Downie, Dennis Fabiszak, Kinky Friedman, Per Gedin, Arthur and Barbara Gelb, Sara Giller, Wendy Glickstein, Geoff and Jean Goers, Robert Gottlieb, Christopher Gray, Elaine Grossinger Etess, Tania Grossinger, Earl Hamner Jr., Alison Harris, Cleve Hattersley, Ted Heller, Christopher Hitchens, Sarah Hochman, Don Imus, Roger Juglair, Dolores Karl, Sarah Knight, Elaine Kremnitz, Estelle Lazarus, Elaine and Gerry Levine, Vicki Levites, Joyce Lapinsky Lewis and Richard Lewis, Molly Lindley, George and Miki Mandel, M. C. Marden, Bob and Abby Mason, Ian McEwan, Jimmy McGovern, Daniel Melamud, Kate Nelligan, Edna O'Brien, Sid and Ronny Osofsky, Maggie Phillips, Richard

Prince, Tony Puzo, Phyllis Raphael, Christopher Rauschenberg, Nancy Robbins, Kristyan Robinson, Aileen Rosen, David Rosenthal, Barbara Ross, Jeff Roth, Nat Russo, Salman Rushdie, Dan and Cyd Seltzer, Deborah Schneider, Harriet Spurlin, Jerome Taub, Rozanne Thornton, A. Robert Towbin, Irene Towbin, Ronald van den Boogaard, Maija Veide, Ed Victor, Lou Ann Walker, and Joe Winogradoff.

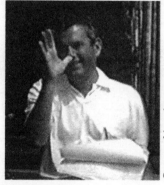

Courtesy of the author

Dad, Beverly Hills, 1963, in one of his favorite poses